The Spanish Language Today

'*The Spanish Language Today* is a lively and valuable addition to the bookshelf of students and teachers in Spanish studies. It is quite unprecedented in the topics it covers and in the authenticity of the materials on which it draws. This book is highly accessible and useful.'

Professor Ralph Penny
Queen Mary and Westfield College, University of London

The Spanish Language Today describes the varied and changing Spanish language in the world today.

As conflicting forces work towards the unification and fragmentation of both Peninsular and Latin American Spanish, this book examines:

- **where** Spanish is spoken on a global scale, from its decline in the Philippines to its vitality in the southern states of the US
- the **status** of Spanish within the realms of politics, education and media, including reference to the English-only movement in the US
- the **standardization** of Spanish
- specific areas of **linguistic variation and change** including: phonetics and phonology, orthography, lexis, and morphosyntax
- the effects of **language contact** on Spanish which is spoken widely in contexts of bi- and multilingualism
- the **linguistic and pragmatic factors** which underlie variation and change
- whether **new technologies** are an opportunity or a threat to the Spanish language

The Spanish Language Today contains numerous extracts from contemporary texts, a glossary of technical linguistic terms and selected translations. It is suitable for those engaged with the modern Spanish language, from beginning students with no prior linguistic knowledge to researchers.

Miranda Stewart is Senior Lecturer in Spanish and Latin American Studies at the University of Strathclyde

The Spanish Language Today

Miranda Stewart

Routledge
Taylor & Francis Group

LONDON AND NEW YORK

First published 1999 by Routledge
11 New Fetter Lane, London EC4P 4EE

Simultaneously published in the USA and Canada
by Routledge
29 West 35th Street, New York, NY 10001

Routledge is an imprint of the Taylor & Francis Group

Transferred to Digital Printing 2003

© 1999 Miranda Stewart

Typeset in Goudy by
J&L Composition Ltd, Filey, North Yorkshire

British Library Cataloguing in Publication Data
A catalogue record for this book is available from the British Library

Library of Congress Cataloging in Publication Data
Stewart, Miranda, 1954–
    The Spanish language today/Miranda Stewart.
        p.   cm.
    Includes bibliographical references.
    1. Spanish language – 20th century.   I. Title.
    PC4087.S84   1999
    460'.9'049 – dc21   98–54089
                        CIP

ISBN 0–415–14258–X (hbk)
ISBN 0–415–14259–8 (pbk)

Printed and bound by Antony Rowe Ltd, Eastbourne

To Ian and Julia

Contents

x   Contents

Preface

The aim of this book is to describe the varied and changing contemporary Spanish language. Given that Spanish is used by approximately 400 million speakers throughout the world, whether as a mother tongue, an official language or a lingua franca in contexts that range from trading in East Africa, through informal conversation in Spain to formal interventions in international organizations, it is quite beyond the scope of this book to be a comprehensive inventory, were such possible, of the enormous variation that exists. Nor do we seek to provide a comprehensive description of an idealized, unchanging, supranational variety of Spanish; indeed, there are many excellent grammars of Spanish which cover the core system of the language and a number which also examine its principal functions. Unlike C. H. Stevenson's book of the same name as the present volume where 'today' is taken to refer to the nineteenth and twentieth centuries' (Hickey 1983/4: 25) we shall endeavour to focus on Spanish at the end of the twentieth century and to describe the current state of the language in terms of the twin phenomena of **variation** and **change**.

We propose to examine the conflicting forces that work towards both unification and fragmentation. On the one hand there is the pressure towards conformity to a common code, which ensures that supranational varieties of the language are available for use in, say, the media, education and administration. At the same time, there is the attraction of diversity, which enables different groups within the Spanish-speaking community to express their individuality through distinctive language usage that may, at extremes, be incomprehensible to a Spanish-speaker from outside that community. We shall look at language **prescription**, whereby a number of agencies ranging from grammarians to press agencies, from letters to the editor to individuals' perceptions of their own language competence, attempt to persuade or even compel language users to speak or write in certain desired and standard ways; we shall also look at how speakers and writers actually **use** the language, on occasion promoting language change through their sheer persistence in using new forms. Such change may, in time and if accepted by the community at large, result in the updating of the prescriptive norm.

The book embraces both Peninsular and American Spanish. There is a proportionately greater focus on Peninsular Spanish principally due to the fact that large areas of the Spanish-speaking world remain seriously under-researched and also to the geographic location of the writer. However, it should be remembered that there may be greater differences between two varieties of Spanish within Spain than between a Peninsular variety and one from a given Latin American country. Indeed, the Spanish spoken in southern Spain and the Canaries has more in common with the majority of Latin American varieties of the language than it has with that of the north of Spain. Therefore, when we provide examples from one side of the Atlantic or the other, they are rarely intended to be representative of the many varieties of Spanish spoken in either Latin America or in Spain respectively. In any case, the geographical dimension is only one of many which underlie language vari-ation. As far as speakers are concerned, factors such as age, sex, social class, level of education are also of prime importance. For example, the resources available to youth subcultures to generate their own varieties of Spanish are remarkably similar across speech communities; the use they are put to, how-ever, may be vastly different. Furthermore, there is the whole, and in our view, under-researched area of language use, that of language functions. That is, usage varies depending on who we are addressing, for what purpose and in what context. Therefore, in *The Spanish Language Today* we shall take as our point of departure the linguistic and pragmatic factors which underlie varia-tion and change and provide examples of these from different varieties of Spanish from both sides of the Atlantic. Consequently, the book should be of relevance to students on courses dealing with the modern Spanish language, to scholars in the language, to those engaged in research in this area and also to those with a more general interest in language variation and change.

It is assumed that many of the readers of this book will have high levels of passive knowledge of Spanish. Therefore, we shall provide translations or glosses of some the Spanish used in the text principally where an understand-ing of context is crucial to an understanding of the language or where im-portant lexis is unlikely to be included in standard dictionaries. These, where appropriate will be included as notes to each chapter. In line with the focus of the book on authentic Spanish used by a variety of speakers and writers at the end of the twentieth century, the vast majority of examples will be taken from naturally-occurring spoken and written discourse and not be confected to illustrate a particular point of linguistic interest. The reader is not expected to have a knowledge of modern linguistics and sociolinguistics although the book will derive its framework from this field. Technical linguistic terms will be explained as they arise and those which are crucial to an understanding of the text will be explained in a separate glossary to be found at the end of the book. Our primary purpose is to use linguistics to provide some insight into Spanish used today rather than to refine categories over which linguists fre-quently disagree, and therefore it may be necessary to simplify the linguistic presentation in certain areas. While specialists may feel that we have failed to represent certain areas of contention, we hope that the approach we have adopted will maintain an acceptable level of rigour while at the same time achieving comprehensibility for a non-specialist readership.

Part I (Chapters 1 and 2) will focus on Spanish as a world language. In Chapter 1 we shall focus on **where** Spanish is spoken in the world today and on the vitality of the different groups which speak it. For example, while Spanish may be a language in terminal decline in Israel or the Philippines, it enjoys conversely undisputed vitality in the southern states of the United States of America. We shall also look at its **status** in the world as evidenced, for example, by its presence in major international organizations, as a second language on the curriculum of non-Spanish-speaking countries and its impact in the audiovisual media.

In Chapter 2 we shall look at the **standardization** of Spanish and in particular at the different agencies responsible for language **prescription** notably the grammarians and lexicographers whether in their old roles as the providers of academic dictionaries and grammars or their newly-acquired ones as consultants to the media, public administration and the professions. One function of language prescription tends towards the conservative and seeks to prevent change from a supposed standard norm; it is interesting therefore to view prescription as providing a window into change currently in progress within groups of speakers of the language, change which this very prescription is designed to arrest. Another role of prescription is, in fact, to promote modernization and renewal of the language by, for example, sanctioning standard neologisms or by proscribing certain archaisms. We shall also examine briefly attempts both in Latin America and Spain to collect language corpora in order to enable linguists to refine their **descriptions** of the language.

Part II (comprising Chapters 3 to 5) will focus on the **system and structures** of the language and examine salient areas of variation and change in its phonetics and phonology, orthography, lexis and morphosyntax. Stevenson (1970) already noted that lexis is the area in which change is most rapid and this is certainly the case in Spanish, a language of considerable vitality. In phonetics and phonology change is considerably slower although variation may be considerable and in morpho-syntax there appears to be comparatively little variation and a very slow pace of change.

Part III (containing Chapters 6 to 8) will focus on the **functions** of the language, on how speakers draw from a common pool of linguistic resources to achieve their communicative ends. How can linguistic politeness be expressed and how might this differ from one community to another, what are the rules in different communities for mutual address, what constitutes a normative telephone call in, for example, Ecuador as compared with Spain, what counts as taboo amongst a given group of speakers today? What are the conventions governing different genres of writing and speaking, for example newspaper headlines or political speeches, in different parts of the Spanish-speaking world?

Spanish is spoken widely in contexts of bi- and multilingualism as well as forming the base for a limited number of Spanish-based pidgins and creoles. After examining the latter, Part IV (Chapter 9) will focus on the effects of **language contact** on Spanish, whether the language in question is cognate such as Catalan or non-cognate such as Maya and Basque, whether Spanish is the dominant language, as it is in its relationship with, for example, Galician or the minority language, as it is in relation to English in the southern states of the United States or on an equal footing as it is with Portuguese on the border between Uruguay and Brazil.

Clearly, within the limits of this book we cannot provide a comprehensive account of each of these areas and the great variety which exists in the Spanish-speaking world can only really be hinted at. However, we hope to have given readers the tools to be able to ask some informed questions about the varieties of Spanish with which they come into contact and some points of comparison when faced with one of the rich varieties of Spanish which does not match the description provided in a standard grammar. We also hope to have demonstrated the current vitality of the Spanish language which continues to be *una lengua en ebullición* ('a language in ferment') (Lorenzo 1966) rapidly changing to meet the newly created needs of an expanding community of users. While these developments can be seen most clearly at the level of lexis, there is also evidence of change in progress in the phonetics and morpho-syntax of Spanish. Furthermore, we hope to show that patterns of use are also evolving to reflect the needs of their users.

Miranda Stewart
Edinburgh, July 1998

Acknowledgements

I would like to thank students past and present who have enthusiastically submitted examples from their own experience for lively discussion. I am also grateful to former colleagues at the University of Newcastle-upon-Tyne, Dr Aidan Coveney, Professor Lesley Milroy, Professor Anthony Lodge and Dr Derek Green, whose enthusiasm for language and linguistics was an inspiration for this book.

I would also like to thank colleagues in the Spanish Division at the University of Strathclyde who covered my teaching for the first semester of 1995–6 to enable me to carry out initial research in Spain, and in particular Professor Eamonn Rodgers whose support has been unstinting. Thanks are also due to the Universitat Autónoma de Barcelona and in particular Professor Seán Golden and Dr Amparo Hurtado for providing me with study facilities and contacts when in Spain. Similarly, Dr Francesc Parcerisas, Dr Mercè Tricás Preckler, Frederic Chaume Varela and Cristina Sánchez were of inestimable assistance. I am particularly grateful to Professors Diarmuid Bradley and Ian Mason for their invaluable help with parts of the manuscript, to Dr Tom Bookless for his helpful comments on my proposal for this book and to Christopher Dixon, Dr Jesús Rodero and Dr Ross Graham for their help. I am also grateful to two anonymous readers whose comments helped to shape this final version. A debt of gratitude is also due to friends and colleagues for their contributions, witting or otherwise, to the data which has been the foundation of the work. All blemishes are entirely my own.

I would also like to acknowledge the help of Ms Julia Hall, who first commissioned this book, and her successors, Ms Louisa Semlyen and Ms Miranda Filbee, who saw the work to completion.

Part I

Spanish as a world language

1 The extent and status of Spanish in the world

1.0 Introduction

At the end of the twentieth century Spanish is spoken by approaching 400 million people throughout the world, and as such is the fourth most widely spoken language in the world after Mandarin Chinese, English and Hindi. It is an official language, generally the sole one, in twenty-one countries. It is spoken not only as a mother tongue but as an important second language (for example in Paraguay where it enjoys co-official status with the indigenous language of Guaraní) and also as a vehicular language or 'lingua franca'. While the Spanish language is most readily associated with its country of origin, Spain, the majority of its speakers live in Latin America where population growth means that numbers of speakers are steadily on the increase. It has a vibrant and rapidly expanding presence in the United States. It is also represented, albeit by small and declining numbers of speakers, in Africa, Asia and the Middle East. In this chapter, we shall look at the Spanish-speaking world and at the current status of Spanish today as a major world language.

It is clear that the number of speakers is but one factor in assessing the status of a language: many other considerations such as its status as an official, co-official or minority language, the economic and cultural potential of the countries where it enjoys official status, the number of those who study it as a foreign or second language, the extent of the domains in which it can be used, its presence in supranational forums, and the efforts expended on its promotion are all factors which contribute to the status of a language.

1.1 The extent of Spanish in the world

1.1.0 Spanish in Latin America

Spanish is the official language of Argentina, Bolivia, Chile, Colombia, Costa Rica, Cuba, the Dominican Republic, Ecuador, El Salvador, Guatemala, Honduras, Mexico, Nicaragua, Panama, Paraguay, Peru, Puerto Rico, Uruguay and Venezuela (see Figure 1.1). In the case of Puerto Rico it shares this status with English, in Paraguay with the indigenous language Guaraní,

Figure 1.1 Map of Spanish-speaking nations of Central and South America (based on Mar-Molinero (1997))

in Peru with Quechua and Aymara and in Bolivia with Aymara. It is also spoken in the former British colony of Belize, on the borders of Guyana and Haiti and in isolated communities in Trinidad. Mexico with a population of some ninety-three million, more than double that of Spain provides the greatest number of Spanish speakers, followed by Argentina and Colombia with approximately thirty-five million inhabitants each. It should be remembered, however, that the process of Castilianization of indigenous populations, while wide-ranging and rapid, is not complete and many countries still have groups of monolingual speakers of indigenous Amerindian languages.[1] Throughout Latin America bi- and multilingualism are commonplace whether between Spanish and the indigenous languages or Spanish and other languages of colonization, for example, Italian and Portuguese. Indeed, care needs to be taken when interpreting figures relating to proficiency in a second language as there may be wide disparities between the literacy claimed for an individual and their ability, opportunity or desire to use that language proficiently. Spanish represents the language of social mobility and functions as the High variety, used, for example, in education and public administration. The indigenous languages serve as the Low variety used, for example, in the home and among the immediate speech community. Interestingly, this is even the case for Guaraní, a co-official national language which enjoys considerable prestige.

1.1.1 Spanish in Spain

In Spain, Spanish is spoken by approximately 40 million people of whom some 40 per cent are bilingual in one of Spain's minority languages (see Figure 1.2). One of the most distinctive features of post-Franco Spain is its emergence as a decentralized and plurilingual country after a period during which severe, albeit lessening, repression of minority languages was exercised in the interests of achieving a centralized, monolingual state.[2] As a reaction against the linguistic illiberalism of this period typified by Franco's vision of national unity, 'la unidad nacional la queremos absoluta, con una sola lengua, el castellano, y una sola personalidad, la española' (Sala 1991), the Constitution of 6 December 1978 sought to redress the balance and offer a measure of protection to minority languages, henceforth seen as part of Spain's rich cultural diversity. Nevertheless, the Constitution clearly established Spanish as the official state language despite the many compromises apparent in its drafting, and in Article 3.1 declares:

> El castellano es la lengua oficial del Estado. Todos los españoles tienen el deber de conocerla y el derecho a usarla.
>
> (Siguan 1992: 75)

Thus, the intention is clear that monolingualism in any language other than Spanish is not permitted to the Spanish citizen and in effect virtually does not

Figure 1.2 Map of Spain showing linguistic and dialect divisions (based on García Mouton (1994))

exist. Article 3.2 provides for the co-officiality of the various minority languages or *lenguas propias* but only within their autonomous communities and not throughout the national territory. Thus Spanish is still very much the language of majority use in Spain and of Spaniards outside Spain despite strenuous efforts by some minority cultures, particularly the Catalans, to express themselves through the medium of their own language nationally and internationally.

1.1.2 *Spanish as the second language in the United States*

Spanish is currently spoken as a first language by approximately twenty-two million people[3] in the United States. Approximately 60 per cent are Mexican in origin and are concentrated in the south west; Puerto Ricans (12 per cent) tend to live in the north east, and principally New York, while the Cubans (4 per cent) favour Florida. The Hispanics are currently America's fastest growing ethnic community and their numbers are set to rise to 96.5 million by 2050 (*The Guardian*, 16.07.98). This is not without problems as the United States does not have legislation which states that English is the official language of the Union; it has always relied on the desire of immigrants for social assimilation and mobility to consolidate the pre-eminence of English. However, friction is now arising between increasingly monolingual Spanish communities and the English-speaking majority, particularly in the southern states where the Hispanic communities are concentrated. In some major cities such as San Antonio and Los Angeles up to one half of the population is of Hispanic descent, and even in New York one tenth of the population is Spanish-speaking.

In the 1990s the Republicans have been active in seeking official status for English and in seeking to limit the use of Spanish mainly outside but also inside the home and they have promoted an 'English only' movement. They are particularly unhappy about the proportion of the state budget devoted to mother-tongue maintenance programmes. However, there has been active resistance on the part of the Spanish-speaking community. In 1994 a federal tribunal ruling in the state of Arizona turned down state legislation prohibiting state employees from using the Spanish language in their official duties on the grounds that it infringed the first amendment of the Constitution. This enabled, for example, administrators in the state administration to deal in Spanish with complaints about healthcare services by Hispanic citizens who were not fluent in English. In San Antonio (Texas), the ninth biggest city in the US, a resolution was passed in 1995 proclaiming the city to be bilingual. In June 1998, however, the Spanish language received a major setback with the United States' most populous state, California, voting for what was called Proposition 227. The effect of this was to end more than twenty years of bilingual education for immigrant children. While the aim is to prevent Hispanic children from being ghettoized and marginalized through lack of proficiency in English, it will be interesting to chart its effects on the use of Spanish amongst the Hispanic community and the status of the language within the US.

1.1.3 Spanish in the rest of the world

Equatorial Guinea

Equatorial Guinea is a fragmented nation on the west coast of Africa with a tiny population which stood, in 1991, at some 335,000 (Quilis 1992: 205).[4]

Spanish was recognized as the country's official language in 1928 and is spoken in general use and as a lingua franca alongside seven indigenous Bantu languages, a Portuguese creole and an English pidgin. After a period under the dictatorship of Macías where indigenous languages, and particularly *fang*, were promoted, independence in 1979 heralded a time of improved relations with Spain and an increase in the use and status accorded to Spanish. However, in the 1990s, there appears to be a rejection of Spanish in favour of French as a trade language, primarily for geo-political reasons; in September 1997 the President, Teodoro Obiang, announced that French would become, in the short term, the official language of the country (*El País*, 23.9.97).

Guam

Guam, a United States colony in the Pacific Ocean, has a Spanish-speaking minority numbering some 780 in 1980 (Rodríguez-Ponga, in Alvar, 1996a: 245) and who are of Spanish, Latin American, United States and Philippine origins. Additionally, some vestigial Spanish is spoken by older speakers of the predominantly Spanish-lexified creole, *chamorro*, used by almost 30 per cent of the population, with further speakers in the northern Marianas Islands and in the United States. On Guam *chamorro* enjoys co-official status with English.

North Africa

Until the independence of Morocco in 1956, Spanish was a co-official language alongside Arabic in the northern part of the Protectorate. Since independence Spanish has ceded ground to French although Quilis (1992: 201–2) has noted a recent slow recovery which he attributes to Spain's policy of creating a number of Spanish-medium primary and secondary schools, to access to Spanish-language broadcast media, and to nationalist feelings in part due to what is perceived as preferential treatment given to French-speaking areas. Radio Rabat provides five hours a day of its broadcasting in Spanish and the French-language newspaper, *L'Opinion* provides a weekly Spanish-language supplement, *Opinión semanal*.

Spanish is also spoken in the Spanish enclaves of Ceuta and Melilla where approximately 15 per cent of the population is Spanish in origin and by a small number of elderly Spaniards resident in Tangier where a proportion of the population is bilingual in French or Spanish and Arabic or trilingual in all three.

Andorra

Here the official language is Catalan which coexists with Spanish, predominantly in the south, and French, predominantly in the north. There are approximately 33,000 users of Spanish.

Ladino or Judeo-Spanish

Ladino or Judeo-Spanish is a variety of Spanish preserved by the Sephardic Jews who were expelled from Spain in 1492 and went to settle not only throughout Europe, North Africa and the Middle East but also further afield, for example to the United States of America. Currently the largest Sephardic communities are located in the United States and Israel. However, in these communities, as elsewhere, *ladino* is being ousted by the dominant language, English or Hebrew, or, in the case of a second language, modern Spanish. Harris (1996) notes that it is used by increasingly fewer speakers, mainly those over the age of seventy, and in increasingly fewer domains, often only with elderly relatives, for entertainment, for example for singing *romanzas* and as a humorous or secret language. She further argues (1996: 45) that 60,000 would be a generous estimate of the number of proficient Judeo-Spanish speakers, of whom none are monolingual speakers of the language and none are passing it on to their children. The United States has given very little institutional support for the language and support in Israel is diminishing. Here, until recent years there had been a thriving press in *ladino* but today this has dwindled virtually out of existence, as have audiovisual broadcasts, with the radio station *Kol Israel* being pressed to give up its Judeo-Spanish broadcasts. There is one journal written completely in Judeo-Spanish, *Aki Yerushalayim*, still in existence mainly due to the efforts of its editor, Moshe Shaul. Indeed, it is to be expected that within a generation this variety of Spanish will disappear as a living language.[5]

Philippines

Spanish in the Philippines is, according to Lipski (1987b), in the process of language death with, already by the 1980s, few proficient speakers under the age of forty. Despite three hundred years of Spanish presence in the Philippines the language did not strike firm roots. It never became a trade language and the Church and the administration preferred to use indigenous languages in pursuit of their goals. From 1898 onwards, the United States, which had won the Philippines from Spain, invested heavily in English-language programmes and precipitated the decline of Spanish. In line with the linguistic reality of the country, the Philippine Constitution of 1987 effectively demoted Spanish from its previous status as a co-official language alongside English and Filipino (Tagalog), stating that it, along with Arabic, 'shall be promoted on a voluntary and optional basis'. It is difficult to obtain the precise numbers of Spanish speakers as censuses do not distinguish between speakers of Spanish and of Spanish-based creoles (*chabacano*).[6] Despite being brought to the Philippines via Mexico, the Spanish spoken here is closest to central and northern Peninsular Spanish and has few features, mainly lexis, from Hispanic America. Interestingly, and unlike the case of Philippines English, there is virtually no geographical variation within Philippines Spanish. It is spoken primarily by Euroasian *mestizos* of Hispanic descent, many of whom have close relations with Spain, who have tended towards intermarriage over the centuries. This group, primarily descended from wealthy landowners, has struggled to keep the language alive but now appears to be losing the battle. In addition to these speakers, there are others who have acquired levels of proficiency through education (until recently Spanish was a compulsory subject at university), profession (many lawyers have high levels of proficiency insofar as the legal code is drafted in Spanish, there are also a number of convents run by Spanish orders), or simply language contact (knowledge, for example, of Philippine Creole Spanish (see 9.0.1), facilitates a passive understanding of the language).

1.2 The status of Spanish as a world language

As we have seen, Spanish is clearly a world language in terms of the number of countries in which it has official status and in terms of the numbers of speakers who use it as a first language or as a prestige variety. Its centre of gravity lies clearly in Latin America where the bulk of its speakers live; in Europe, in terms of native speaker numbers it comes after Russian, German, French and English. Nonetheless, it should be recognized that Spain, one of the faster developing economies of Europe (*The Economist* 1996: 93–100), is proportionally much stronger economically than any of the other countries where Spanish is an official language. Spanish has been and is being developed to cope with virtually all fields of knowledge[7] and the rapid assimilation of foreign forms into the language allows speakers to use Spanish in domains such as information technology, where speakers of other languages (e.g. German, see Clyne 1995: 9) are more constrained to use English. Nonetheless, if we look at its presence in the international arena where English has long been dominant, we are struck by the fact that the use of Spanish is much less prominent than French, which has considerably fewer native speakers worldwide. Nonetheless, French is present as the official language in a larger number of countries (see Ball 1997: 6) and France itself has always been active in promoting the language. As we shall see, the use of Spanish is declining within the major international and European organizations and efforts to promote the language have been restricted by economic constraints.

1.2.0 Economic and cultural potential

While Spanish does not enjoy the economic potential of the English, German and Japanese language communities, it does enjoy a significant cultural presence. The Nobel prize for Literature has been won on ten occasions by Spanish speakers (José Echegaray y Eizaguirre (Spain, 1904), Jacinto Benavente (Spain, 1922), Gabriela Mistral (Chile, 1945), Juan Ramón Jiménez (Spain, 1956), Miguel Angel Asturias (Guatemala, 1967), Pablo Neruda (Chile, 1971), Vicente Aleixandre (Spain, 1977), Gabriel García Márquez (Colombia, 1982), Camilo José Cela (Spain, 1989) and Octavio Paz (Mexico, 1990). Spanish language literature and most significantly the Latin American literature of the 'boom' generation of writers of the 1960s and 1970s has been widely translated, for example, Mario Vargas Llosa, Gabriel García Márquez. Furthermore, foreign-language production ranging from influential academic writing through computer software to world literature is often rapidly translated into Spanish and there is a thriving industry of film subtitling and dubbing into Spanish.

1.2.1 *Supranational organizations*

French and English always 2 princ. language.

International organizations

Despite being one of the six official languages, along with English, French, Russian, Chinese and Arabic, used by the major international organizations such as the United Nations, the World Health Organization, UNESCO, NATO, there is evidence that these organizations increasingly work in the two main languages of English and French.[8] Furthermore, it appears that budgetary constraints are frequently responsible for limiting the quality and quantity of translation into the other official languages (*El País*, 27.4.95) and the time it takes for the translations to become available. In the OECD the two working languages are English and French and only occasionally are translations commissioned into Spanish. In the FAO, where the countries of Latin America have a particular interest and where the third working language is Spanish, there have been cuts in staffing which had a proportional effect on the quantity of translation into Spanish. Similar cuts have affected the WHO. As regards those organizations where the principal working languages are English and Spanish, for example, the Pan American Health Organization and the International Organization for Migration (*El País*, 27.4.95) there is increasing computer-assisted translation which, despite post-editing, produces a variety of Spanish which is structurally calqued on English.

The European Union

As in the case of the international organizations, those languages which are deemed official, twelve with the accession of Austria, Finland, Norway and Sweden to membership on 4 May 1994, in theory enjoy equality of status. Nonetheless, the EU tends to work in six of the Union's languages, English French, German, Spanish, Italian and Dutch with, here again, the two principal working languages being English and French. Interestingly it is French which figures most prominently in European bureaucracy and which frequently provides the source text from which translations are made into Union languages. In 1986 and 1998 Spain actively protested about the inclusion of German as a third principal language, boycotting the work of the Union. The Spanish position favours the use of either two, six or all of the languages of the EU. In Chapter 7 we shall investigate the influence of French and English on the Spanish of officials and parliamentarians.

Latin America

Mar-Molinero (1997: 26) notes the use of Spanish in the promotion of a supra-national identity of *Pan-Hispanidad* through organizations such as the *Comunidad Iberoamericana de Naciones*, the aim of which is to provide a counterweight to the economic and cultural power of the United States and also the emerging European Union. The *Instituto de Cooperación Iberoamericana* similarly promotes a panhispanic identity.

1.2.2 The promotion of the language

While Spanish is the first foreign language in schools in the United States where it is studied by more than 60 per cent of pupils, it is much less widely studied in Europe where English and French followed by German have been the principal foreign languages studied and where organizations such as the British Council, the Alliance Française and the Goethe Institute, with considerable financial backing from their respective governments, have been active in promoting the the study of their language. In effect it is the fourth most studied language after English, French and German, although less than 5 per cent of secondary school pupils studied Spanish compared with approximately 60 per cent studying English and 40 per cent studying French. However, according to Moreno, in Marqués de Tamarón (1995: 211), these figures appear to be on the increase. In 1991, in anticipation of the *Quinto Centenario*, the Spanish government decided to follow suit and made a heavy investment in improving and consolidating its promotion of Spanish abroad, which had previously been the responsibility of three different ministries. Indeed, a number of the pre-existing centres dated from the time of the Franco regime when they were set up to meet needs generated by emigration in the 1960s. Thus, the government created thirty *Institutos Cervantes* throughout the world, ranging from New York through Cairo to the Philippines. Since 1991, financial constraints have proved a curb on expansion. Nonetheless, thirty-five centres are projected to be in operation by the millenium and a *Centro Virtual Cervantes* is available on the World Wide Web, widening access to the centre's resources.

Outside Europe and the United States, Spanish is taught at secondary and in some cases tertiary level in a number of African nations south of the Sahara (Cameroon, Ivory Coast, Gabon, Senegal, Mali, Benin, Burkina Faso, the Central African Republic and the Republic of Congo). It is expanding, from a narrow base, in Australia and New Zealand. It is also taught in Asia, in the Republic of Korea, in Taiwan and enjoys a particularly strong presence in Japan. In Brazil, in the southern cone of Latin America, mainly as a result of the creation of the economic alliance Mercosur and the general economic upturn of the region, it is the second foreign language studied after English. Despite a shortage of qualified teachers, the study of Spanish is rapidly expanding (Moreno in Marqués de Tamarón 1995: 219–23).

1.3 Conclusion

Otero, in Marqués de Tamarón (1995: 267), on the basis of six indicators which have broadly been dealt with above, ranks Spanish as the third most important language in the international arena after English and French.

We have seen that the main strengths of Spanish lie with its number of speakers worldwide, who are to be found in their vast majority in the Americas, with its rich cultural and publishing traditions, and also with the willingness of its speakers to adapt and use it for an ever-increasing number of purposes. The Spanish-speaking world, within the limits of its resources, has promoted language change in the field of new technologies. This is in striking contrast with France which initially did little to promote the development of French to meet the language needs generated by the expansion of the Internet while at the same time proscribing borrowing from English through its language-planning law, the *Loi Toubon*. This led to language innovation emanating from the competing standard of Quebec. The weaknesses of Spanish lie in its inability to compete with the dominant languages, principally English, within international organizations and in the modest economic circumstances of many of the countries where it is spoken. Future economic growth in Latin America could prove to enhance the status of the language; similarly it will be interesting to monitor developments in the status of Spanish as a minority language in the United States. Providing that the 'English only' lobby fails in its objectives to relegate Spanish to an increasingly marginalized position, it is in the United States where there is the greatest potential for a real increase in the status accorded to the language, with individuals of Hispanic descent coming to occupy positions of power in politics and industry.

2 The standardization of Spanish

As it is our aim in this book to look at variety and change in the Spanish language it is appropriate to start by examining the process of language standardization. This process has the aim of uniting the Spanish-speaking world around agreed usages, thereby standardizing *el español culto*, or educated Spanish, wherever it is used.[1] It is certainly an area in which speakers and writers of the language feel they have a stake, if we are to judge by the frequency with which issues to do with language 'correctness' are debated in the public domain and the strength of feeling shown by participants. Language standardization can never, in a sense, be complete and it is only in the area of written language, particularly orthography, that an appreciable measure of standardization has been achieved. Nonetheless, as Butt and Benjamin (1994: vii) note, Spanish is relatively unstandardized compared to, for example, French and German, where the metropolitan French and west German varieties have hitherto functioned as the international standard, and even to English, where there are the two principal competing norms of US and British English. In the case of Spanish, whose speakers span a greater part of the world than any other language but English, the official language of twenty-one countries, a minority language of considerable and rapidly increasing presence in the US, and third working language in the United Nations, as Lipski (1994: 136) notes, there is no one agreed panhispanic norm. While Castilian might once have enjoyed considerable prestige, in educational and literary circles, as 'the language of Cervantes', this has long ceased to be the case. Over recent decades it has been the literary boom in Latin America which has produced the most influential Spanish-speaking authors whose distinctive voices are adding to the rich variety of written Spanish. Indeed, in the field of literary Spanish the differences between the Spanish on either side of the Atlantic can be so great that the Chilean writer, Jorge Edwards, has been led to use George Bernard Shaw's dictum to refer to Spanish as '*el idioma común que nos separa*' (in El País, 11.6.94: 37).

Moving from the written to the spoken language, what is considered standard spoken Spanish admits of a good deal of variety in practice, with, here even more so, the existence of competing **prestige norms** being evident. As Lipski[2] notes, while the prestige norm is frequently based on the speech of the educated inhabitants of the capital, in larger, more complex societies where there is greater fragmentation, the norm may be located elsewhere. This is the case in Spain, where the educated, urban Spanish of Old Castile and principally of the cities of Burgos and Valladolid is more likely to be adopted as a standard than that of the capital Madrid, where high inward migration from other parts of Spain and population mobility in general lead to the co-existence of many varieties of Spanish. As for Latin America, Lipski notes that the speech of the Colombian capital Bogotá is losing much of its former prestige and that, in Peru, while the prestige norm of the capital Lima is still implicit in news media and education, in reality this norm has ceased to exist and there is a fragmentation into popular varieties. Mexico City and Buenos Aires manage to impose their prestige norm over considerable heterogeneity. Once we reach the level of non-standard spoken Spanish, divergences may be such that certain varieties are mutually incomprehensible.

A positive attitude on the part of a particular speech community towards a given variety is crucial in its establishment and maintenance as a prestige norm. Consequently, it is instructive to sketch a broad overview of attitudes towards different varieties of Spanish. In 1985 Lucinda Hart-González, working amongst the Spanish-speaking population of Washington DC (USA), comprising nationals from a wide number of Spanish-speaking countries, explored the attitudes of two groups, on the one hand South American and on the other Central American and Caribbean, towards eighteen national varieties. Both groups coincided in placing Argentinian and Castilian [3] as the varieties with highest prestige and Salvadorian as that which enjoyed least prestige; however, there were considerable disparities in between with the Central American group rating Colombia highly and Cuba towards the bottom of the scale, and the South American group reversing this rating. Solé (1991), however, shows that the inhabitants of the capital city of Argentina accord their own variety low prestige, especially when compared with the Spanish of Castile.

Notwithstanding this diversity in varieties and attitudes, authorities in language, whether socio-political or linguistic, are active in determining the 'correct' spelling, grammar, vocabulary and pronunciation of the language with the aim of maintaining one variety of the language which will function as a common currency throughout the Spanish-speaking world. The *Real Academia Española* (RAE) was set up in 1713 to define a prestige standard and was to be joined, over the next two centuries, by academies representing other Spanish-speaking countries. However, in the twentieth century these academies have been perceived to be out of touch with actual language use. Their gradual loss of prestige and influence, and with it the role of Spain as the arbiter of internationally 'correct' Spanish, has not left a vacuum. The last three decades have witnessed the rapid rise of the *libro de estilo* (style guide) which attempts to regulate Spanish usage in the media in general and, in the case of the audiovisual media whose viewing public is drawn from across national boundaries, to delimit a mutually comprehensible variety of Spanish. Commercial interests clearly also play a role in the unification of Spanish as it is a desire to market their product as widely as possible that has prompted the producers of *culebrones* (television soap operas) to employ language consultants who, in the words of the Spanish linguist Gregorio Salvador (*El País*, 29.1.94: 55) '*están haciendo mucho por preservar la unidad lingüística*'. And in the 1990s, in the age of the electronic book, it may be the producers of computer software, such as Microsoft based in the US, who will determine language standards as they produce on-line dictionaries, grammars, spelling and style checkers designed to capture the widest possible market share (see J. A Millán, *El País*, 10.10.92).

At the same time, a changing social reality has led public institutions to question their discourse practices in an attempt to bring them more into line with the image they wish to project. Thus, in Spain, for example, guidelines have been produced to enable the public administration to project a new democratic relationship between the individual and the State and avoid the archaic and formulaic jargon of the state bureaucrat with its unfortunate Francoist associations. Language lobbies, such as those advocating, for example, non-sexist discourse, have also had a not inconsiderable role to play in language standardization and the issue of 'political correctness' is as alive in the Spanish-speaking world as it is elsewhere.

It is therefore interesting to look more closely at these authorities and the elements of variability in Spanish that they are trying to suppress, for a knowledge of what is currently held as standard is a useful yardstick against which to examine non-standard forms of language. Moreover, a knowledge of what is currently proscribed, or what was proscribed yesterday but no longer is today, can often provide a window into the changes which are currently taking place in the language. It is not, however, the aim of this chapter, or of this book, to replicate unnecessarily information easily available in dictionaries, grammars and histories of the language and which is amply covered elsewhere.

In this chapter we concentrate on what is considered to be 'standard Spanish' and examine common deviations from this using exemplification from the style guides which are principally, albeit not exclusively, concerned with **prescribing** usage in the written language. We also briefly concern ourselves with language description by providing an overview of a number of projects which have been concerned with collecting language data to enable linguists to refine **descriptions** of language in use. These will provide some of the examples examined in later chapters.

2.0 Language Prescription: from the academy to the style guide

2.0.0 *The rise and fall (and rise?) of the academies*

The standardization of Spanish arguably goes back to the endeavours of the thirteenth-century scholar and king of Castile, Alfonso X.[4] During his reign he promoted a variety of Castilian, probably based on the speech of the educated speakers of Toledo, raising its prestige by using it exclusively for affairs of state and extending its functions for use in new domains by developing its grammar and vastly increasing its vocabulary. This was done externally through borrowing from Latin and Arabic and internally through word formation. Thus it became the medium for scientific, legal, administrative and other writings. Antonio de Nebrija's *Gramática de la Lengua Castellana* (1492), written during a period of relative calm in the development of the language, provides a summation of the Spanish of the Middle Ages and predates a period of rapid expansion and change in the Spanish language over the sixteenth and seventeenth centuries. It should nonetheless be noted that this regional norm, which in the sixteenth century passed from Toledo to Madrid, has ever since been in competition with that of Seville.

The next major reform of the Spanish language took place in the eighteenth century with the creation in 1713, in the service of the Crown and hence the State, of the *Real Academia Española* (RAE) whose role was to purify and preserve the Spanish language in the words of its crest, '*limpia, fija y da esplendor*'. In a spirit of linguistic purism, the RAE was to reform the spelling of Spanish (*Orthographía Española* first published in 1741), provide a grammar of the language, the *Gramática de la Lengua Española* (first published in 1771), and produce and periodically update a dictionary, the *Diccionario de la Lengua Castellana*, more commonly known as the *Diccionario de Autoridades* (DRAE), first published, in six volumes, between 1726 and 1739. Since its inception, the RAE has counted on support from notable Latin American philologists, and independence from Spain did not break these links. Thus the nineteenth century saw the creation of associated national *academias*[5] in Latin America and the Philippines which continued well into this century. In 1951 Mexico was a prime mover in attempting to bring together the *academias*, and these, in 1961, formed the *Asociación de Academias de la Lengua Española*. In 1985 its ranks were swollen by the acceptance of the first *academia* from a country where Spanish was not an official language, the *Academia Norteamericana de la Lengua Española*.

The *Asociación*, which meets quadriennially, provides a more powerful forum than those provided by its constituent *academias* in which to promote the use of the Spanish language internationally and to preserve its unity. It also acts as a conduit for lexical items frequently used in member states to be proposed for inclusion in the DRAE. Thus, it has been active, for example, in supporting the *academia* of Colombia in its successful attempt at lobbying for the enactment of a *ley de defensa del idioma* proscribing the use of foreign language terms in official documents. Similarly, it supported the *academia* of Puerto Rico in its, initially successful but later overturned, attempt to have Spanish declared the sole official language of that country. At the same time, it appears to be the most trivial issues which create the greatest amount of debate within the association. For example, a debate raged for a number of years over whether to align Spanish alphabetical practice with that of the international community, rather than retaining 'ch' and 'll' as separate letters of the alphabet.[6] Its resolution required, in 1994, a change in the Association's Constitution in order to impose the majority view that, at a time of increasing globalization, alignment was indeed necessary. However, the decision was taken in the face of intense opposition by a number of Central and South American states who viewed the issue in terms of United States cultural hegemony. Indeed, until the right of veto by any member state was abolished in 1994, most proposals for change could easily be blocked, making the Association a force for conservatism rather than change.

The selection and 'authorization' of those elements of the Spanish language considered suitable for use by the educated speaker might have appeared a realistic task in the eighteenth century when there was still a relatively small number of educated speakers of Spanish and when the authority of the *madre patria* was unquestioned. However, it is clearly untenable in the twentieth century when, in the field of science and technology alone, some 30,000 new terms are introduced annually (Sánchez Albornoz, *El País*, 12.9.94) and when Spanish is spoken by approximately 400 million individuals throughout the world. While the DRAE has never been as prescriptive as its name *Diccionario de Autoridades* implies, it has, in the minds of many, become a byword for prescriptivism and this has often shaped the debate surrounding it.

The DRAE is undoubtedly considered to be the most authoritative dictionary in the Spanish-speaking world and remains a reference point, for good or ill, for the work of a majority of lexicographers of Spanish. Haensch (1997: 162) observes that this is in direct contrast with France where authority lies with dictionaries produced by private publishers such as Larousse, Hatier, Hachette and Robert and not with the dictionary produced by the *Académie Française*.

The DRAE, currently in its twenty-first edition, has come in for a great deal of criticism over recent decades from language purists and non-purists alike: from the purists because it is seen as admitting to the hallowed ranks of authorized language elements of the vernacular considered unseemly, for example, the inclusion of *gilipollas* (silly bugger) in its special 1992 centenary edition; and from the non-purists, because it is seen as completely out of touch with current language practice. According to its current director, Fernando Lázaro Carreter who was appointed in 1991, it continues to include language which no one has ever actually used while the language that speakers and writers do use is only very partially covered (Lázaro Carreter (1985) quoted in M. García-Posada, *El País*, 9.11.92). However, with the appointment of this director who is convinced of the need to work towards a descriptive rather than a prescriptive grammar, based on the teamwork of full-time specialists along with the application of information technology, it would appear that the 1992 edition marks the end of an era. For Spain, following the example of countries such as Britain, Germany and Italy, has invested heavily in the creation of a *Corpus de Referencia del Español Actual* (CREA) and aims to create a database of some 200 million words by the year 2000. Thus the CREA will provide examples and frequencies of current usage, primarily written but also spoken, from Spain and the countries of Latin America on which descriptive dictionaries and grammars of usage can be based. It is hoped that CREA will thus aid lexicographers working on future editions of the DRAE to address what is perceived in Latin America as a bias towards Peninsular Spanish; not only is common usage in the Latin American countries poorly represented in the DRAE but the dictionary takes Peninsular Spanish as the norm and marks certain items as *americanismos*, failing to mark equally items restricted to the Peninsular as *españolismos*, such as *ordenador* (*computadora* in Latin America), *judías* (*alubias* in Latin America).

As regards the *Gramática*, the Academia's most recent complete grammar dates back to 1931. This was followed with the publication in 1973 of an updated outline grammar, *Esbozo de una nueva gramática de la lengua española*. Finally 1994 saw the publication of the *Gramática de la lengua española*, the result of ten years' work by the linguist Emilio Alarcos Llorach. Within the confines of prescription inherent in a grammar of this kind, the DRAE's most recent authorized grammar declares itself, in the words of its author, to be '*sin espíritu dogmático*'. The most recent orthographic reform dates back to the publication, in 1952, of the *Nuevas normas de prosodia y ortografía* which were made prescriptive in 1959.

It was partly because of the deficiencies of the DRAE, that the other major dictionary of the Spanish of Spain has enjoyed such a degree of success. It was the work of one woman, published for the first time in 1966, the *Diccionario de uso del español*, more commonly known by the name of its author, the *María Moliner*, which provided a far more thorough description of the Spanish language despite its obvious idiosyncrasies, for example, the decision to group references by families rather than strictly alphabetically. Indeed, Gabriel García Márquez has said that María Moliner '*había sido capaz de convertir un diccionario en una obra del realismo mágico*' (quoted by G. Salvador, *El País*, 30.4.94). However, given the nature of the enterprise, this dictionary has not been updated and consequently its usefulness is diminishing with time. Other influential monolingual dictionaries have been the *Diccionario ideológico* by Julio Casares and the *Vox* series, the first in Spain to use computerization.[7]

In addition to general monolingual dictionaries, there is for Spanish, as is the case for all major languages, an abundance of more specialized works ranging from the bi- and multilingual dictionary through dictionaries of place names or technical terms to dictionaries of euphemism and taboo. One area of particular concern to us here is that of neologisms, where two principal volumes can be cited. In 1994 the *Diccionario de voces de uso actual* (Alvar) appeared in Spain in an attempt to remedy one of the most pressing shortcomings of the DRAE, that is the absence of many frequently used neologisms, such as *hora feliz* for 'happy hour', and the lack of information about contemporary semantic extensions, for example, *canguro* to refer to a babysitter or child-minder. The dictionary, based on a corpus from a variety of newspapers and journals (e.g. *El País, ABC, Cambio 16*) has the virtue of providing the lexical items in context and attributing them to source. There is also the Italian-Spanish bilingual dictionary *Nuevas palabras-Parole nuove* (Calvi/Monti) which, according to Haensch (1997: 84) has the merit of including a number of lexical items which are no longer strictly neologisms but which have failed to be included in standard dictionaries.

In Latin America, the weight of a prescriptive tradition appears to have been less constraining although a lack of financial resources has limited lexicography in large parts of the subcontinent and meant that much work on Latin American Spanish has often been carried out by projects financed elsewhere. Already in 1973 the preparation of a major *Diccionario del español de México* was set in train based on a corpus of over two million words taken from the speech and writing of Mexicans of different socio-economic groups and different geographical areas. Computerization has allowed frequency counts and concordancing resulting, in 1982, in a *Diccionario fundamental del español de México* (2,500 entries) with a new edition in 1993 and, in 1986, in a *Diccionario básico de México* (7,000 entries). A complete dictionary is currently awaited.[8]

Outside Latin America, since 1976 the University of Augsburg in Germany has, under the direction of Günther Haensch and Reinhold Werner, been engaged in the preparation of a series of dictionaries, coming under the generic title of *Nuevo diccionario de americanismos*, covering the different national, and within this, regional, varieties of Spanish in the nineteen Spanish-speaking countries of Latin America. These are to be descriptive with ample information on current usage, and at the same time contrastive insofar as they will focus on elements which present a contrast with Peninsular usage, providing Peninsular synonyms where such exist.[9] In 1993 dictionaries for Colombia, Argentina and Uruguay were published with the fourth volume, on Cuban Spanish, in preparation. In addition to this major German project, in Tokyo an ambitious project entitled *Proyecto Internacional: Español del mundo* or VARILEX directed by Hiroto Ueda and Toshihiro Takagaki aims to compile a dictionary of the different lexical varieties from a number of cities from Spain and the Spanish-speaking countries of Latin America.

Perhaps it is not surprising, given the great variety of Spanish and its rate of change, that there should be a strong desire for clear prescriptive statements on issues concerning modern usage of educated Spanish in the form of 'diccionarios de dudas'. The two most influential of these guides are Manuel Seco's *Diccionario de dudas y dificultades de la lengua española* (first edition in 1961, tenth edition in 1998) and Francisco Marsá's *Diccionario normativo y guía práctica de la lengua española* (first edition, 1986). Seco clearly sees his role as that of a linguistic policeman patrolling the linguistic unity of the Spanish-speaking world, advising on which regional and idiosyncratic uses of the language must henceforth be eradicated and ensuring that those neologisms and borrowings which are accepted meet appropriate criteria of Spanishness (1986: XIV). Marsá's book is a clear reaction to the trend away from prescriptivism towards descriptivism. For example, he is disturbed that the RAE does not prescribe pronunciation and indeed gives no guidance on the thorny issue of /ll/ versus /y/ (1986: 28).[10] Indeed, what he does provide is an up-to-date statement of linguistic purism. In this, deviations from the norm are seen as defects. One such defect is argued to be *seseo* (1986: 30), the majority pronunciation in the Spanish-speaking world and accepted into the norm by the *II Congreso de las Academias de la lengua española* in 1956. He is also an advocate of conservative spelling and maintains, for example, against majority usage throughout the Spanish-speaking world, that the 'foreign' letter 'k' should be rendered by the Spanish 'qu', for example, *quilo* and not *kilo* (1986: 37).

Butt and Benjamin (1994: vii) note the loss of prestige of the RAE in the second half of the twentieth century and point to correctness being decided by the consensus of native speakers. However, it must be noted that this consensus is actively influenced by other agencies for prescription, notably the style guide for the media, administration and the professions. Not only has this form of prescription constituted a growth area in the latter part of the twentieth century but it is interesting to note that it is customary to find members of the discredited RAE playing a prominent and authoritative role in this new field of publication, the area which will provide the focus of the following section of this chapter.

2.0.1 Standardization and the media

The need to avoid the fragmentation of Spanish and to staunch what is frequently viewed in fairly militaristic terms as an invasion of foreign items has, for many years, been a concern of the Spanish-language press. Not surprisingly, given the proximity of its northern neighbour, the United States, the first Spanish-language style guide was brought out in Cuba.[11] While its principal aim was to provide a standard translation of neologisms and to alert the reader to potential problems caused by false friends, for example, the need to translate 'editor' by *director* (*de un periódico*) and not *editor* (publisher), it also sought to advise on the use of grammar. Nowadays, most major press agencies have Latin American desks, increasingly located in Latin America. A number of these, in recent years, have responded to the need for standardization by producing in-house style sheets or guides. One of the first and certainly the most influential attempt to standardize news production was initiated by the Spanish-language press agency EFE, which has since become the leading press agency in the Latin American subcontinent (*El País*, 16.10.95) in conjunction with the *Instituto de Cooperación Iberoamericana* (ICI) in 1980. In addition to providing general guidelines for the presentation of items of news in its handbook *Normas básicas para los servicios informativos*, EFE created in 1980 its own *Departamento de español urgente* (DEU) which would: examine a selection of news output, identify grammatical, lexical and orthographical errors and advise on correct usage, supply transcriptions and transliterations of foreign terms, propose Spanish equivalents for neologisms originating from outside the Spanish-speaking world, and generally respond to queries from users of EFE's press services. The result of their work was the *Manual de español urgente* (MEU), a style guide which was to be updated annually on the basis of the weekly reports the Department would supply to the various organs of the media. The influence of the Academy on the Department, made up of a permanent staff of philologists and a Style Advisory Council (*Consejo Asesor de Estilo*), is considerable. Three of the seven members of the Council are drawn from the RAE, with its director, Lázaro Carreter, occupying the chair, and one from the *academia* of Puerto Rico, the two remaining members being a practising journalist and an academic. The general usefulness and quality of this style guide as well as the need to cater more comprehensively for the needs of Latin America were recognized in 1989 in the *Declaración de Madrid* (Fundación Germán Sánchez Pérez 1990: 257) signed by representatives of the world's major press agencies where participating bodies were encouraged to contribute to the updating of MEU and where there was a call to produce a style guide for use by all agencies. This call has since been re-iterated in the 1998 Zacatecas Congress held in Mexico.

In *Normas básicas para los servicios informativos* EFE had provided journalists with a number of brief rules-of-thumb regarding language usage: they were to use the DRAE, or the dictionaries by María Moliner and Julio Casares and they had to avoid using terms which did not appear in them. In the field of radio broadcasting, where, especially with the use of satellite broadcasting, the target audience may be drawn from across national boundaries, they were to avoid country-specific terminology. For example, *coche* (Pen.) and *carro* (L.A.) were to be avoided in favour of the neutral *automóvil*. Such concerns are of particular relevance to Latin America where the role of radio broadcasting, particularly in rural areas with high levels of illiteracy, takes on an importance unimaginable in Europe[12] and where a clear need is perceived to avoid the use of terms which not only might not be comprehensible in certain countries but which might actually cause offence. For example, the use of the verb *coger* is considered taboo in a number of countries, Mexico, for example, where its use is reserved for acts of fornication.

In the MEU there is a clear recognition of the pace of language change and the role of the media in promoting and disseminating new forms. It is of the view that indispensable neologisms abound even though they have not yet been admitted by the Academy. In line with the principal aim of the Cuban volume, a major concern of the DEU is to regulate the use of Anglicisms and Gallicisms. For example, in the field of sports lexis, the creation *antidoping* (drug testing) should be avoided in favour of *antidopaje* or *control de estimulantes*; *por contra* (from the French *par contre*) should be replaced by *por el contrario* or *en cambio*. Other major areas of concern include standardization of place reference, transcription and transliteration of foreign words and phrases, use of acronyms and advice on selected areas of grammar. For example, journalists should avoid what is seen as an excessive use of the gerund, particularly the 'State Gazette gerund', such as *Mañana se publicará un informe* **regulando** *la exportación de vinos* and the 'weather report' gerund, such as **mejorando** *en el transcurso del día*. Similarly, journalists are enjoined to avoid the use of what is known as the *condicional de rumor* or 'conditional of allegation', such as *El gobierno* **estaría** *dispuesto a entablar negociaciones con ETA* (Agencia EFE 1989a: 58), a construction imported from the French press and also used in Italian.

Over a similar period, in Spain, individual organs of the press have also felt the need to have their own style guides in order to maintain and promote their own distinctive image. The national daily *El País*, was only two years old in 1977 when it produced its first *libro de estilo*. Other major dailies such as ABC (first edition of its style guide, 1993), *El Mundo* (first style guide, 1996), regional newspapers, the Basque *El Correo español* and *El pueblo vasco* and the Catalan *La Vanguardia* (first style guide, 1986) and sports papers such as *El Mundo Deportivo* have produced style guides which are periodically updated. Radio Televisión Española (RTVE), the State television service, produced its *Libro de estilo de los servicios informativos de TVE* in 1985 and the Andalusian channel Canal Sur updated its own style guide in 1997.

Advice ranges from the mandatory, in the case of *El País*, to the strongly recommendatory in the case of ABC. *El País's* style guide, for example, takes a strong line on the use of the conditional of allegation, prohibiting its use outright and sees fit to offer alternatives, for example, '*el ministro parece estar dispuesto . . .*', '*según indicios, el obispo ha establecido . . .*', '*parece ser (o tal vez) que han sido detenidos siete grapos . . .*' (1990: 8). In contrast, ABC's style guide has more modest aspirations, aiming to provide a checklist of standard journalistic usage. While there is a large measure of agreement between the style guides on issues such as the use of the conditional, the over- and misuse of the gerund, and Anglicisms and Gallicisms to be avoided, it is interesting to see how they seek to differentiate themselves from each other in certain crucial areas. Let us take, as examples, the issues of regional politics and non-sexist language use.

While all three newspapers see themselves clearly as Spanish-language newspapers, they show differing levels of acceptance of the use of words and phrases drawn from minority languages, principally Catalan, Basque and Galician, in their reporting. *El País* will accept those which have entered general usage, those which cannot be translated and those which would lose certain connotations if translated (1990: 79). Thus, while in 1980 reference to the autonomous government of Catalonia was to be rendered by the Spanish translation *La Generalidad*, by 1990 *El País's* readership was considered sufficiently acquainted with the institution for it to be called *La Generalitat* with the proviso that journalists should make it clear whether they are referring to the Catalan or Valencian government, both of which use the term. Similarly, in 1980 *abertzale* (Basque nationalist) was to be translated as '*nacionalista*' and by 1990 could be retained in the original form, albeit italicized. The traditionalist ABC, on the other hand, prefers the Spanish translation wherever possible. Interestingly, the *El País* style guide provides a particularly complete reference guide to words and phrases in Basque with suggested translations and cultural notes. In reality, the number of Basque terms with which the general reading public of *El País* is deemed to be acquainted is on the increase, as evidenced by the number of terms which appear without explanation and even without italicization such as *batzoki* (meeting place of the Basque Nationalist Party), *lehendekari* (President of the autonomous government), *ikurriña* (Basque flag). As might be expected, the readership of the Catalan daily *La Vanguardia* is deemed to be acquainted with the Catalan terms used for the institutions within the autonomous community, and therefore the newspaper's policy is to publish in Catalan terms referring the organs of regional government which appear in the Statute of Autonomy (*La Vanguardia* 1986: 176). Nonetheless, the newspaper retains the Spanish translation for words and phrases the use of which is not exclusive to Catalonia alone, for example, 'El Presidente (not President) de Cataluña (not Catalunya)' (*La Vanguardia* 1986: 174) and while it states that Basque should receive the same treatment as Catalan, it nonetheless recommends the use of translation in many instances to avoid miscomprehension. It recommends, for example, the easily intelligible expression *policía vasca* to *ertzaina* or *hertzaina* which are terms which their readers might not know. Thus we are faced, here as elsewhere, with the competing needs of establishing an individual identity through language, leading to greater fragmentation, and that of reaching the widest possible readership, leading to greater unification. At the same time the ideological dimension of language becomes apparent; just as journalists in Latin America may wish to avoid borrowings from English because of the connotations of United States hegemony that are attached, so too within Spain the choice of including or avoiding borrowings from the different minority languages acts as a powerful semiotic, indicating where the newspaper's sympathies lie.

The use of non-sexist language[13] has been a live issue in Spain since the *Transición*[14] and this is also an area where newspapers have adjusted their language use to reflect changes in society at large. Already in 1980 *El País* showed its liberal colours in its attitude to the then vexed question of how to refer to women who occupied what traditionally had been seen as male jobs. It prescribed that terms denoting occupations and professions should agree in all cases with the gender of the person occupying the post, for example, '*la doctora*' (*El País* 1980: 17). The 1990 edition repeats this injunction but warns against what it sees an an over-extension of these principles, i.e. the tendency to make neutral terms such as *modista* agree with a male referent (i.e. to use *el modisto* for *el modista* when journalists would not dream of saying *el periodisto* for *el periodista*). They similarly attacked the tendency to impose agreement on linguistically neutral but semantically marked terms such as *el juez*, advocating *la juez* and not *la jueza*. Interestingly the frequently used '*el modisto*' has now entered the DRAE. Indeed, in a relatively short space of time the usage prescribed above has become standard, with the traditionalist *ABC* espousing the same linguistic policy. However, as we shall see later (2.4), there continue to be wide divergences for a variety of motives from what is currently prescribed as standard. For example, the conservative Spanish Minister of the Environment, Isabel Tocino has invoked her right to be called *el ministro* and not *la ministra*, aligning her language use with her politics.

Interesting as these norms are, it is even more interesting to examine to what extent they are observed in practice. Already, in the late 1970s a widening gulf was opening up between the language used in the press and that codified in the dictionaries of the time. While there has been a considerable effort in the intervening years to bring the main sources of reference into line with current linguistic practice and while the DEU carries out an inestimable service with its updates on a weekly basis, journalists, even from *El País*, where adherence to house norms is mandatory, do not, for whatever reason, necessarily seek guidance at all times. In his brief survey of style guides and their observance, Smith (1995) records a substantial list of anglicisms. In some cases he records borrowings (*los box office*, *los raids*, for example) where a Spanish equivalent is easily available (*las taquillas*, *los ataques*). In others he notes occurrences of what, in the case of *El País*, are proscribed grammatical structures, for example, *en base a* (*hacer la guerra **en base a** consideraciones morales*), non-standard use of the preposition *a*, (for example, *precauciones **a** tomar*), the presence of the conditional of allegation, such as *Savimbi **habría** justificado su ausencia por razones de seguridad*), and the use of the past subjunctive *-ara* (*-ase*), *-iera* (*-iese*) not as a subjunctive but as a stylistic variant of the preterite tense (*. . . la actriz que protagoniz**ase** Flashdance . . .*) (Smith 1995: 83).

Audiovisual broadcasting has also provided a fertile ground for style guides. Like the press, radio and television are often the butts of harsh criticism for their alleged abuse of language, and in Spain the situation is no different although the terms in which the debate is couched reflect national concerns. For example, Fontanillo and Riesco justify their 1994 critique of the media's (mis)use of the spoken language in the name of preserving democracy claiming that '*esforzarse por mejorar el lenguaje y el estilo equivale a crear condiciones más democráticas*' (1994: 8) and maintaining that the future of the *cultura hablada* in Spain is threatened by the twin enemies of *pasotismo* and television. The evidence for their work is taken from the media in the 1980s and provides an ample insight into not only the performance errors common in the spoken language, such as lack of agreement between verb and noun, but also areas where change may be in progress[15] and areas where stylistic preference may conflict with normative syntax (for example, Fontanillo and Riesco do not accept '*la derecha ha llegado a decir que la izquierda no **sabíamos** gobernar*' 1994: 36 where the choice of the first-person plural rather than the grammatically standard third-person singular *sabía* allows the speaker to include him- or herself as part of the referent).

The national television broadcasting company, Radio Televisión Española (RTVE), brought out its own style guide in 1985 under the supervision of V. García Yebra of the RAE with a prologue by Fernando Lázaro Carreter, much of which is a repetition of the advice currently available in other style guides with very little relating specifically to the spoken language. However, with regional broadcasting, the question soon arose of how to express spoken norms for those channels which chose not to adopt the prestige norm of Castile. Canal Sur Televisión, based in Seville and serving all eight provinces of the autonomous community of Andalusia first brought out its own style guide in 1991 in which it seeks to allay feelings of linguistic insecurity which might be felt by its broadcasters. For example, Canal Sur advises its broadcasters not to imitate the pronunciation of Valladolid, given that not only is Andalusian not an inferior variety of Spanish but rather the one of majority use. It urges them to guard against **hypercorrect** pronunciation with the reminder that there is no difference between /b/ and /v/ and rarely one between /ll/ and /y/. While newscasters should not play up *andalucismos*, they should not avoid them either in the interests of a supposedly neutral Spanish. Andalusian should be seen as a repository of many fine turns of phrase of, on occasion, more distinguished ancestry than the standard Spanish equivalent. The guide is a model of tolerance of language variety. It rejoices in the wide variety of accents and only proscribes a limited number of pronunciation variants on account of their stigmatization, for example, metathesis of /l/ and /r/, *branquear* for *blanquear* (1991: 64).

The broadcasting company of the autonomous community of Madrid, Telemadrid, in its 1993 *Libro de estilo de informativos* takes a much more prescriptive approach when it addresses, in considerable depth compared with the other guides available, the issue of what constitutes neutral or standard spoken Spanish in terms of its own audience. It provides an extremely complete guide to prosody and pronunciation, for example, it recommends the retention of intervocalic and word-final [d]:

> En ningún caso el redactor de Telemadrid utilizaría las terminaciones en *-ao* sustituyendo a las de en *-ado*, aunque es un uso frecuente entre políticos, empresarios, deportistas y personajes políticos, quienes habitualmente constituyen la fuente de información. (. . .) No es correcto, por tanto, pronunciar Madrid como Madriz.
>
> (Libro de estilo de informativos 1993: 122)

It also proscribes the reduction of complex consonantal clusters (*solemnidad* not *solenidad*) and its counterpart, hypercorrection (*discreción* not *discreción*), bans synaeresis (*país* not *pais*), and prohibits *seseo* (*ciencia* not *siensia*), *ceceo* (*Casa Blanca* not *Caza Blanca*) and *yeísmo* (*pollo* not *poyo*) with the justification that anyone who engages in public speaking should be able to use both pronunciations correctly.[16] Telemadrid is aware of many differences between spoken and written language and gives guidance on issues which do not bear comment in the written style guides. For example, in hypothetical clauses, broadcasters are to use the *-ra* imperfect subjunctive (*Si yo estuviera en tu lugar* not *Si yo estaría/estuviese en tu lugar*); they are to avoid colloquial fillers such as *y tal y tal* and *y demás*, they are to avoid the non-standard second-person singular familiar ending (*hiciste* not *hicistes*) and they are to use the correct disjunctive pronoun (*detrás de ti* not *detrás tuyo*). As regards intonation, newscasters are to avoid affections such as *el dejo* and *el tonillo*, two non-standard intonation patterns commonly adopted by broadcasters.

Telemadrid is aware that one area of language where the broadcast media come in for a great deal of criticism is that of live sports broadcasting, where the broadcasters are frequently sports and not media professionals and where the heat of the game may do violence to the language. Thus they have devoted a section of their guide to advice for use during repeat broadcasts of sports events. This guide contains, for example, listings of clichés to be avoided, for example, '*el maillot amarillo da alas*' (1993: 282). While recognizing that foreign sports terms are frequently much more easily understood by the viewer, it recommends that during replays broadcasters should introduce the Spanish equivalents suggesting, for example, that terms such as *albatros* (golf) should be rendered as *tres golpes menos que el par* and *green* (golf) should become *césped cercano al hoyo*. Castañón Rodríguez (1997) has identified three phases in the standardization of sports terminology: the first, between 1976 and 1992, related to the inclusion of sports-related advice within more general style guides; the second, between 1992 and 1996, saw the publication of sports-specific style guides under the aegis of Agencia EFE and the Barcelona daily *El Mundo Deportivo*, helped in large measure by work which had gone into preparing for the 1992 Barcelona Olympics, and culminating in the production of *El Mundo Deportivo*'s own style guide; finally, from 1997 onwards, there is the part of the *Proyecto Zacatecas* which aims to create a common sports style guide for the Spanish-speaking world which will be accessible from the Internet. *Proyecto Zacatecas*, in its initial stages, has brought together fifty-one style guides (twenty-one from Latin America) in conjunction with works on the use of Spanish in journalism with a view to achieving a greater degree of panhispanic standardization in the media (*El País*, 10.4.97).

What is interesting about a study of these style guides is not so much the variety of language which they purport to attempt to unify but more the window they provide onto the changes which are currently taking place in the language of the media and to a greater or lesser extent, depending on the particular feature, in the language outside it. For there to be such common accord in combating the 'invasion' of, for example, the conditional of allegation, the excessive use and misuse of the gerund, the prepositional use of *a* (for example, *avión a reacción, en base a*), indiscriminate use of foreign lexis where Spanish terms already exist (such as *fan* for *hincha* in the case of sport if not in that of music), new and unsanctioned usages for Spanish lexis (for example *agresivo* in the sense of *emprendedor* calqued on the English usage), there must indeed be significant numbers of journalists who persist in using them. Indeed, subsequent editions of a style guide can serve to show which battles are being lost and where there has been relative victory. It is significant that, with the exception of changes internal to the Spanish language such as the issue of *leísmo, loísmo* and *laísmo*, or the phenomenon of *dequeísmo*, the two main areas of influence on Spanish appear to be French and English. Furthermore, it is important to note that the change affects not only determined areas of lexis such as, for example, those of sport or financial institutions, but the structure of language itself.[17] What is more, in the case of the Spanish national daily *El País* which espouses the greatest degree of prescription, actual practice is not always aligned on the injunctions of the style guides. Indeed, the whole area of borrowing, not only from the minority languages of Spain, but more importantly from English, is one where journalists deviate widely from recommended practice.

2.0.2 Standardization in public administration

One domain in Spain where change in the use of the Spanish language has been actively and effectively promoted at institutional level has been within the Public Administration, whose use of language under the Franco regime had become a byword for verbose obfuscation of an archaic variety and a butt of humour for satirists. As Tinsley (1992: 24) notes, historical factors compounded by the ideology of the Nationalist regime had produced a 'highly centralized organization which valued hierarchy, position, and strict adherence to regulations as a safeguard against corruption' and which expressed its relationship with the public (the citizen in a position of dependence on a superior authority) through a variety of language characterized, amongst other features, by set formulae, archaisms, excessive use of honorifics and contorted syntax.[18] Furthermore, citizens faced the added barrier of having to adopt this register themselves in their dealings with the Administration. For example, they were expected to end requests and applications with the following set formula:

> *Es gracia que espera alcanzar del recto proceder de V.I. cuya vida guarde Dios muchos años.*

(Tinsley 1992: 24)

As Tinsley notes, the formula abounds in religious overtones with the citizen firmly placed in the position of a supplicant before a quasi-divine authority.

In other western countries there had already been significant institutional reform with a view to achieving the democratic ideal of an administration which would act as a public servant to citizens who had rights as well as duties. Furthermore, during the 1960s and 1970s there had been major language reform designed to reflect this changing reality. The Plain English movement had had a significant impact in English-speaking countries and France had seen fit to reform the use of French in its public administration. One of the challenges which faced Spain during the Transition was to create a new relationship between the citizen and the state which would reflect new democratic procedures. With the adoption of a new constitution in Spain (1978) and devolution of powers to the autonomous communities (1981), those communities with a minority language rapidly drafted guidelines regulating the use of their language in public administration. However, during this period the central government expended its energies on modernizing the institution itself and neglected, to a large extent, the reform of its discursive practices, assuming that these would simply, in time, come to reflect this new social reality.

However, as Tinsley notes (1992: 29), whether due to inherent conservatism, laziness or a desire for self-aggrandizement, these changes failed to materialize as quickly or as systematically as might have been expected. Thus, during the 1980s administrative documents drafted in Spanish looked increasingly archaic and out of tune with modern aspirations.

This mismatch between the new 'corporate image' and the language used to express it entered public consciousness to the extent that repeated complaints brought the issue to the attention of the *Defensor del pueblo* (Ombudsman). His 1988 report to Parliament was severely critical of the language used by Spain's administrative services and called for a thoroughgoing reform of its discourse practices, not least to ensure that information of a public nature was much more intelligible to the average citizen.

The direct result of this damning report was the publication, in 1990, of the *Manual de estilo del lenguaje administrativo* by the *Ministerio para las Administraciones Públicas*. The style guide, based on the analysis of a corpus of 302 representative documents produced by the Public Administration, constitutes a compendium of what is considered to be good practice. Essentially, it follows the outline of the style guides for journalism we have looked at previously – i.e. it deals with orthography, grammar, lexis and style, as well as including a whole, separate section on the use of non-sexist language[19] – and uses many of the same sources (for example, the DRAE). However, unlike the media style guides, one of its primary functions is not to regulate an influx of neologisms into the language but rather to eradicate a whole range of archaisms rarely found nowadays in Peninsular Spanish other than in administrative texts. Further functions, as we have mentioned above, are to achieve greater economy of expression, greater clarity and to project a more acceptable relationship with the average citizen.

Thus, for example, in the fight against archaisms, forms of address such as *Vuestra Ilustrísima* (*V.I.*) and *Vuestra Senoría* (*V.S.*) are to be replaced by plain *Vd.*; the use of the future subjunctive is discouraged, for example, *para la sanción administrativa que* **procediere** in favour of the present subjunctive (*que* **proceda**); overuse of the conjunction *y* is to be avoided, such as *Deberá hacer efectiva la multa en papel de pagos al Estado y en esta Delegación* where the conjunction is superfluous; a pseudo-legal use of participles, particularly the present participle, is similarly discouraged, for example, *Que en los antecedentes* **obrantes** *en la secretaría . . .*; likewise, the so-called '*gerundio del B.O.E.*' is to be avoided (for example, *Escrito* **recogiendo** (= **que recoja**) *la firma de todos . . .*; and, furthermore, the tendency to create, willy-nilly, adjectival neologisms with archaic overtones, such as *las listas* **cobratorias** (= **de cobro**) is to be curbed. The lexical section clearly marks what are considered to be archaisms, for example, the use of the impersonal pronoun *ello* as in **ello**, *no obstante*.

As regards economy of expression and consequently the streamlining of correspondence, superfluous administrative formulae and rhetorical flourishes are to be eschewed. For example, writers should plainly state that they have made an error rather than recur to the verbosity of, say, *En relación con la reclamación que, con fecha . . ., formula Vd. . . . me cumple participarle, después de . . ., que, efectivamente, no fué correcta la forma de entrega . . . toda vez que . . .* Similarly, circumlocutions such as *Se procederá a **dictar resolución de revocación*** be replaced by the simpler *Se procederá a **revocar*** and, indeed, verbal rather than nominal forms are to be preferred throughout, for example, *avisar* is better than *dar aviso*. **Muletillas**, or empty formulae, such as *Lo que se hace público para su general conocimiento . . .* and superfluous adjectives such as *la **(preceptiva o necesaria)** autorización* are to be avoided.

In the interests of clarity officials should endeavour not to deviate from standard word order, avoiding, for example, *Comunico a Vd. que **por esta dependencia se han dictado con esta fecha**.* The guide notes the tendency in administrative documents to prepose adjectives more frequently than is habitual in other documentation, such as *normas legales de **pertinente** aplicación*, and to use an abundance of adjectives in sequence with no punctuation. Thus it provides the recommendation that, for example, *cuota íntegra ajustada positiva* should appear as *cuota íntegra, ajustada y positiva*. The guide also warns against an overuse of weak personal pronouns, for example, *Para hacer constar que la presente solicitud se recibe sin exhibirse ni acompañarle todos los documentos.* The lexical section provides plain language alternatives for what it considers *cultismos administrativos*. For example, ***tomar** una medida* is recommended for ***adoptar** una medida*.

In terms of the relationship to be projected between citizen and State, as personified by the Public Administration, officials are recommended to avoid the depersonalization of, say, *Esta delegación . . .* and to opt, for example, for the more direct first person *Le comunico . . . .* We have already mentioned the injunction to avoid the use of archaic honorifics such as *V.I.* in favour of the more egalitarian *Vd.* to be used for high-ranking officials and public alike. In instructive documents, officials are required to avoid the overuse of the present subjunctive and the infinitive as imperatives (e.g. *Procédase a la celebración de la misma . . .* and *Señalar con una cruz*), and use instead more direct forms such as *tener que* + infinitive and *deber* + infinitive. The lexical section marks, as affectations to be avoided, formulae such as *En relación con la reclamación, me cumple participarle . . .* and *Suplico a Vd. (que) se digne dar las órdenes*; these express an assymetrical power relationship which the administration is anxious not to project.

The guide also includes a section on the use of non-sexist language drafted in line with the Economic Community Action Plan for Equal Opportunities for Women (1988–90) and the guidelines published by the *Instituto de la Mujer* in 1988.[20]

Unlike articles in the daily press, administrative documents for public consumption and pro-formas for internal use typically have longer production deadlines and therefore a more systematic adherence to guidelines might be expected. However, as Tinsley notes (1992: 28), referring to non-sexist language, recommendations are 'employed patchily and very much according to individual conviction', and elsewhere she makes the point that many of the characteristics of administrative language, for example, the *muletillas*, may serve the function of creating in-group solidarity and an idea of separateness amongst those who work for the institution. This, she says, could explain why, for example, the use of *muletillas* has taken so long to decline despite repeated pressure, including an order issued as far back as 1958 instructing officials not to use them.

In Chapter 7 we shall look at two degree certificates, written twenty-five years apart, in order to see what evidence there is of actual change in discourse practices. We shall also examine a number of administrative and official texts to gauge the extent to which obscure 'officialese' is still to be found.

2.0.3 Guidelines for non-sexist language use

The research conducted in the 1970s into the concept of sexist discourse gave rise in the 1980s, in the industrialized world, to a number of changes in discursive practices, brought about, for example, by the production of publishers' guidelines regulating desirable practice, and Spain was no stranger to this process. It should nonetheless be noted that, once again, it appears to be the autonomous communities of Catalonia and Valencia which were leading the way. However, it was the Council of Europe Programme for Equal Opportunities for Women for 1988–90, approved by the Council of Ministers in September 1987, which provided the major spur to the public sector with its call for all documentation to be reviewed for possible discriminatory linguistic practices.

In the following year, the *Ministerio de Educación y Ciencia* produced, for publishers, materials developers and teachers alike, its own recommendations for the preparation of non-sexist teaching materials, which, while focusing largely on content, also contained a number of recommendations pertaining to linguistic practices, for example, avoidance of the masculine as generic. These recommendations were broadly in line with its perception of the constitutional role of public education as an instrument of social change.

In 1989 the *Instituto de la Mujer*, part of the *Ministerio de Asuntos Sociales*, in line with the same EC initiative, produced, for a wider public, a series of proposals for non-sexist language based on the rationale that, as participation in the job market evolved, linguistic change should accompany it in order to avoid possible discrimination.

However it was not until 1991, when the *Ministerio para las Administraciones Públicas y Asuntos Sociales* launched separately a section of its style guide which was devoted to guidelines for non-sexist language use to be incorporated into Ministry documents from 15 April 1991, that the issue really reached the public domain. The linguistic engineering proposed by the guide was denounced by some: it was '*una perversión sexista del lenguaje*' (J. Aguilar, *Diario 16*, 11.2.91), and the now Nobel Prize winner Camilo José Cela (*El Independiente*, 13.2.91), after satirizing the 'slash form' (*la/el pareja/o*), saw fit to deplore the whole venture in the following terms:

> – Reconforta, es un decir, y también estremece, la verdad es que estremece más que reconforta, la idea que mientras el hombre se mata y mata todo lo que tiene en torno, la administración pública espanola quiere reinventar la gramática, recomponer el espíritu de la lengua y reestructurar los usos léxicos del funcionariado.[21]

Others saw in it a timely document:

> La verdad es que hacía falta. Cuesta poco introducir femeninos en las solicitudes, desterrar la identificación unilateral masculina de cabeza de familia, incluir a la mujer como algo más que cónyuge, etc.
>
> (R. M. Rodríguez Magda, *Las Provincias*, 8.2.91).[22]

However, most ink was expended in lengthy debate about the fine detail of the proposals. So, what were the proposals for non-sexist language use contained in these guidelines? What interests us here is how proposals which have been adopted to a greater or lesser extent throughout western society have been applied specifically to the Spanish language.

The proposals can be broadly grouped into three categories: the use of the masculine as a generic, the assymetical treatment of men and women, and, the most contentious of all, the choice of terms for referring to the professional status of women.[23]

Masculine as generic

In line with the view that the use of the masculine as a generic can lead to the invisibility of women in the public domain, all the guidelines recommend the avoidance of this form. Thus the MAS recommends the substitution of *hombre(s)* by any of the following: *persona(s), ser(es) humano(s), humanidad, hombres y mujeres/mujeres y hombres*, for example, *la inteligencia del hombre* should become *la inteligencia humana*. Similarly, the use of the masculine plural to refer to mixed sex rather than exclusively male groups, obscures the presence of women and consequently should be replaced either by the repetition of both masculine and feminine forms or by the appropriate collective noun, for example, *los profesores* should be replaced by *las profesoras y los profesores* or *el profesorado*). The systematic use of the masculine to refer to the public (e.g. *El abajo firmante . . ., Si se solicita al mismo tiempo el permiso de trabajo (. . .) para él y los familiares que de él dependen,. . .) 'Observaciones del solicitante'* should be avoided through a combination of the above strategies and also through the use of the slash or brackets, such as *Si es separado/a o divorciado/a . . ., . . . o está casado (a) con un (a) español (a) . . .*

Assymetrical reference to women

Sexist discourse practices also lie in the ways in which reference is made to men and women. For example, there is the use of different terms to refer to men and women of otherwise equal status, for example, *Se designa Instructor a **Don** José . . . y Secretaria a la **Sta.** Alicia . . ., jefes de Sección y Negociado, respectivamente, del Gobierno Civil de . . . .* The honorifics *Señora* and *Señorita* define the women in terms of their relationships with a man (only *Señor* (and not *señorito*) is used to refer to the man), as does the use of *Señora de* + husband's surname rather than *Señora* + own surname. There is also the systematic tendency to refer first to the man and then to the woman, such as *Ponga una V, M o una X, según sea **varón, mujer** o razón social.* The recommended forms are: the observance of strict symmetry of reference (e.g. *Don/Doña*); the use of *señora* + surname for all women regardless of marital status (the abbreviation *Sa.*, an equivalent of the Anglo-Saxon Ms, is proposed, in a footnote, by the *Instituto de la Mujer*, but would appear not to have caught on), and alternation in the order of referring to males and females. Traditionally, the terms *varón* and *hembra* were used to refer to specific men and women; while *hembra* has fallen into disuse, *varón* is commonly used. This being the case, the guide condones its alternation with *hombre*, despite any resulting dissymmetry.

Terms referring to the professional status of women

Traditionally, terms used to refer to high-status professional posts were masculine, essentially because their incumbents were male. Thus, for example, *el alcalde* was used to refer to the (male) mayor and *la alcaldesa* to refer to his wife. This used to be the definition provided by the DRAE. As women increasingly entered the professions, they tended to be referred to by the masculine form, *el médico*, in some cases to differentiate their professional status from that of the wife of the professional and in others to avoid the pejorative or colloquial overtones attaching to the feminine form (*la poetisa, la estudianta*). In time this usage came to appear anachronistic, and the feminine form started to be used (*la médica*) as well as a hybrid form (*la médico*), linguistically anomalous but retaining the distinction between woman as professional and as wife of a professional. The guidelines all recommend the systematic use of feminine forms, such as *Juana Valmez, médica, o Secretaria de Estado, o directora de orquesta o Embajadora, o gobernadora, o concejala, o alcaldesa* when the postholder is a woman. Here is where the guides have come in for the greatest criticism; while it appears perfectly acceptable to feminize masculine forms, the feminization of forms not linguistically marked for gender, for example, *juez, gerente, jefe, conserje*, is seen by some, although not the DRAE, as doing violence to the language. It is interesting to note that forms like *jueza* were standard in a number of countries, such as Peru, long before the current debate arose.

All the style guides we have looked at have acknowledged a need to address the question of non-sexist discourse, ranging in their response from the inclusion of a separate section (public administration) to declaring it, along with dehumanizing discourse, such as the use of *caso* for *paciente*, a matter of personal style (medicine). However, let us look at some instances of current language use to see what changes there have been in practice.

Non-sexist discourse practices

Guidelines of this kind generally follow, to a certain extent, changes in discourse practices and are only ever as successful as their practitioners are willing for them to be. Some, such as the feminization of terms referring to the professional status of specific women have permeated society as a whole, including many of those which originally provoked the greatest protest, although their application may be haphazard. Fuertes Olivera (1992: 161) points to linguistic turbulence in the press where masculine, feminine and 'mixed' forms may be used, sometimes within the same article or within the same paper, for example:

> *Margaret Thatcher . . . continuaba como* **primer ministro** (*El País*, 24.11.90)
> **La Primer Ministro inglesa** *visitó . . .* (*El País*, 23.11.1990)
> **La Primera Ministro británica** *inauguró . . .* (*El Norte de Castilla*, 23.11.90)
> **La primera Ministra británica** *calificó . . .* (*El País*, 2.3.1990)
>
> (Fuertes Olivera 1992: 160)

Indeed, the expectation is that terms denoting professional status should reflect the sex of their referent (thus *el modisto* is frequently preferred to *el modista*) and it is now newsworthy that a woman student of information sciences in the Universidad Complutense in Madrid is unable to obtain a copy of her degree certificate with the title *licenciada*, rather than *licenciado*, despite a ministerial decree of 28 March 1995 requiring faculties to adopt non-sexist practices (*El País*, 21.11.95). Newspapers such as *El País* tend to ensure that terms which are marked for gender (i.e. ending in 'a' or 'o') reflect the gender of their referent although unmarked terms such as *concejal* show greater variability (*la concejal/la concejala*).

However, the generic masculine still abounds in commercial and semi-administrative literature and terms such as *el abonado, Sr. Propietario, el usuario, el representante, el cliente, apreciado* GM (*Club Med*) abound. Indeed, as we have already seen in the case of the press, it is possible to find examples of sexist and non-sexist practice in the same document. For example, on a certificate attesting the periodic inspection of gas installations, the customer is referred to throughout as *el usuario* while the person who has carried out the inspection is referred to as *la persona competente*.

Other uses, for example, parallel terms such as *los profesores y profesoras* and the alternation in precedence between masculine and feminine, while being adopted in some official documents, have not generally become part of the discourse practices of a wider public, no doubt due to their general unwieldiness. However, they do, in some contexts, enjoy a semiotic value of progressiveness and allow, for example, politicians to appeal directly to, say, the woman voter through *Ciudadanas, ciudadanos*. In addressing Parliament, members, for example, will use the non-gender-specific, and elsewhere archaic, *Señorías*, or alternatively, *Señoras y señores diputados* and rarely the masculine generic *Señores diputados*.

Dictionary entries have changed significantly over the past four decades, and the sexism inherent in the following definitions *comadrón: cirujano que asiste a la mujer . . ./comadrona: mujer que tiene por oficio asistir . . .* has, in general, been replaced by parallelism. Similarly, feminine forms of the nouns now appear and in the case of terms unmarked for gender the designation 'f.' appears in addition to 'm.'

While change is, by the nature of things, patchy and more readily adopted by some sectors of the speech community than others, it can be said that there has been considerable effective change regarding the terms used to denote professional status. We shall return to considering this issue in our examination of language in use in Chapters 6 to 8.

2.0.4 Standardization in science and technology

A significant area where language change appears to be taking place rapidly due to the influence primarily of English, but also, to a much lesser extent, French, is that of science and technology. We have already mentioned (2.1) the potential role of information technology in imposing new standards through on-line language services such as style-checkers. Now that computers are no longer a domain for specialists, language innovation from this field is permeating general language use. Medicine is also a field where the language of a specialism undergoing rapid development is similarly in a process of ferment and where there is popularization of this change whether through the media or through direct contact of the public with medical services. We shall briefly examine these subject areas, as the issues they raise can be easily applied to the wider domain of science and technology.

In the field of medicine, as in the case of the media, a perceived need to standardize usage and the absence of external authorities (the DRAE, as might be expected, lags significantly behind change in this field) has generated the production of style guides by the profession itself. Its style guide, *Medicina clínica: manual de estilo*, contains a lengthy section on medical language and, in addition to dealing with standard problems of written expression, tackles a number of areas of particular relevance to the profession.

For example, where the norms of Spanish orthography (see 3.2) come into conflict with WHO norms for naming pharmacological products, it is the latter which hold sway, for example, *ketoconazol* and not *quetoconozol*. Indeed, in the case of new medicines, the authors of the guide note the difficulties inherent in attributing gender and suggest, as a rule-of-thumb, masculine if the word ends in *o*, as in *el ciprofloxacino*, feminine for *a*, as in *la zidoviduna* and, in most cases, masculine if the word ends in a consonant such as *el diázepam*.

A further problem for the profession is what to do with calqued adjectival and nominal compounds, derived from English constructions, such as *estafilococos meticílin-resistentes* (methicillin-resistant staphylococci). Although, according to the guide, these should be adapted to Spanish syntax, for example, *los estafilococos resistentes a la meticilina*, the authors are realistic about the likely success of this strategy and concede that if they are used they should not be hyphenated, for example, *insulinodependiente* (as is the case in Spanish in general, e.g. *drogodependiente*) unless they contain an acronym such as *cromosoma-Ph-negativo*, or a proper name, e.g. *Coombs-positivo*, although the hyphen may disappear over time as the proper name is lexicalized such as *gramnegativo*. Whether this reflects lexicalization within Spanish itself or a calque of a process already complete in English is questionable. Another 'problem' of wider relevance than merely the domain of medicine is that posed by the English prefix 'non-' and the suffixes '-free' and '-like'. The solutions suggested by the guide are in line with Spanish syntax: *linfoma no hodgkiniano* ('non-Hodgkins lymphoma'), *libre de enfermedad* ('disease-free'), *similar al lupus* ('lupus-like').

In the area of lexis, while the guide supplies Spanish equivalents for a number of commonly used borrowings from English and French some of which have been naturalized such as *randomizar* from English (they suggest *aleatorizar*) or *despistaje* from French (they suggest *detección, hallazgo*), it also recognizes that a number of borrowings have already entered Spanish and are no longer amenable to hispanicization such as *proteínas de shock térmico, test* (plural, *tests*), *spray*. As we shall see in Chapter 4, the features we have discussed here are not restricted to this field alone but parallel trends within the Spanish language in general.

In the field of computer terminology, change is much more rapid and much less standardized than in the case of the professional field of medicine. At the time of writing approximately 90 per cent of communication on the Internet takes place through the medium of English and a fraction of the remainder through that of Spanish, with the result that many Spanish-language users are operating through what some purists refer to by the derogatory *ciberespanglish*. It is true that even the most widely used terms such as 'the Net' give rise to a wide variety of Spanish terms ranging from *(el) Internet*, through *la malla* and *la red* to the inventive *la urdimbre*. The *-(e)ar* ending (see Chapter 4) has generated verbs such as *printear, deletear, down/uplodear* and the auxiliary verb *hacer* has provided *hacer clic* and *hacer exit*. Given the need, in the first instance, to promote a common equivalent for frequently used terms such as 'the Net' and the desire, in the second, to promote words which are Spanish rather than English in origin, there are constant attempts to channel usage. For example, in 1987, the Spanish Ministry, *El Ministerio de Relaciones con las Cortes y de la Secretaría de Gobierno* produced a *Vocabulario normalizado de informática* which remains a major resource for the DEU along with the more recent *Glosario básico de Internet* (Fernández Calvo 1996). However, these works are, given the pace of change, inherently obsolescent, and glossaries are increasingly becoming available on line where they can be updated on a regular basis.

2.1 Language description: oral and written corpora

It is clear from these style guides which, in the majority of cases are of similar utility either side of the Atlantic, that there is a panhispanic educated norm with only slight variation. This means that, for example, the Spanish used in a quality daily newspaper in Mexico, such as *Excelsior*, differs little from that of one from Spain, for example, *El País*.[24] What is more, the audiovisual media can appeal to audiences throughout the Spanish-speaking world using a norm which is being strengthened rather than weakened by facility of communications and globalization in general. Alongside this, there is a whole mosaic of varieties of Spanish, many of which are under-researched to the extent that, even simply in geographical terms, there is little agreement on boundaries between principal dialects.

With the advent of technology, principally the tape recorder, the task of documenting the many different varieties of Spanish has become incomparably easier, more comprehensive and more reliable than the efforts of the early dialectologists who relied on memory and written notes or those linguists who relied on stylized representations of speech in the novel or the play. At the same time there has been a move away from a concentration on the written language and on an idealized model speaker, which largely informs the **prescriptivist** view of language which we have examined in the preceding section, to investigating actual speakers in actual communicative contexts and to **describing** their behaviour. The RAE's *Corpus de Referencia del Español Actual* (CREA), composed of written texts from journalism, literature, science and technology as well as recordings of naturally-occurring and broadcast speech, is testimony to this change of focus.[25]

Of course, there had always been an interest in the spoken language, but this had mainly been the preserve of traditional dialectologists who sought out the 'purest' varieties of the language in remote rural areas where their informants tended to be elderly, illiterate male peasants whose language had not been affected by contact outside their own village. The early linguistic atlases (e.g. *Atlas Lingüístico de la Península Ibérica* (ALPI) (1962) were based on interviews with informants such as these while later ones broadened their scope to include female and urban informants. ALPI, which only gave rise to one published volume (1962) mainly devoted to phonetic variation has been followed by a number of more influential regional studies, principally the *Atlas lingüístico y etnográfico de Andalucía* (ALEA) which has been the reference point for studies of southern Spanish and also atlases for the Canaries, Aragón, Navarra and Rioja, Cantabria, Castilla-La Mancha and Castilla y León.

In Spanish-speaking America there have been a number of atlas projects, principally the *Atlas lingüístico de México* (1990) as well as atlases for Puerto Rico, southern Chile and Colombia, with work in progress on Uruguay, Argentina and Ecuador. There is also a major project, the *Atlas Lingüístico de Hispanoamérica*, directed by two Spanish linguists Manuel Alvar and Antonio Quilis, which aims to use the same methodology throughout Latin America.

However, in addition to primarily rural dialectology there has been increasing interest in urban varieties of Spanish. Foremost amongst studies of urban Spanish has been the ambitious *Proyecto de estudio coordinado de la norma lingüística culta de las principales ciudades de Iberoamérica y de la Península*

Ibérica. The idea for this project, presented by the distinguished Puerto Rican linguist Lope Blanch in 1964, was initially to address what was seen as a neglect of Latin American urban varieties of Spanish, although soon Spanish cities were also included amongst the urban centres to be investigated. As Lipski (1994: 155) notes, the vast majority of Spanish-speaking Latin Americans are urban dwellers. The cities participating in the '*norma culta*' project were finally to be Barcelona, Bogotá, Buenos Aires, Caracas, Havana, La Laguna/Santa Cruz de Tenerife, La Paz, Lima, Madrid, Mexico, Montevideo, Panama City, Quito, San José, San Juan de Puerto Rico, Santiago de Chile, Santo Domingo and Seville, and the corpora obtained have in many cases provided a basis for numerous studies of spoken Spanish. In the case of Spain, the work carried out in Seville has generated the most complete studies. While the methods for obtaining the corpora were virtually identical for all the participating cities, although the methodology used then does not always find favour with linguists today, the use made of them has responded to the different needs, resources and interests of researchers involved. According to Cortés Rodríguez (1994: 62), while principally Mexico but also Madrid and to a lesser extent Buenos Aires and Caracas have focused on morpho-syntactic features, Cuba, Puerto Rico, the Dominican Republic and Panama have preferred to focus on the phonetics of their variety of Spanish, particularly the pronunciation of /s/. There has been a limited amount of work on lexis, principally on terms imported from French, English or the indigenous languages of Latin America.[26]

Despite limited resources, work is still going on to fill in the gaps left by the *norma culta* project; the concentration on selected cities has left others uncharted, such as those in the southwestern United States, and has neglected the vast rural areas in between both in rural United States and in regional Mexico, the concentration on the educated speaker has meant the exclusion of other groups. These new studies are in a position to exploit improved technology, for example, better quality and more durable recordings than those of the *norma culta* project, and to learn from some of the methodological shortcomings of previous works.

Other studies include the *Atlas Lingüístico de Hispanoamérica*, currently under preparation under the direction of Manuel Alvar and Antonio Quilis, and a number of smaller-scale linguistic atlases (Mexico, Costa Rica, Ecuador, Uruguay and Argentina).

These corpora concentrate primarily on user variation and seek to enable investigation of differences and similarities between speakers from different geographical areas and, in some cases, different socio-economic and socio-cultural groups. More recently, there have been attempts to build corpora on the basis of variation in use. Such is the case of the *Val.Es.Co.* (*Valencia español coloquial*) group's corpus,[27] which provides a rich sample of primarily informal conversational Spanish as well as material for those interested in user variation.

Notwithstanding the limitations of these ambitious corpora, they have proved the basis for considerable study of Spanish spoken in the late twentieth century and a number of the works derived from them will be cited in the pages that follow.

2.2 Conclusion

From what we have seen in Chapter 2, it would appear that the style guide and the desire for standardization which it represents are a major defining feature of the Spanish-speaking world in the late twentieth century. Leading professions ranging from the media to medicine espouse the need to standardize practice within their field. Even the Roman Catholic church in the United States, where those of Hispanic origin make up more than a third of practising Catholics and constitute a fast-growing community, has, after fourteen years of work, agreed on a common prayer book for its Spanish-speaking faithful using shared Latin American norms, such as the use of the address form *ustedes* rather than the Peninsular *vosotros* (*El País*, 18.11.97). The focus of this chapter has been mainly on the pressures for conformity with a number of imposed norms; yet at the same time it has enabled us to gain some insight into the tensions towards fragmentation which exist. It has also principally been focused on the use of written Spanish, primarily in formal situations. However, we have also given a brief account of a number of projects which seek to describe the language, mainly in its spoken form and by a wide range of speakers. Some of the data from these projects will resurface in Parts II and III where we look respectively at variation and change in the language system and how this system is exploited by speakers and writers.

Part II

Spanish: variation and change

In Chapter 2 we saw how Spanish, like many other world languages, is subject to a number of competing prestige norms relating to where the 'best' Spanish is considered to be spoken. These are generally located in the principal centres of influence of the Spanish-speaking world, i.e. the capital cities of its major countries. The differences between these varieties, while significant in distinguishing one from another and as markers of national identity, may not be very great indeed in terms of their phonology, lexis or syntax. And yet there may be quite considerable disparities between the different varieties in terms of status, whether internationally or within their own countries. Alongside a broad uniformity in educated Spanish, there is considerable diversity in the Spanish spoken and also written by the different speech communities which make up the Spanish-speaking world. We already saw how the codified norms which do exist come under pressure to change from the actual discourse practices of language users and also how, in many instances, attitudes towards this change may be negative even well after the change in question has entered the standardized code.

In the chapters which make up this part of the book we shall look at the phonetics and phonology, the orthography, the lexis and the morphosyntax of Spanish, not to describe in detail each of the principal standards (at this level of analysis, these are amply described in other works) but rather to look at the main axes of **variation** in the standard, which may or may not coincide with national boundaries, and also to examine salient variants which may in time affect the standard code promoting language **change** as well as other variants which, being stigmatized, are unlikely to enter the standard code. It should be borne in mind, nonetheless, that this focus on difference rather than similarity will mask what these standards have in common. Some readers may feel that disproportionate attention is paid to non-prestige varieties, or what is commonly known as 'bad Spanish'; nevertheless many of the forms discussed in these chapters are used by countless speakers of the language on a daily basis. Nonetheless, this book could usefully be read in conjunction with a grammar of standard Spanish (such as Butt and Benjamin 1994; Alarcos Llorach 1994).

The pace of language change and the extent of variation depend on the level of language examined. **Phonetically**, it is possible to detect change over a period of some decades; the pronunciation, for example, of newsreels of the 1940s can easily be distinguished from that of today. Studies of speakers, aided by the tape recorder, whether in real or 'apparent' time can reveal change in progress. **Orthographically**, change tends to occur in the wake of spelling reforms which may take place at an interval of hundreds of years or mere decades. What is more, prescriptivism appears to have been at its most effective in the standardization of spelling with virtually no variation between educated writers throughout the Spanish-speaking world. It is in the **lexicon** that change is most evident and most rapid, for, in an era of rapid cultural and technological change, neologisms are constantly in demand. Of course, while many of these may be ephemeral and may never enter the standard lexicon of the language, there are nonetheless very many which do. Also geographical variation is extensive and regional idiom abounds in literature. However, with increasing globalization and dialect levelling there may be a greater uniformity of lexical use. Finally, in the area of **morphosyntax** change is slowest and variation least apparent, for example, the verbs *ser* and *estar* have been in competition for centuries with the latter only very gradually eroding the functions of the former. While language contact is frequently adduced as a reason for language change, it is interesting to note that many of these changes appear to be affecting not one, but a significant number of regional varieties of Spanish at the same time.

3 The phonetics, phonology and orthography of Spanish

In this chapter we shall be concerned with the **phonology** and more specifically with the **phonetics** of Spanish insofar as it relates to the **pronunciation** of different varieties of the language. As Lipski (1994: 9) points out, '[t]o the Latin American person on the street', it is the *acento* which most readily identifies Spanish dialects, . . . '. He also points out that despite this diversity 'even the most rustic and isolated dialects spread out over thousands of miles share a greater similarity (and almost mutual comprehensibility) than Peninsular dialects circumscribed by a tiny radius' (1994: 45). Nevertheless, with dialect levelling in Spain this must be the case to a lesser and lesser extent.

Factors related to speakers – such as their geographical provenance, socioeconomic group, gender, ethnic group, level of education, rural/urban, age – and to the circumstances in which they speak – formally or informally, to in- or outgroup members, and so on – may explain variations in pronunciation not only between different speakers but within the same speaker. In the light, therefore, of the enormous variation which does exist, all we can do here is to examine primarily the educated norm (*norma culta*) mainly in a formal context but also in informal speech and make the most general of observations about the principal differences between the Castilian norm, located by some in urban Madrid and by others in Valladolid/Burgos, and the variety shared to a greater or lesser extent by the vast majority of Spanish speakers who do not share this norm. We shall make reference to broadcast speech while at the same time recognizing that as a speech style it differs substantially from everyday speech both in pronunciation and in its characteristic intonation patterns. Nonetheless, the disparities between the broadcast word and everyday speech of a particular country can give some insight into what features are thought particularly desirable. We shall also focus on some salient areas of difference, particularly where there is evidence that change is in progress.[1] In the second part of the chapter, we shall focus on the **orthography** of Spanish and on recent and proposed spelling reforms. For although Spanish is arguably one of the major languages where spelling most closely reflects pronunciation, there are constant demands for this correspondence between orthography and pronunciation to be made even closer.

3.0 The phonology of Spanish

It is useful, at this point, to provide a brief **phonological** description of Spanish which respects the two main varieties of Spanish, Castilian and Latin American, the latter also shared by most of southern Spain and the Canary Islands. In doing so, it is important to point out that a phonological system seeks to describe patterns of functionally distinctive sound found in a language and, as such, is necessarily an idealization of one particular variety. We shall use as appropriate the symbols of the International Phonetic Alphabet (see Figure 3.1) and conventionalized spelling. We shall represent phonemes (i.e. the minimal sounds in the language system) by the use of slashes, /f/, use square brackets to represent pronunciation, [f], and use underlining to represent spelling, f.[2]

Both Castilian and Latin American Spanish have a relatively simple system of vocalic phonemes just with five (as opposed to six for Catalan, seven for Italian and sixteen for French).[3] In both systems there are two semi-vocalic glides [j,w]. As regards the consonant system, the now generalized loss of /ʎ/, retained as an allophone of /j/ by some speakers in some contexts, has, brought the Castilian system into line with that of Latin America. However, unlike Latin American Spanish, Castilian provides for a distinction between the fricative dento-alveolar [θ] and [s]. Thus Castilian allows a distinction to be made between, for example *caza* and *casa* and between *cocer* and *coser*, which are pronounced identically in say, Mexican Spanish. The latter has generated alternative terms (respectively *acoso* and *cocinar*) to allow the distinction to be maintained.

It should be apparent from Figure 3.2 that there are only two principal phonological differences; between those varieties which distinguish /θ/ and /s/ (mainly Castilian) and those which do not; and between those which distinguish /ʎ/ and /j/ (currently very few) and those which do not. Indeed, the vast majority of speakers of Spanish share a system which excludes both of these variants. Therefore the main distinctions of note, those that make up the *acento* to which Lipski (1994) refers, are at the level of phonetics, i.e. of the distinct realizations that different speakers make of these phonemes. To illustrate this point, let us consider some examples. As we saw earlier, the distinction (in Castilian) between *coser* and *cocer* is a phonological one, as is that between *pollo* and *poyo*. However, the distinction between, say the n of *vengo* and that of *nada*, while phonetically important, is not phonological; nor is the wide variety of pronunciations available for word initial 'y' such as *yo*.

	Vowels		Glides	
High	i	u	j	w
Mid	e	o		
Low		a		

Figure 3.1 Vowels and semi-vocalic glides

	Bilabial		Dento-alveolar			Palatal	Velar
Oral stops							
[− voice]	p		t				k
[+ voice]		b		d			g
Affricates							
[− voice]						tʃ	
[+ voice]						[dʒ]	
Fricatives							
[− voice]		f	θ*		s		
Nasal stops	m				n	ɲ	
Laterals					l	ʎ	
Vibrants							
[+ tense]					r		
[− tense]					ɾ		

Figure 3.2 Consonants (based on Green (1990a: 81, 85))
(* = Castilian only)

3.1 The phonetics and phonology of Spanish: variation and change

As we have said, the phonemes detailed above are obviously not representative of any particular variety of speech and therefore mask a certain degree of variation at the level of realization of actual speech sounds. Research into variation and change in the pronunciations of different speech communities in the Spanish-speaking world is relatively recent, helped of course by the advent of the tape recorder. Given the importance of social as well as geographical factors in this variation, it is hardly surprising that attitudes towards pronunciation are strongly held and influence many of the prescriptive statements made about this area of language use. The subconscious belief, which we shall examine in 3.2, that careful speech ought to reflect as closely as possible the written form and vice versa is widespread. Indeed it figures prominently in the defence of prestige norms against, for example, reduced or eroded variants such as the case of *-ado/ao* or the consonantal clusters discussed below which tended initially to be associated with regional, rural or working-class speech communities. Yet the RAE has never imposed the same norms in the area of pronunciation as it has attempted to do in other areas and in its 1973 *Esbozo* limits itself to providing a description, and not a prescription, of '*los usos que han predominado en Madrid dentro de los últimos cincuenta años en el seno de familias burguesas de antiguo abolengo madrileño y en gran parte de los medios universitarios y cultos*' (Marsá 1986: 25–6).[4]

In this section, we propose to limit ourselves to the discussion of some of the more salient areas of variation and/or change, certainly in terms of the perceptions of the speech communities involved, while recognizing that this can only provide a small snapshot of the immense variety and flux to be found throughout the Spanish-speaking world. The features we shall examine in this section include the realization of intervocalic and word-final d̲, the realization of *s*, *yeísmo*, *seseo/ceceo*, the realization of consonantal clusters, of word-final n̲, and the dipthongization of hiatus. We shall also examine the **suprasegmental** features of stress and intonation.

/d/

The intervocalic /d/ in the variable *-ado* has long been recognized as a particularly salient site for phonetic change in Peninsular Spanish (Díaz-Castañon 1975), and there is evidence that even at the beginning of the century the variant *-ao*, previously associated with the uneducated speaker, was penetrating the informal speech of the educated speaker.[5] Nowadays, the inroads made by *-ao* into standard Spanish are such that *-ado* has become a marker of extremely careful speech and, according to Green (1990a: 82), *-ao* has become standard pronunciation among younger speakers. One of the principal contexts where *-ado* still survives is in the language of the broadcast media although the variant *-ao* does surface here as we noted in 2.0.1. In practice it is not uncommon for newcasters in Spain to weaken and even on occasion to delete intervocalic /d/. Telemadrid's injunction to combat the disappearance of [d] in past participles ending in *-ado* is, in a sense, a last-ditch attempt to halt a process of change which has been affecting Spanish for some time now. While the use of the variant *-ao* may attract considerable opprobrium as it has long been considered vulgar, this has not halted its expansion through speech communities (from the uneducated to the educated, from women to men, etc.) and situations (from the familiar to the formal) and to other linguistic contexts (such as the participle *-ido* or nouns ending in *-ado* such as *Estado*). The change has been such that, in many contexts, speakers view the pronunciation of *-ado* as excessive and even pedantic (Williams 1987: 78). Nonetheless, the social stigma traditionally attaching to the use of *-ao* can lead to **hypercorrection**, where a speaker of a non-standard variety suffering from linguistic insecurity and aiming at producing the prestige norm will overgeneralize rules and produce inappropriate corrections to their speech, the example frequently given being *bacalado* for *bacalao*.

There is also a geographical dimension to the spread of the variant *-ao*. In the Catalan-speaking parts of Spain and in Mexico, Argentina and Uruguay, for example, the pronunciation of *-ado* is standard usage with *-ao* a feature of rural speech. In most of the Caribbean, in Chile, on the Pacific coast of Colombia and in coastal Ecuador there is the tendency for intervocalic /d/ to weaken or disappear entirely (especially in past participles) in standard speech. In some areas, such as Yucatán in Mexico, contact with indigenous languages causes intervocalic /d/ to be realized as a plosive and in parts of the

Colombian Pacific Coast, African influence causes its substitution by /r/ (see Fontanella de Weinberg 1995: 140).

Word-final <u>d</u> is also realized in a variety of ways ranging from its stigmatized (in formal speech) elimination or substitution by /θ/ – whereby, for example, Madrid is pronounced Madrí, or Madriz – to, in Catalan-speaking parts of Spain, its realization as [t], Madrid being pronounced as Madrit. In southern Spain its loss appears to be the norm in all but the most careful speech with *pared*, *red*, *verdad* and *voluntad* being pronounced *paré*, *ré*, *verdá* and *voluntá* (Narbona *et al.* 1998: 163). Both in Spain and Latin America its weakening or loss occurs most frequently in informal speech and amongst speakers from lower socio-economic groups.

/s/

This variable is significant in non-Castilian varieties both within Spain (principally in Andalusia and the Canary Islands) and in large parts of Latin America (for further details see, for example, Alcina and Blecua 1980). As López Morales (1989: 86) notes, it is the most widely studied phonetic element of Spanish. Its principal variants are aspiration (e.g. *lah casah*) or omission (e.g. *la casa* (plural)) in which case there may or may not be a lengthening of the vowel which precedes it.

Variation depends on linguistic factors (for example, the position of <u>s</u> within the word and its function) and on social and stylistic factors (such as geographical provenance, social class and education of the speaker, formality of the speech situation). It is particularly salient in word final position (*la casa* vs. *las casas*) and in contexts where the presence of *s* is clearly functional, marking the difference between singular and plural. However, it is also to be found word-finally in non-plural contexts (*tos*) and word-internally (*mismo*).

Within Spain, aspiration or deletion is predominantly a feature of southern Spanish and in Latin America they are widespread with the exception of the north and central meseta of Mexico, the mountainous regions of Central America, Colombia, Ecuador and Bolivia, most of Peru and parts of north-western Argentina (see Fontanella de Weinberg (1995: 136)).

In many varieties of Spanish, such as that spoken in Las Palmas in the Canary Islands, the position of s within the word is clearly extremely important for determining whether it is retained, aspirated or eliminated. Here, for example, aspiration is the preferred option word-internally (*mihmo*) while in word final position speakers tend towards either aspiration or elimination in broadly equal measure (Samper 1988, in López-Morales 1989). Cedergren, in her study of Panamanian Spanish has shown that one speaker may, indeed, use all three variants:

toaø lah cosah que se habían hecho   everything that had been
                                                      done

se dehpidió de la mamá y de los hijitoø   he said goodbye to the
                                            mother and the little
                                            children
consistía en que los otroø   meant that the others
                                    (Cedergren in Silva-Corvalán 1989: 62)

In southern Spain and Latin America aspiration and particularly the loss of s̱
have tended to be seen as a social class marker with the upper and educated
classes seeking to preserve s̱. Cedergren has shown that in Panama it is age as
well as socio-economic group which determine the use of /s/: speakers who are
over fifty and come from the highest socio-economic group tend to retain s̱;
aspiration is favoured among younger speakers and those from middle-income
groups; elimination is favoured primarily by men from the lowest socio-
economic groups living in rural areas.[6] Sex is also important in determining
the use of /s/. Fontanella de Weinberg (1973), in her study of Buenos Aires
Spanish, found that women were more likely than men to retain the prestige
variant s̱ in word-final position, a finding which has been repeated in other
communities in Latin America.

Thus it is apparent that in certain contexts considerable stigma is attached
to the loss of /s/, which in turn may lead to speakers indulging in hypercorrection and restoring the /s/ to contexts where it never existed in the first
place. Colloquially and jocularly, these speakers are referred to as speaking
'*muy fisno*' (i.e. *muy fino*) (Lozano Domingo 1995: 115).

Lipski (1985: 223) has studied the aspiration and deletion of /s/ in United
States and Latin American broadcasting and notes that nationals from Cuba
and Puerto Rico who frequently weaken or drop the /s/ (this is a characteristic
of even highly educated speakers) will endeavour to retain it when broadcasting. This evidently causes sharp contrasts between their speech and that, for
example, of their interviewees or those who participate in phone-in shows. This
artificial form of speech is relaxed somewhat in sports commentaries due to the
speed of delivery. Interestingly, in the case of Cuba, while the international
broadcasts of Radio Havana retain what Lipski calls the 'homogenised s̱-laden
pronunciation' of the traditional style of announcer, the broadcasts directed at
the domestic market contain similar proportions of deletions as would be
found in the speech of the people. Under Sandinista Nicaragua, no doubt for
ideological reasons of the same order, similar practices obtained.

Yeísmo

Yeísmo or the delateralization of the liquid /ʎ/ to [j], where *pollo* and *poyo* are
pronounced identically, is to be found in most of Latin America. Exceptions
are the whole of Paraguay where the distinction is retained and shows no signs
of disappearing (Lipski 1994: 307), most of Bolivia and parts of Colombia,
Ecuador, Peru, Chile and Argentina although in some of these areas, Bogotá,
for example, it is in swift decline (see Fontanella de Weinberg 1995: 134).

Yeísmo is also standard in southern areas of Spain (according to the *Esbozo*, almost all Andalusia and Extremadura, Ciudad Real, Madrid, Toledo and south of Avila), although the distinction still persists in parts of the Canary Islands, for example the hinterland of Lanzarote. Its spread is, in fact, much wider than grammars such as the *Esbozo* suggest, with [j] having become the standard pronunciation except in some particularly formal contexts or in some rural areas. For example, in some rural villages in the Spanish province of Granada women, and frequently older women, appear to retain /ʎ/ while men tend to adopt a *yeísta* pronunciation (Lozano Domingo 1995: 101–10). Interestingly /ʎ/ continues to be perceived by language purists in Spain as the prestige form (Marsá, 1986: 27–8). For example, as we saw in Chapter 2, the Spanish capital's television channel *Telemadrid* insists that presenters distinguish between /ʎ/ and /j/. However, in practice this is not always the case. It is interesting to note that this is in contrast with Canal Sur's 1991 style guide which enjoins presenters to avoid '*excesos en la corrección; la diferencia fonética entre /ʎ/ y /y/ ya casi no existe*' (1991: 67). In the south, *yeísmo* is so alien to most speakers that the prestige form 'mandatory' in Madrid does not enjoy prestige in, say, Seville, and would be out of keeping with the identity of the regional channel. Similarly, in Latin America, as Lipski notes (1994: 139) '*lleísmo* or the maintenance of the /y/–/ʎ/ distinction is rarely regarded as prestigious or worthy of imitation, despite the fact that this distinction was once part of all "Castilian" dialects'.

What is interesting in Latin America is the wide range of **allophones** available to realize /j/. Lope Blanch detects up to eight alone in the different varieties of Mexican Spanish (Fontanella de Weinberg 1995: 135). In parts of Latin America and amongst some speech communities in Spain, there has been a strengthening of [j] to the fricative [ʒ] or the affricate [dʒ]. Green (1990a: 84) points out that in Spain this strengthening is usually stigmatized: a speaker who pronounces *calle* as [kaʒe] is often regarded as uneducated; one who pronounces it as [kadʒe] is vulgar. The strengthening of [j] (here not a derivation of /ʎ/) is particularly evident, and less stigmatized, in certain initial positions. For example, the first person singular pronoun 'yo' may be pronounced for emphasis as [dʒo].

In Uruguay and southern and eastern Argentina the groove fricative [ʒ] predominates (*zeísta* pronunciation). Lipski (1994: 140) points out that a national/regional pride in this distinctive pronunciation is accompanied by an element of linguistic insecurity. This pronunciation is gaining ground; indeed a study by Fontanella de Weinberg of the inhabitants of Buenos Aires in the mid-1970s showed that women were promoting this change (Fontanella de Weinberg 1995: 136).

Seseo/ceceo[7]

As we mentioned earlier, the prime distinction which can be made between the standard phonologies of Castilian and Latin American Spanish is that the former provides a distinction between /s/ and /θ/, as in *casa* /kasa/ and *caza* /kaθa/, while the latter employs a single sibilant, which depending on geographical area may vary, for example, being a (alveo-) dental fricative /s/ or an apicoalveolar /s/. The term *seseo* refers to the use of /s/ in all contexts. It is the norm in Latin America, in most of Andalusia and in the Canary Islands. In some parts of Andalusia and in some rural communities of Central America and Mexico *ceceo* is found, that is, the use of /θ/ in all contexts but its use is not part of a prestige norm.

In Andalusia existing norms are currently under pressure. In the first place, there are two competing prestige norms, that of Castile which distinguishes between /s/ and /θ/, and the local Seville norm (*seseo*) which does not. The Castilian norm has long enjoyed considerable prestige in Andalusia, particularly among the educated classes and women. In Cordoba, for example, research amongst young people has shown that the Castilian norm is more highly valued (Uruburu 1990: 140); similarly, in Granada it is the prestige norm (Moya Corrall and García Wiedemann 1995: 113). Second, the presence of *ceceo* leads to a complex linguistic situation where in the same city there may be speakers who make a distinction, those who are *seseante* (use *seseo*), those who are *ceceante* (use *ceceo*) and those who are in the process of transition between one system and another. In this case they are generally moving from the non-standard *ceceo* towards the Castilian norm. They use both /s/ and /θ/ but make inappropriate distinctions (e.g. they may pronounce *sucia* /θusia/ (dirty)). This phenomenon, found elsewhere in Andalusia, is called *seceo* or *ceseo* (Narbona *et al.* 1998: 134). The city of Granada, traditionally within the

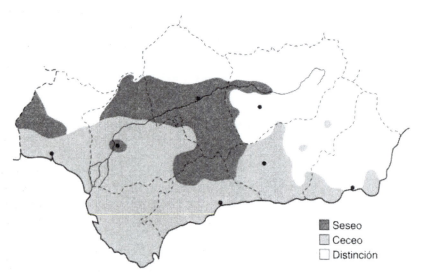

Seseo
Ceceo
Distinción

Figure 3.3 Distribution of *seseo/ceceo* in Andalusia (based on Moya Corral and García Wiedemann (1995))

zone of *seseo* would appear to be moving towards the Castilian norm for a variety of reasons. Moya Corral and García Wiedemann (1995: 208) suggest that in addition to the influx of immigrants from θ/s areas, the flight from the land and the consequent desire of the newcomers to the city to lose their stigmatized rural *ceceo* and adopt the language of social mobility, as well as deepseated feelings of rivalry with Seville, which is now the capital of the autonomous community and which employs *seseo*, all contribute to this interesting change in progress.

Consonantal clusters

In informal speech, there is a tendency in a number of varieties of Spanish to simplify complex consonantal clusters by eliminating or modifying the initial consonant. For example, [ks] may be reduced to [s], e.g. *auxiliar* 'ausiliar' or [gs] *excelente* 'egscelente'; [k] may be reduced to [θ], e.g. *aspecto* 'aspezto', or eliminated altogether, e.g. *doctor* 'dotor'. Mexican Spanish, which, as we have already seen, retains *-ado* as educated usage, similarly retains complex consonantal clusters and stigmatizes their erosion.

Velarisation of final /n/

This is a process which affects significant areas of Peninsular Spanish, particularly Andalusia, as well as parts of Latin America, particularly Central America and the Caribbean. Here word-final, and sometimes syllable-final, n is realized as /ŋ/ and the preceding vowel is nasalized. Thus *jamón* is pronounced as /xamoŋ/. Cedegren has shown that this pronunciation is gaining ground in Panama (in Silva-Corvalán (1989: 75)). Nonetheless, it is to a certain extent a stigmatized pronunciation. This is corroborated by the fact that Latin American broadcasters tend to avoid it to a much greater extent than is the case in popular speech (Lipski 1985: 227).

Other pronunciations generally stigmatized are:

- the **metathesis** of preconsonantal r and l where *una falda larga* may be pronounced *una farda lalga*. In some varieties these phonemes may be omitted altogether (e.g. the final r of infinitives may be omitted); may be aspirated similarly to preconsonantal s (for example [kahloh] *Carlos*); or, when preceding l and n, may be assimilated through gemination, as in [kanne] *carne*. This neutralization of syllable-final l and r is virtually never found in radio broadcasting in Latin America (Lipski 1985: 227) and is, as we have seen in Chapter 2, a practice which Spanish broadcasters are enjoined to avoid.
- the aspiration of word-initial silent h (derived from the Latin f) which leads to, for example, *hambre* being pronounced *jambre*. In some varieties, Aragonese for example, it may even be pronounced as /f/. All these pronunciations, which occur to a greater or lesser extent in many parts of the

Spanish-speaking world, are common in parts of Andalusia and are amongst the very few features of Andalusian dialects proscribed by the regional television service.

It is interesting to note that while there are some features which are stigmatized as non-prestige forms of Spanish throughout the Spanish-speaking world such as *ceceo*, metathesis, and the aspiration of word-initial silent **h**, most being pronunciations used by the rural and urban poor, the vast majority can only be judged within the context in which they are used. For example while *-ado* may still be seen as standard usage in certain formal contexts in northern Spain, in other contexts, far from being a prestige variant, it is merely perceived by many as a pedantic archaism. Similarly, while the ability to distinguish between /ʎ/ and /j/ may, in the ear of some, still retain its role as a powerful social signifier, for the vast majority of speakers of varieties of Spanish it is of no consequence whatsoever and /ʎ/ is certainly not perceived as a prestige variant and in some areas may even connote rustic backwardness. As we have seen, there exist a number of competing norms in Spanish whether at international level (where the Castilian norm appears to be preferred in numerous international organizations), at national level (e.g. the Mexican norm versus the Argentinian one), intranationally (e.g. the northern versus the southern Spanish norms) right down to the norms of the particular subgroups which individuals may belong to. Here it is interesting to note the way non-standard pronunciations are exploited as 'anti-language' by youth and underworld subgroups (see 4.1.3). We have noted, as in the case of *-ado* above, that while certain pronunciations do not enjoy prestige in formal contexts, they may be the preferred pronunciation of educated speakers in all other contexts. We have also alluded to the awareness of prestige norms among speakers, even though these may not be reflected in their own forms of speech, which may give rise to degrees of linguistic insecurity. Indeed, it is such an awareness allied with a lack of knowledge of the prestige variant which gives rise to hypercorrection.

Suprasegmentals: stress and intonation

In the concluding part of this section, we shall look at what are known as **suprasegmentals**, that is features which continue over several successive phonemes and which mould for the hearer the meaning of an utterance. Principal amongst these are intonation and stress.

Stress

Stress refers to the prominence of a particular syllable or syllables within an utterance and is achieved usually by an increase in loudness of the syllable but also by increases in length and pitch. Grammatical stress refers to that stress which is determined by a series of linguistic constraints and over which the speaker has no control. There is also emphatic stress whereby a speaker may choose to give prominence to a particular word (e.g. '*Era GUAPITA pero no guapa*' (She was attractive but not pretty.) Briz 1995: 216, '*una bodega qu'estoy montandoo que va a quedar de puta madre*' (a bar which I'm setting up and which is going to be bloody brilliant. (Briz 1995: 186)). In this section we shall focus on grammatical stress.

A certain amount of variation and change relates to stress assignment.[8] In Spanish, stress falls on the penultimate syllable where the word ends in a vowel, a dipthong, n̲ or s̲. In words which end in a consonant other than n̲ and s̲ stress tends to fall on the last syllable. In effect, there are many exceptions to this tendency, and in orthography (see 3.2) these are marked by an accent on the stressed syllable. When two vowel sounds occur together, their pronunciation as two separate syllables depends partly on whether they are strong vowels (a, o and u) or weak vowels (e and i). In standard Spanish, two strong vowels occurring together are pronounced as two separate syllables for example, *el caos* while other combinations give rise to dipthongs such as *la rabia, la ruina, oigo* although there are many exceptions to this rule which are marked as such in spelling by accentuation. It is common to find in Spain and Latin America dipthongization in what would normally be bi- and trisyllabic words, especially in colloquial and informal speech. For example, *país* may be pronounced *pais, maestro* as *maistro* and *estropearon* as *estropjaron*. It is frequent in Mexico, even amongst educated speakers, to find the dipthongization of /ea/, /eo/, /oa/, /oe/ as in /tjátro/ (*teatro*), /pjór/ (*peor*), /twáya/ (*toalla*) and /pwéta/ (*poeta*), a practice which is stigmatized elsewhere (Lope Blanch, in Alvar 1996b: 82). There are also a number of words where there is no clear standard regarding stress. Such is the case of *período* versus *periodo*. In the audiovisual media there are frequent accusations on the part of media watchers that foreign intonation and stress patterns are affecting those of broadcasters, causing stress to fall on unaccustomed syllables. Fontanillo and Riesco (1994: 175–85) identify, amongst others, the following anomalies: the replacement of a dipthong by two syllables, e.g. *süeco* (for *sueco*), *püesto* (*puesto*) *que está jugando*; change in the placement of stress, e.g. *chóferes* (for *choferes*); and placement of stress on more than one syllable, e.g. *la clásificación* (*clasificación*), *El gobierno tiene la résponsabilidad* (*responsabilidad*) *última de la fínanciación* (*financiación*) *interna*.

Intonation[9]

The term **intonation** refers to the distinctive use of patterns of pitch and it performs a role broadly similar to that of punctuation in writing by indicating grammatical structure. Another function of intonation is that of conveying the attitude of the speaker, for example, surprise, ironic disbelief, polite attentiveness, humour or sarcasm. Intonation patterns and rates of delivery vary widely throughout the Spanish-speaking world and the 'machine-gun' high speed delivery of parts of Castile where the register, as Green notes (1990a: 80), 'is confined to little more than an octave' is very different from say, the melodious patterns and more leisurely rates found in the speaker from Mexico City. Nonetheless, the delivery of Spanish is regular (Green prefers to call it a segment-timed rather than a syllable-timed language because, while noticeably regular, its basic rhythm is not imposed by the syllable). This regularity affects its intonation patterns, which can accommodate melodic units of up to fifteen syllables. Similar intonation patterns occur in all varieties of Spanish to distinguish between declaratives, questions, enumeration, clause boundaries and exclamations.

Simple declaratives share a rising–falling pattern:

e.g. *Ha venido a clase.*

Interrogatives are marked by a sustained rise:

e.g *¿Ha venido a clase?*

unless they are preceded by an interrogative pronoun such as *quién, qué, cómo, cuánto, dónde* which have a sharp rise followed by a prolonged fall:

e.g. *¿Quién ha venido a clase?*

Enumeration or pausing within the utterance is marked by level or rising intonation, the latter signalling clearly that the speaker does not wish to relinquish a turn:

e.g. *Los que han venido a clase, y que quieren entregar el trabajo, pueden . . .*

Exclamations and interjections may be marked by a sharp rising tone on the initial syllable followed by a falling tone:

e.g. *¡Hijodeputa!*

However, the above is clearly a simplification and the wide range of feelings, such as surprise, irritation, relief, impatience, polite interest, sarcasm, regret, which can be expressed in Spain, by interjections such as *¡vaya!* or *¡por favor!* depending on subtle differences in intonational contours is ample testimony of this.

For example:

por favor (please)
por favor (come off it)

3.2 Orthography

The Spanish alphabet[10] today consists of twenty-seven letters (or **graphemes**), of which six, A, E, I, O, U, Y are used as vowel letters and twenty-one are used as consonant letters: B, C, D, F, G, H, J, K, L, M, N, Ñ, P, Q, R, S, T, V, W, X, Y, Z. In addition Spanish has three **digraphs**, CH, LL and RR, the first two of which occupied a separate place in the alphabet, after 'C' and 'L' respectively, from the time of a reform brought in by the RAE in 1803. However in 1994, after much debate, the *Asociación de las Academias de la Lengua Española* decided to bring the alphabetical ordering of Spanish into line with that of other countries using Roman script. Additionally, Spanish uses the following **diacritic** symbols: the stress accent (´), the diaerisis, (¨) and the tilde (~) to provide the following seven graphemes: á, é, í, ó, ú, ü, ñ. The combination of N and the diacritic tilde (~) to form Ñ is particular to the Spanish language alone. Ñ is generally considered to be a letter in its own right and occupies its own space in the alphabet after N. The diacritic (´) serves two functions: to distinguish between **homonyms**, for example *mi* (possessive adjective) and *mí* (disjunctive pronoun), and to mark **stress** when it diverges from the expected patterns (see 3.1.3). The function of the diacritic (¨), only used with the vowel U before the vowels E and I, is to convey the sounds **[gwe]** and **[gwi]** (e.g. *agüero* compared with *guerra*). The letters W and K are not considered to be indigenous. W is only used in words of foreign provenance and tends to be replaced by V, or more infrequently by G/GÜ as these words become assimilated into Spanish, such as *vagón* from the English 'waggon', *güisqui* from the English 'whisk(e)y'. Similarly, K is frequently replaced by C before the vowels A, O and U and by QU before E and I, as in *quiosco* (kiosk).

The first written texts in Spanish, as opposed to Latin, date back to the eleventh century when spelling systems began to be adopted by local scribes to convey vernacular pronunciations. However, it was not until the late thirteenth century that, largely under the endeavours of the scholar-king, Alfonso X, a standardized supraregional variety of Spanish began to emerge.[11] Marcos Marín (1979: 101) provides the following text to illustrate how the orthographic norms adopted by Alfonso X in his *General Estoria* (General History) closely reflected the phonology of the period:

> *E quando caualgaua, por encobrir ensi las cosas dond ella aurie uerguença, si paresciesse al caualgar, ouo a buscar manera poro las encobriesse, por que quando caualgasse que sele non estoruasse por esta razon delo fazer ligera mientre; . . .*[12]

What is immediately apparent is the wider range of **sibilants** represented. For example, a distinction is made between the sibilant represented by s̲ (*las cosas*) and that represented by s̲s̲ (*caualgasse*) now both conveyed by S, and between that represented by ç (*uerguença*) and that represented by z̲ (*fazer*) now both represented by Z and C respectively.[13]

The next major reform of Spanish orthographic norms came in the eighteenth century when the RAE, driven by a need to bring Alfonsine norms into line with the pronunciation of the time while at the same time respecting etymological concerns, undertook to simplify norms of spelling. Thus, in the reforms of 1746, 1763 and 1815:

- *ç* is removed;
- *qu* becomes C before A and O;
- X replaces *k*;
- *ph*, *ss* and *th* are replaced by F, S and T;
- silent H is maintained for etymological reasons;
- word initial *s* is eliminated;
- Z is used to represent /θ/ before A, O and U, and C before E and I.

The RAE also put an end to confusion between U and V and I and J, reserving U and I as vowels and V and J as consonants.[14] It was at this time that today's orthographical norms of Spanish were largely established; subsequent reforms have primarily dealt with issues of punctuation and accentuation. For example, the most recent reform which took place with the publication by the RAE, in 1952, of its *Nuevas normas de prosodia y ortografía*, made prescriptive in 1959, was not substantial, and consisted primarily in relaxing standards of accentuation where these did not distinguish homonyms or indicate stress. For example, the third-person singular preterites of the verbs *dar, ver* were no longer required to be accentuated (*dió* was henceforth *dio* and *vió* was to become *vio*), *solo* neither as an adjective (*llegó solo*) nor as an adverb (*solo tengo dos*) was required to take an accent except in the case of possible confusion; nonetheless, acceptance of these norms is far from complete and these accents are still used by some, and in the case of, for example, *solo/sólo*, many writers today.

In Spanish, there is a relatively close correspondence between the graphical conventions used and the phonemic reality they convey. Indeed, this is perhaps what gives rise to the widespread belief, in the Spanish-speaking world, that the two should in fact coincide, a concern which does not arise in similar measure for the other main European languages.[15] Nonetheless, as Green (1990a: 90) points out, standard orthography is biased towards the Castilian norm and therefore poses problems for the vast majority of speakers in the Spanish-speaking world, who, for example, have no phonological opposition between [s] and [θ]. Furthermore, while speakers may find it relatively easy to read aloud the written language, they experience considerably greater difficulty in transcribing from the spoken language. The writer Enrique Jardiel Poncela uses this to humorous effect when he reproduces a letter purportedly written by one Ceferino Mogaz, a man of scant learning:

> *Me cerido hamigo: Su carta que e rrecibido en el momento enque estaba sakando hagua del filtro del komedor de la fonda, me a producido gran contrariedad. La verdaz es qüe yo no hesperava por-parte de Ustez un trato tan desconsiderao . . .*
>
> (*Mi querido amigo: Su carta, que he recibido en el momento en que estaba sacando agua del filtro del comedor de la fonda, me ha producido gran contrariedad. La verdad es que yo no esperaba por parte de usted un trato tan desconsiderado . . .*)[16]

(De Bruyne 1995b: 26)

These very difficulties have lain behind various attempts, originating primarily in Latin America, further to reform orthographic norms, for example, to remove the silent 'h' and to standardize the representation of *jota/ge*. Already in the nineteenth century, the distinguished Chilean grammarian Andrés Bello proposed major orthographic reforms and more recently, in Cuba, the literacy campaigns of the 1950s and 1960s, and the perceived need to teach as simple a representation of the spoken language as possible, led to the Cuban Academy's proposal to the Third Congress of the Academies in 1961 to reform further spelling norms. These proposals have so far been rejected. Nonetheless, debates around the future of the Spanish language are frequently articulated in terms of spelling reform. In 1997, the Nobel prize-winning author Gabriel García Márquez's heartfelt plea for a thorough-going spelling reform whipped up debate throughout the Spanish-speaking world.

The Spanish alphabet has in recent years been the focus for acrimonious debate between the different national *academias* as increasing internationalization and the need for computer compatibility has brought external pressure to bear on it. For example, the need was perceived to eliminate 'ch' and 'll' from their internationally anomalous positions in the alphabet and to include them after 'cg' and 'lk' respectively, where María Moliner had already decided it was logical to place them in her 1966 dictionary. This reorganizational move, which did not involve either the loss of the phoneme or the letter, was supported by the RAE but heatedly opposed by some Latin American *academias* who saw in this reform cultural colonization. In the words of the representative of the Guatemalan *academia* '*estas dos letras han sido asesinadas a causa de la presión o la colonización económica del mundo anglosajón.*' (*El País*, 28.4.94).[17]

However, the pressure brought to bear by UNESCO, in the interests of keyboard compatibility, to remove an actual letter, Spain's distinctive 'ñ', and to replace it by, for example, 'ny'[18] has so far been resisted; here Spain is united with the rest of the Spanish-speaking world in its defence of the letter. This issue has unleashed a torrent of 'letters to the editor' in recent years. In 1998 the outcry which followed the Spanish Ministry of Health's ill-judged acquisition of 17,512 computers devoid of this letter testified to the strength of public opinion which this issue can generate (*El País*, 16.3.98).

Another, older debate, is still evident in the retention, by Mexico, of the 'x' of the nation's name and nationality which was inherited from the Nahuatl /sh/ (Meshico). The RAE standardized the spelling to 'j' (*Méjico, mejicano*), spellings which were resisted for reasons of national pride by the Mexicans in this instance, although they were accepted in respect of other place names (e.g. Guadalajara, Jalisco). In Peru, for similar reasons, the letter 'z' finds little favour in certain contexts and in the 1990s the country's national telephone company was fined for spelling the name of Peru's second city with a 'z' (*Cuzco*) rather than with an 's' (*Cusco*) which would relate more closely to the Quechua roots of the name.

Despite this, what is interesting is the extent to which the same conventions of spelling are adhered to throughout the Spanish-speaking world. In contrast, the one variety of Spanish which has undergone a thoroughgoing reform in the direction of phonemic orthography, *Djudeo-espanyol* (Judeo-Spanish), otherwise known as *ladino*, appears at first sight, as Green (1990a: 92) observes, a different language.

Ladino has the most phonemic orthography of any variety of Spanish. It is a dying variety which nonetheless has undergone a modernizing spelling reform when it is written in Roman letters. The following extract illustrates to what extent it is distinct from standard Spanish spelling.

> . . . *500 anyos despues de la ekspulsion, el djudeo-espanyol es ainda una lengua ke puede ser entendida bastante fasilmente por los ispanoavlantes en las diversas partes del mundo. No solo esto sino ke eya desperta tambien onde eyos un grande intereso, a kavza de su fonetika partikulara i de su reushidad a konservar munchos elementos del espanyol medieval anso ke numerosos kantes, kuentos i refranes ke konstituyen un verdadero trezoro para los ke se okupan de la istoria de la lengua espanyola i de su literatura.*

(Shaul 1996: 74)[19]

The orthographic simplification which provides an even more phonemic transcription than standard Spanish orthography is noticeable in the use of K for QU and C (e.g. *ke*, *kon*), the use of V for V and B (e.g. *ispanoavlantes*), the use of S and Z for two distinct sibilants (e.g. *trezoro* and *fasilmente*), the replacement of LL by Y (e.g. *eyos*), the elimination of diacritics e.g. *fonetika* and consequent transcription of Ñ as NY, as in *espanyola*.

Returning to standard Spanish, it is easy, against a background of such conformity, for letters and combinations of letters which are considered to be nonstandard to acquire distinct semiotic values of their own. For example, while the letter combination 'th' was lost in the RAE's early reforms, its use can convey a certain exoticism in, for example, words such as *Thailandia*. Thus, while style guides, such as the *Libro de estilo de El País*, recommend the Castilianized *Tailandia*, writers persist in using the proscribed form, such as *thriler*, and it is common practice amongst travel agencies to use *Thailandia* and its derived adjective *thailandés* in their promotional literature (De Bruyne 1995b: 19).

Similarly the use of the letter K is considered by the RAE and the style guides to be non-standard and they recommend that it be replaced by C before the vowels A, O and U and QU before E and I. Nonetheless, it appears that K is being used with increasing frequency in Spanish as injunctions to Castilianize, for example, international weights and measures fail to achieve the desired effect with *kilo* being preferred to *quilo* (we have already seen how, in the field of pharmacology, the imperative of international standardization has led to the adoption of K rather than QU in the designation of medical products). K also has a role to play in 'anti-languages' (see 4.1.2), varieties shared by those who reject the values of mainstream society, for example by squatters, *okupa(nte)s*. Thus it is frequent to see K used in anti-establishment graffiti in Spain. For example:

> *No keremos karceles*
> *keremos lokales*

(De Bruyne 1995b: 61)

An additional value attached to K in the Spanish context is its ability to connote 'Basqueness', as Basque is the only minority language in Spain to include
K in its standard alphabet. Thus, for example, the adoption of the spelling
euskera (or especially of the more Basque-influenced *euskara*) to refer to the
Basque language, rather than the retention of the *qu* in accordance with
Spanish norms as in *eusquera*, can convey the writer's, probably nationalistic,
feelings towards the Basque country.

Punctuation and capitalization

Perhaps the most distinctive feature of Spanish is the use of upside-down
question (¿) and exclamation (¡) marks to signal the beginning of a question or
exclamation regardless of whether this occurs sentence-initially or not. For
example, *Pues fíjate ¿qué voy a querer yo para mis hijos?* In Spanish, chevrons « »
are used to indicate quotations within a text, to mark 'deviant' forms and
occasionally to mark dialogue, for example, *el autodenominado «Bloc de
Progrès»*. These are all areas of punctuation likely to be affected by the internationalization of the computer keyboard. This is particularly the case for the
chevron, for, while inverted commas (") are included as standard, the chevron
is harder to access. Similarly, the Academy's injunction to write accents on
capital letters can also cause keyboard difficulties.

In writing figures, most of the Spanish-speaking world, with the exception
of Mexico, in common with the languages of Continental Europe, uses the
point to mark thousands (e.g. 3.406) and the comma to mark decimal points
(e.g. 5,2) but there is evidence that with increasing internationalization, this
practice is ceding ground to the conventions adopted by the wider international community. The punctuation of dialogue may be achieved through
the use of the dash (–) which may precede new dialogue and which surrounds
any intrusion of narrative into the body of dialogue. For example, 'Yo tuve el
honor de conocerle –recuerda Nicolás Franco– cuando mi padre era . . . '
(Prego 95: 161).

Capitalization is relatively infrequent in Spanish and is not used, for
example, for months, seasons, days of the week, names of religions, points
of the compass, adjectives derived from capitalized proper nouns or titles of
books or films with the exception of the first letter as in *El bueno, el feo y el
malo*.[20] However, there is evidence that under pressure from English these conventions are being eroded. For example, film titles such as the one above are
increasingly found in capitalized form as are days of the week and months of
the year.

The writing system of Spanish, therefore, can be seen to be highly phonemic, especially so with regard to standard Castilian, and also extremely

standardized across all varieties. This very standardization allows deviant spellings to be highly semiotically charged, carrying, for example, connotations of nationalism or of anti-establishment feeling. The principal pressures towards change come from the globalization of communications and in particular from the limitations imposed on the language by the standard computer keyboard and communications software, such as that enabling e-mail communication. Behind this, is of course the more general phenomenon of the pressure from English which, as we have seen, has particular implications for punctuation.

The highly phonemic nature of Spanish spelling when compared with careful formal educated speech is a striking feature of the Spanish language, notwithstanding ongoing debates seeking to render it even more so. The symbolic power of orthography often provides a window into the power struggles involved in creating and maintaining a national or regional standard. Behind this impression of uniformity however, lies considerable variation, particularly at the level of spontaneous informal speech reflecting the speaker's provenance (in terms of geography, class, education, etc.) and the purposes for which the language is used (e.g. formal speech, informal conversation). At the same time change is clearly taking place and new prestige standards are being defined; for example, the once-stigmatized *yeísmo* is becoming standard usage in Spain.

4   Spanish lexis

In this chapter, I intend to deal with the two main areas of interest in the Spanish lexicon today: its unprecedented rate of change and the mechanisms that exist which allow speakers to create neologisms; and the resulting variation which exists across the Spanish-speaking world.

4.0 Lexical change

When, in 1966, the Spanish philologist, Emilio Lorenzo, coined the phrase *lengua en ebullición* (language in ferment) he was referring to the rapid pace of lexical creation and change occurring in the Spanish language. While there is much to be said about the lexical stock of Spanish prior to the late twentieth century, ranging from pre-Roman items through extensive borrowing from Arabic, Latin and Greek to colonial assimilation from the Amerindian languages, it is my intention in this book to look at the processes of lexical change and creation taking place today. Rapid social, political and economic change in the twentieth century, such as advances in the fields of science and technology, sport and medicine, has prompted equally rapid lexical change, with concepts and vocabulary being absorbed into Spanish, primarily from English and French, at an unprecedented rate. In post-Francoist Spain, in particular, there is an openness to foreign influence which may be seen partly as a reaction to the inward-looking, deeply xenophobic regime which preceded it. Multinational corporations such as IBM and Coca-Cola, international organizations such as UN, NATO, EU, NAFTA and the vast amounts of translation that they generate, the internationalization of certain cultures such as pop music and the technologization of communications with, for example, the expansion of the Internet all bring Spanish into contact with other languages, principally English, and are all factors which precipitate change. Added to this is the fact that English is the principal second language studied in the Spanish-speaking world, and exposure to it through, for example, satellite television is widespread. While the media are undoubtedly the greatest force for the dissemination of neologisms and borrowings, in speech communities where there is direct and everyday contact with a powerful contact language, such as in Mexico and the Spanish-speaking communities of the United States, borrowing may take place directly.

Undoubtedly, many of the neologisms and borrowings which arise from cultural contact and technological progress fulfil only a temporary or highly specialized need and fail to enter the lexicon of the great majority of speakers; nonetheless, it is at the level of lexis that the greatest enduring variation and change can be detected.

What is of interest here are the productive resources of the language that allow willing speakers and (principally) writers of Spanish both to generate neologisms from indigenous Spanish stock and at the same time to absorb a vast number of borrowings and make them their own through, for example, the processes of assimilation to Spanish orthography, phonology, morphology and syntax. For example, 'scanner', which entered Spanish as the loan word *scanner* has since been adopted by the Academy and the style guides as *escáner* (thus adapting the loanword to Spanish phonology which does not accept position initial [s] followed by a consonant) and has generated a number of **derivations** for example *escanear, escaneo, escaneado* (DB), and so on. At the same time, speakers of Spanish are able to expand the lexicon through means such as affixation (e.g. the use of the prefix *euro-* as in *eurodiputado*), compounding (such as *salvapantallas* (screensaver)) and acronymic derivation (e.g. *renfista* = an employee of RENFE (*Red Nacional de los Ferrocarriles Españoles*), the Spanish state railway company). While in more prescriptive quarters there is frequently disquiet about what is perceived as an 'invasion' of foreign terms into Spanish, the Spanish-speaking world – unlike, for example, France with its *Loi Toubon* – has, in the main, not looked to legislation to impose linguistic purity. Rather, it has permitted usage and advice, from the style guides, for example, to channel change and has allowed borrowing to be a source of enrichment of the language. Indeed, Green (1990a) observes that through the indigenous creative mechanisms outlined above the Spanish language is actually becoming more rather than less Romance in its lexical structure.

In this section we shall concentrate, first, on the **creation of neologisms** from indigenous Spanish-language stock and, second, on **borrowing** and **calquing** from other languages with which Spanish is in contact, although there is much overlap between both processes. Borrowing and calquing are undoubtedly the principal channels by which the Spanish lexicon is expanding; nonetheless, it is the productive mechanisms within the language which allow borrowings to be assimilated and subsequently to generate related forms, and thus we shall deal with these first.

4.0.0 *Creation of neologisms from Spanish-language stock*

Very few words are created *ex nihilo* but rather draw on elements previously available within the language or import elements from outside. The processes of word formation in Spanish which we shall deal with here are **affixation** (prefixation and suffixation), **compounding**, **conversion**, the use of **acronyms/alphabetisms** and **abbreviation**.

(i) Affixation

Affixation, through the use of prefixes and suffixes, is an extremely productive derivational mechanism in Spanish. Azevedo (1992) provides the following example of the extent to which affixes can be used to build on a root lexeme, in this case *caj-* (box). Prefixes are morphemes which precede the root, while suffixes are endings which attach to roots:

prefix	root	suffix	
	caj-	*a*	box
	caj-	*ero*	cashier
	caj-	*ista*	typesetter
	caj-	*eta*	small box
	caj-	*et-illa*	small box
	caj-	*uela*	boot (of car)
	caj-	*ón*	big box
	caj-	*on-cito*	(small) big box
en-	*caj-*	*ar*	to insert
des-en-	*caj-*	*ar*	to dislocate
des-en-	*caj-*	*a-dor*	a person who dislocates
des-en-	*caj-*	*a-miento*	the action of dislocating/ dislocation

Thus it is possible on the basis of elements already existing within the language and easily identifiable by the listener and reader to extend an existing lexical network to meet new needs, or, on the basis of a new root lexeme, for example *fax* to create, element by element, a new lexical network (e.g. ranging from the standard verb *faxear*, to fax, to the instantly understandable and jocular *faxitis*, pathology deriving from overdependence on the fax machine).

(a) Prefixation

While prefixation has always been a productive source of neologism in Spanish, in the latter part of the twentieth century it appears to have taken on a new lease of life with a number of traditional prefixes taking on new vitality. For example, as has been the case in other languages, the prefixes *super-* and *hiper-* have proved particularly productive in recent decades with, for example, *mercado* becoming first *supermercado* and later *hipermercado*. Fashions in prefixes may be relatively fleeting but can have a lasting impact. Such was the case of *mini-*, imported from English in the 1960s; in contrast, the prefix *maxi-*, the revitalization of which dated from the same period, has enjoyed much less success. The even more recently revitalized prefix *mega-* similarly has created a legion of new lexical items, such as *el mega-ordenador Pixar* (*Cambio 16*: 15.4.96: 66). Bookless (1994: 15) notes that in Spanish, prefixes which are favoured at the end of the twentieth century are: *eco-*, *neo-*, *bio-*, *euro-*, *multi-*, *micro-*, *macro-*, *hiper-*. Some traditional prefixes have acquired new meanings, for example, *pro-* is now commonly used in the sense of 'favourable to' such as *proiraquí*. Others, such as the prolific *des-*, are so transparent in meaning that they are used in a multitude of creative ways which are unlikely to enter a formal dictionary, for example, *desdonjuanizar* (the action of stopping someone behaving in a manner appropriate to a Don Juan). Prefixes may also be combined as in *autodesmitificación* (self-debunking).

Prefixes can be added to nouns (e.g. *previsión*, foresight), to adjectives (e.g. *previsible*, forseeable) and to verbs (*prever*, to forsee). While the majority of prefixes are derived from Latin and Greek and are similar to those used in the languages with with Spanish has the most contact (English and French), there are some which are specifically Spanish, for example, the primarily colloquial prefixes of intensification of *re-*, *requete-* and *recontra-* (*rebueno*, *requetebién*, *recontrabueno*), the latter being more specific to Latin America. In some instances there are two variants, an educated one (*prefijo culto*) and one derived from the vernacular (*prefijo popular*). This is the case with *inter-* and *entre-* (*interviú* vs. *entrevista*, and *super-* and *sobre-* (**supermercado** and **sobrealimentador**). In other cases there are variant spellings: the etymological prefix and a phonetic simplification as it is assimilated to Spanish orthography and phonology, for example, *pos-* or *post-* (**posmoderno**, **postfranquista**), *tras-* or *trans-* (**traslúcido/translúcido**), *deo-* or *deso-* (**deodorante/desodorante**), *sico/psico* (**sicología/psicología**). In the case of *linfo-* or *lympho-* (**linfoma/lymphoma**) we have a prefix which is not fully assimilated and which may have remained so under the pressure of English (DB). In most cases the reduced form is becoming the standard form, although there is a tendency in the style guides to recommend the use of the form *post-* before a vowel and, in medicine, to use the etymological *psico-* to permit differentiation between homonyms such as *psicosis* (a mental disorder) and *sicosis* (a skin complaint).

In this section we shall concentrate only on those prefixes which are particularly productive at the moment. The following semantic fields are based on Guerrero Ramos (1995):

Number or quantity
multi- *póliza multirriesgo* (fully comprehensive policy), *edificio multifamiliar* (block of flats).
pluri- *pluriempleado* (having more than one job), *estado plurilingüe* (state where more than one language is spoken).
poli- *polideportivo* (sports centre), *politraumatismo* (multiple injuries).
mono- *monomando* (mixer tap), *monofamiliar* (attributive. single-parent family).
uni- *unicameral* (single chamber (legislature)), *calle unidireccional* (one-way street).
bi- *bipartidismo* (two party system), *bimensual* (twice-monthly).
tri- *tridimensional* (three-dimensional), *trifásico* (three-phase).
cuatri- *cuatrimotor* (four-engined), compare with the competing form **tetra-**, *tetramotor* (DB).

Importance
super- *supersecreto* (top secret), *superlight* (ultra low in nicotine and tar). *Super* is particularly productive as an emphatic device in informal spoken language in Spain, for example, '*yo tengo una cosa que va superbién (. . .) no perjudica y es superbueno*' (Briz: 1995: 114), '*ahora hay, hacen operaciones con rayos láser super-limpias*' (Briz, 1995: 159).

hiper-/o- *hiperactivo, hipocalórico* (low calory).

macro- *macroconcierto* (huge concert), *macropuente* (a succession of public holidays).

sobre- *sobrecapacidad* (excess capacity), *sobrecualificación* (being overqualified).

ultra- *ultraconservador* (hardline conservative), *ultraligero* (microlight aircraft).

mini- *minigolf* (miniature golf-course), *minicalculadora* (pocket calculator).

micro- *microbus* (minibus), *microcirugía* (micro-surgery).

infra- *infrautilizar* (to under-use), *infravivienda* (sub-standard housing).

vice- *vicerrector* (vice-chancellor (of a univerisity)).

Time
pre- *premamá* (mum-to-be), *comidas precocinadas* (cook-chill meals).

pos(t)- *posindustrial* (post-industrial), *posfranquismo* (period after the death of Franco).

neo- *asistencia neonatal* (post-natal care), *neonazi* (neo-nazi).

For and against
anti- *tratamiento antidroga* (treatment for drug addiction), *anticoncepción* (contraception), *antideportivo* (unsporting attitude). According to Lorenzo (1995), this is a particularly productive prefix in the Spanish language today.

contra- *aparato contraincendios* (fire-fighting equipment).

pro- *proetarra* (pro-ETA) (DB).

Exclusion and negation
des- *desregulación* (deregulation), *descafeinado* (decaffeinated). According to Lorenzo (1995), *des-* is probably the most productive prefix in the Spanish language today.

in-/il- *ingobernable* (ungovernable), *ininflamable* (fire-resistant), *ilocalizable* (unavailable).

There is also a tendency, under the influence of the English prefix 'non-' to prepose the negative particle *no*, for example, *Demuestra la no existencia de Parkinson, el acuerdo de no proliferación*. This form is currently competing with the existing prefix *in-* and the construction *sin* + infinitive, for example, *inconformista/no conformista, un niño no escolarizado/sin escolarizar*.

Collaboration
co- *copatrocinador* (joint sponsor), *cogestión* (worker participation).

inter- *interbancario* (between banks), *interregional* (between regions).

Reiteration

re- *reeducar profesionalmente* (to give industrial retraining to), *reinserción social* (social rehabilitation).

Positions

extra- *actividad extraescolar* (out-of-school activity), *extraconstitucional* (unconstitutional).
sub- *subacuático* (underwater).
intra- *intrarregional* (within the region).
supra- *suprarregional* (above the level of the region).

Other

auto- *autogestión* (self-management), *autoedición* (desktop publishing), *auto-handling* (baggage handling service provided by the airline itself). For *auto-* meaning 'car', rather than 'self', see under blends.
bio- *biodiversidad* (bio-diversity).
ciber- *cibercafé* (Internet café) (DB), *ciberespanglish* (a variety of Spanish used on the Internet).
eco- *ecoturismo* (eco-tourism).
euro- *eurófilo* (Europhile).
para- *paranormal* (paranormal) (DB), *paramédico* (paramedic) (DB).

(b) Suffixation

Suffixation can be divided into two main types: non-emotive and emotive. Non-emotive suffixation is a particularly productive mechanism in creating neologisms. Emotive suffixation (diminutives, augmentatives and pejoratives), rather than creating neologisms which can then be shared by a speech community, expresses the speaker's attitude towards the lexical items and frequently towards the addressee and may be used extensively in informal conversation and in politeness in its widest sense.[1]

Non-emotive suffixation

A suffix can be applied to a verbal, nominal or adjectival root and the neologism created in this way may remain within that grammatical category or it may change category. For example, while the noun *golpista* has been derived from the noun *golpe*, the verb *reinsertar* has been derived from the noun *reinserción* and the verb *golear* from the noun *gol*.

According to Guerrero Ramos (1995) the suffixes which are currently most productive in the Spanish language are: *-ionar*, *-izar*, *-ción*, *-ado*, *-ismo*, *-ista*, *-al*, *-ano*, *-oide*, *-able*. However, we shall look at a wider selection than this as many less frequently used suffixes have nonetheless had considerable impact on the development of the Spanish language. We shall, for convenience, look in turn at suffixes which are primarily affixed to **verbs**, **nouns**, **adjectives** and

adverbs although some suffixes may be affixed to more than one category of root.

New **verbs** are almost exclusively in the first conjugation, i.e. *-ar* verbs. This development has led in a significant number of cases to the existence of duals where new *-ar* verbs are taking over from competing verbs in the other conjugations, for example:

> *promocionar* for *promover*
> *ejercitar* for *ejercer*
> *fusionar* for *fundir*
> *influenciar* for *influir*
> *ofertar* for *ofrecer*
> *imposibilitar* for *impedir*

The influence of English and French has been arguably the most important factor in the rapid creation and dissemination of the suffixes *-izar* and *-ización* which can be attached to a nominal and an adjectival base, for example:

> *un espónsor*   *esponsorizar*
> *un escándalo*   *escandalizar*
> *la derecha*   *derechizar*
> *el guión*   *guionizar*
> *normal*   *normalizar*
> *privado*   *privatizar*
> *rentable*   *rentabilizar*
> *vital*   *revitalización*

In some cases the suffix *-izador* (the person responsible for) can also be added, for example:

> *organizador*

Bookless (1994: 15) notes that while newly created verbs such as *traumatizar, dramatizar, visualizar, globalizar* owe their existence to the prior creativity of English, this suffix can also be found in neologisms which are not derived from English such as: *mentalizar, responsabilizar, autonomizar, compatibilizar, alunizar, climatizar, inertizar, verbalizar una duda, popularizarse* as in 'Audi se "populariza" con el A3' (*El País*, 7.7.96).

Guerrero Ramos (1995) notes that such has been the success of the *-izar* ending that it is currently displacing other *-ar* variants, for example, *culpabilizar* for *culpar*, *valorizar* for *valorar*, *optimizar* for *optimar*.

The verbal suffixes *-ar* and *-ear*, also undoubtedly under the influence of English, have proved particularly fertile, with many of the new forms created being obvious calques of English, for example, *piratear, programar, filmar* (cf. *rodar*), *faxear, escanear, tipear* (LA). Nonetheless, as Bookless (1994: 144) notes, the tendency appears to have taken on a life of its own, not only influencing the creation of verbs from nouns ending in -*ión* (where a different verbal suffix (e.g. -*er*) might be expected), such as *erosionar, distorsionar, presionar, anexionar* (replacing *anejar*), *conexionar* for *conectar* but, more interestingly, allowing for the creation of semantically complex verbs which are not directly calqued from elsewhere. Bookless gives the example of *colapsar* now used transitively to mean 'to cause to collapse', particularly as regards transport systems, as shown in his example, '*Los trabajadores de Spantax colapsaron el acceso al aeropuerto*' (*El País*, 9.11.87). *Simultanear* and *mentalizar* also show this process at work.

The suffix -*ificar* has also been the source of recent verbal creation as in *tonificar los músculos, dignificar, mistificar*.

While there are a large number of suffixes which may be used to create new **nouns** from verbal and adjectival roots, our intention here is to concentrate on those which are enjoying vitality in the Spanish language today and therefore we do not intend to be exhaustive in their treatment.[2]

The suffixes listed below have enjoyed renewed vitality in recent years:

-*abilidad* normally expresses the notion 'to be able to be' or inherent quality, for example, '*permitir (. . .) que aumentase el volumen de* **edificabilidad** *de una construcción en Marbella*' (*El País*, 7.7.96).

-*ción* is a particularly productive suffix, meaning action or effect, e.g. *desforestación, digitalización*. This suffix is particularly salient in technical and scientific language and interestingly continues to oust its equivalent -*miento* (e.g. *estancamiento*) (Alvar Esquerra 1995: 56).

-*ado*, along with -*aje*, is a suffix which allows the creation of nouns which express a process, e.g. *el blanqueado de dinero, etiquetado, recalentado*. As such its function differs from that of the verbal participle which implies perfective aspect. It can also be used when the base is a noun to refer to groups, e.g. *estudiantado*.

-*aje* for example, *trucaje* (special effects, from *truco* (a trick)), *dopaje, frenaje, equilibraje* (wheel-balancing). There are also a number of duals where both -*aje* and -*ado* are used, e.g. *equilibrado/equilibraje*.

-*amen* has been revived recently and denotes quantities. As it is frequently used in spoken language for jocular effect, it could also be classified under emotive suffixation, e.g. *papelamen* (masses of papers), *juergamen* (tremendous binge), *cuerpamen* (beefcake (of a body)).

-*ata*, -*ota*, -*eta* the suffix -*ata* constituted one of the defining features of a particular youth variety of Peninsular Spanish, *cheli* (see 4.1.2) and, over the 1970s and 1980s, has extended beyond this speech community. Casado Velarde (1985: 71–80) notes how current uses of this suffix differ from traditional uses, principally Italianisms (e.g. *serenata, sonata*), feminines of -*ato* and -*ate*, and terms derived from Latin (e.g. *separata*). Examples of the new ways in which -*ata* is used which are recognized by and may even be used by the wider speech community in Spain include, *cubata* (from the drink *Cuba Libre*), *bocata* (from *bocadillo*), *drogata* (from *drogadicto*), *fumata* (from *fumador* (de droga)), *tocata* (from *tocadiscos*). Much less commonly used are the suffixes *-ota* and *-eta* (e.g. *pasota, chuleta*). Occasionally they exist as variants of *-ata* (e.g. *drogota* and *fumeta*). Given that the revitalization of these suffixes took place initially in the language of marginal communities before being adopted by subgroups of young people, it is not surprising that they are generally associated with vocabulary relating to the basics of life and with jargon associated with drugs and prison. This association also allows for their use as pejorative affixes in colloquial language, e.g. the use of *sociatas* to refer to the *socialistas*, and as such they overlap with the emotive suffixes discussed later. An interesting case is to be found in *azafata* derived from Arabic and used typically to refer to an air hostess. The form *azafato* can be found in parts of Latin America to refer to an air steward. Diarmuid Bradley (personal communication) notes that *azafata* is increasingly used to refer to ground hostesses in, say, trade fairs and is being replaced by *auxiliar de vuelo* in the context of air travel.

-azo can be used as an augmentative with neutral, positive or negative connotations. However, its most salient use in Spanish today is to denote an action or result of an action as in *tejerazo* (coup d'état by Tejero in Spain), *fujimorazo* (re-election of Fujimori in Peru/his suspension of democratic liberties), *pantallazo* (abuse of television time by a politician), *avionazo/bolazo* (plane crash), *dedazo* (action by outgoing Mexican President in designating (unofficially) his successor), *champanazo* (a binge on champagne/cava), *un auténtico bombazo* (a real bombshell). As it can convey the attitude of the speaker it will also be dealt with under emotive suffixation.

-cida expresses the notion of killing and has extended from its traditional domain e.g. *homicida* to attach to a much wider variety of roots, e.g. *plaguicida* (insecticide), *raticida, bactericida* (DB), *arboricida* (DB).

-dromo expresses the notion of place, e.g. *velódromo, patinódromo, rocódromo* (climbing wall) (DB), *canódromo* (greyhound track) (DB) and can also be used creatively as in *Va a ser un manifestódromo* (It's going to be one big area for demonstrating) (Videotaped corpus of Spoken Spanish from Valladolid (Val.)).

-e provides a noun from a verbal root, e.g. *el tueste* from *tostar* (to torrefy) and has given nouns such as *desfase* as in *el desfase horario* (jetlag), *el destape* (state of undress, period of liberalization post-Franco), *un ligue* (a date) (DB).

-eo is used to refer to an activity, e.g. *el chateo* (going for a drink) (DB).

-ero/a provides a noun from a noun base and is used generally to refer to a place, a receptacle or an agent. The choice of feminine or masculine may be selected on a regional basis, for example *azúcar* produces *azucarero* in Spain and *azucarera* in Latin America (Lang 1990: 134). Yet in Spain the feminine is also used for domestic items such as *tetera, cafetera, yogurtera* (DB).

-ería has two primary senses, that of the inherent quality of the nominal or adjectival root, e.g. *matonería* (thuggishness) and that of location or 'a place where', e.g. *washetería* common in the Spanish of Mexico and the US, *liguería* (pick-up joint), *cruasantería* (shop where you buy croissants), *bocatería* (DB).

-idad is added to an adjectival root to create an abstract noun signifying quality, e.g. *españolidad* (Spanishness), *consideró aquellas fotografías como un atentado contra su privacidad* where *privacidad*, a calque from English, is currently displacing Spanish equivalents such as *intimidad* (DEU, Jan. 95). This suffix competes with **-ía**, for example *asturianía* (the quality of being from Asturias in Spain) (DB).

-ígeno/-ógeno express the notion of causation, particularly in the field of medicine, and have become detached from their more common roots, e.g. *un material cancerígeno, acidógeno* (DB) to be applied creatively elsewhere, e.g. *anorexígeno* (causing anorexia) (DB). Diarmuid Bradley (personal communication) notes a shift in meaning for this suffix in certain contexts: for example, the adjective *plumígeno* (feather-producing, i.e. fowl) can now be applied to duvets acquiring the sense of 'feather-containing'; similarly, *rocas petrolíferas* have been followed by *compañías petrolíferas*, a different sense of production altogether.

-ismo, -ista can express the idea of ideology/belief and supporters of that ideology/belief, and are particularly common in the field of politics. They can be used pejoratively or amelioratively depending on context. For example, in Spain while *el felipismo* (cult of/belief in the ideas embodied by the Prime Minister, Felipe González, 1982–96) may have had positive connotations for those on the left in the early years of his premiership, towards the end of his period of office, it had acquired pejorative overtones in virtually all contexts. Other examples are *yuppismo, sandinista, somocista* (supporter of the former Nicaraguan President, Somoza), *madridista* (supporter of the Spanish football club, Real Madrid), *euroescepticismo* (feelings against further integration of Europe), *fundamentalismo/integrismo islámico*. Lang (1990: 136) notes that *-ista* is the suffix most amenable to foreign bases, e.g. *crolista* (someone who swims the crawl), *waterpolista* (DB) and *surfista* (DB).

-itis has extended its usage from the field of medicine where it is used to refer to a pathology, e.g. *tendinitis*. It can also be used jocularly to imply a pathological condition, e.g. *titulitis* (an obsession with paper qualifications).

-landia perhaps calqued on the English 'land' used in a commercial sense, notably 'Disneyland', or perhaps taken directly from the names of countries such as *Finlandia, Islandia* is currently a particularly creative suffix in Spanish. In Spain this tends to be used to refer to retail outlets, e.g. *fotolandia* (a shop where you can buy photographic equipment), *zumolandia* (a fruit juice outlet), *bricolandia* (a DIY outlet). However, on both sides of the Atlantic it can be used with humorous and pejorative overtones, e.g. *gringolandia/yanquilandia* (a place where the Yanks hold sway).

-manía is another suffix imported from English expressing the notion 'to be crazy about', e.g. *atlantamanía* (obsession with the Olympic Games held in Atlanta 1996), *beatlemanía*.

-cracia meaning 'rule by' tends to be used with pejorative overtones, e.g. *la psoecracia* (autocratic rule by the Spanish socialist party, PSOE), *dedocracia* (see *dedazo*, arbitrary use of power), *eurocracia* (Eurocracy, or all power in the hands of Brussels) (DB).

-oide/-oidal are suffixes, generally used pejoratively, which can be applied to adjectives and nouns and which express the idea of similarity to, and often a debased form of, someone or something, e.g. *fascistoide* (quasi-fascist), *infantiloide* (infantile rather than childlike).

-ólogo denotes 'a person who', e.g. *agresólogo* (specialist in conflict), *politólogo, alergólogo* (DB).

-osis like *-itis* also implies a pathological condition e.g. *acidosis* (DB), *adiposis* (obesity) (DB) and can also be used for jocular or humorous intent.

Where Spanish does not have a lexicalized **adjective** it uses a prepositional phrase. In the following examples no appropriate adjective exists derived respectively from *hueso* and *vestimenta*, and therefore a prepositional phrase is used: *lesiones articulares y de huesos, las barreras arquitectónicas y de vestimenta.* However, there is currently a tendency in Spanish to move away, where possible, from the use of adjectival phrases and to create new adjectives through suffixation. Many of them enable the creation of an adjective from a nominal root. Some of the most productive suffixes currently in use in Spanish are described below:

-able, -ible meaning 'capable of being' is generally added to a verbal root, for example, '*El, con otros **extraditables**, (el helicóptero) tiene flotadores **hinchables** en el caso de amerizaje*' (El País, 7.7.96), **urbanizable, deducible** *de la base* **imponible.** This suffix can form the base for *-ibilidad* a suffix denoting an abstract quality, e.g. *la* **imbatibilidad,** *la* **asequibilidad** (DB).

-ador e.g. *la primera etapa* **privatizadora.**

-al is a particularly productive suffix in Spanish today. Examples of its usage are: *degradación* **medioambiental** rather than *degradación del medioambiente.* Other examples are *argumental* (relating to the plot), *una explicación* **documental,** *carga* **frontal** *de documentos, un choque* **frontal,** *zona* **peatonal,** *la incorporación* **laboral,** *un testigo* **presencial.**

-ante e.g. *Trajes de charol de* **impactantes** *colores* (El País Semanal, 14.7.96), *adelgazante* (DB), *acojonante* (DB).

-ario/orio e.g. *política presupuestaria, plazas hospitalarias, política monetaria, participación comunitaria* (participation in the European Community/Union).

-ativo e.g. *la democratización* **informativa,** *transporte* **corporativo,** *imperio* **especulativo** *inmobiliario.*

-ero is a widely used adjectival and nominal suffix, e.g. *el colectivo* **batasunero** (the Herri Batasuna (a Basque political party) group), *los* **jamoneros** *españoles, los* **peperos** (members or supporters of the Partido Popular).

-esco expresses the notion 'in the manner of', e.g. *abuelesco* (grandfatherly) (DB) and is often used to humorous or ironic effect in journalism, e.g. '. . . *el líder del PP, con modales* **versallescos,** *pidió una política española consensuada en Europa.*' (Cambio 16, 11.7.94).

-iano expresses quality and is frequently found with common names, e.g. *thacheriano* (Thatcherite), 'A *los Stones se les exige ser cada día más* **stonianos**' (*Cambio 16*, 11.7.94), ' . . . *los festivales (. . .) que organizó el* **bocacciano** *Regàs*' (*ABC*, 6.5.94).

-icio e.g. *el sistema* **crediticio**, *la dieta* **alimenticia**.

-ista e.g. *los liberales* **occidentalistas**, *una vuelta* **ciclista**, *una senda claramente* **alcista**.

-ístico e.g. *su actividad* **propagandística** . . . , *guía* **turístico**, *la afición* **futbolística**, *la carrera* **armamentística** (DB).

-ivo e.g. *instalaciones* **deportivas**, *una sociedad* **permisiva**.

-izante can be used with pejorative overtones, e.g. *academizante* (DB), *anarquizante* (DB), *teorizante*.

Additionally, there is the whole question of *gentilicios* or toponyms. Suffixes can be used with the names of countries, towns and other geographical areas. According to Lang (1990: 191) about a dozen suffixes are commonly used, and these vary in their productivity. Examples include:

-aco (*polaco, cosaco* (DB), *canaco* (Kanak) (DB), *bosáico* (Bosnian) (DB)) a suffix which Lang (1990) notes as relatively unproductive. Nonetheless, the last two examples above point to some recent productivity.

-ano (*peruano*), a very productive suffix covering countries, towns and geographical areas.

-ense (*costarricense*), the most productive suffix of all.

-eño (*salvadoreño, acapulqueño* (DB), *alasqueño* (DB)), particularly productive in Latin America.

-ero (*cartagenero*) much more productive in Latin America than it is in Spain.

-és (*ampurdanés*) most widely used with countries but also in the designation of towns and regions.

-í (*marbellí, ceutí* (DB)), derived from Arabic and principally associated with Middle Eastern and North African names (however, *nepalí* has taken over from *nepalés* (DB)). The masculine plural is *-íes*. In a number of instances it co-varies with *-ita*, e.g. *saudí/saudita*.

-ino/ín (*argentino, mallorquín*), *-ín* attaches to Balearic place names.

-ita (*vietnamita*), of very restricted use.

-teco/a (*guatemalteco, chiapateco* (DB)) this suffix is derived from the nahuatl (*-ecatl*) and is found especially in Mexico and Central America, e.g. *yucateco, tolteco*.

There are other rare suffixes which occur occasionally; Lang (1990: 192) mentions *ibicenco* (Ibiza), *nizardo* (Niza) and *ciudadrealengo* (more commonly *ciudadrealeño*) (Ciudad Real).

Diarmuid Bradley (personal communication) also identifies the following suffixes of interest:

-ata croata
-ar kosovar

-arra *gazteiztarra* (inhabitant of Vitoria in the Spanish Basque country)
-én/ena *chechén*
-eno *esloveno*
-is *kirguis*

Suffixes are not always attached to the Spanish toponymic but may attach to an alternative formulation, whether in the original Latin, for example, *hispalense* (Seville), or in a minority language, such as Basque, for example *donostiarra* (San Sebastián). Thus some cities have alternative forms, for example, in the case of Seville, the 'learned' *hispalense* and the 'popular' *sevillano*.

There are also regional preferences. For example, Van Dijk (Herranz in Alvar (1996b: 109)) has noted that the most common place name suffix in Honduras is *-eño*, as in *hondureño*.

It is very difficult to predict which gentilic suffix will attach to which place name. Thus the same place name may attract a different gentilic depending on the country in which it is generated. Lang (1990: 192) gives the following examples:

Santa Fe	*santafecino* (Argentina)
	santafereño (Colombia)
Santiago	*santiagués* (Spain)
	santiaguero (Cuba)
Barcelona	*barcelonés* (Spain)
	barcelonense (Venezuela)

Given the frequency with which new place names from all over the world are temporarily the focus of the news, one of the tasks of the *Departamento de español urgente* (DEU) is to propose to the international news media, or remind them of, an appropriate gentilic in the interests of standardization. For example, when Kashmir came into the news in 1995, the DEU proposed the use of *Cachemira* for the country, *cachemira*, *cachemir* or *casimir* (in preference to, for example, *cashmeer* or *kachmir*) for items made with wool from the country and the alternative forms *cachemirí* or *cachemirano* as the gentilic and to refer to the language spoken in that country.

Diarmuid Bradley (personal communication) notes the tendency for tribal names to be treated as invariable, in line with Lorenzo's (1966) observation that new borrowings may be left invariable, and provides the following examples showing the plural both marked and unmarked:

> Los **hausa**, *agricultores musulmanes muy tradicionalistas* (. . .); *los* **yoruba**, *un sector social más evolucionado* (. . .) *y los* **ibo** . . .
> . . . *dos pueblos,* **ibos** *y* **hausas** *de culturas ancestralmente distintas.*

Adverbs are formed in Spanish by the addition of the suffix *-mente* to the feminine form of the adjective. However, in the case of longer or more infrequently used adjectives, speakers and writers tend to prefer to use adverbial phrases, although the adverbial form can be used for humorous purposes.

However, recent trends in journalism, football commentating and advertising have led to increased use of adverbial forms where they previously would not have occurred, for example:

> Un jamón controlado **nutricionalmente** para tener menos sal,
> . . . Corea del sur y España son los países que más han mejorado **deportivamente** . . . ,
> **Militarmente** no fue una operación muy sangrienta asesorar . . . ,
> **Futbolísticamente**, recuerdo que . . .   (all from *El País Semanal*, 14.7.96).

Emotive suffixation

As we saw earlier, emotive suffixation[3] conveys the attitude of the speaker towards the noun or adjective to which it attaches. It is also used, particularly in casual or intimate conversation, to convey the speaker's attitude towards other speakers and as a marker of informal speech. Thus the terms **diminutive** (conveying the idea of smallness, positive affection or belittling), **augmentative** (conveying large size, impressiveness or general ugliness) and **pejorative** (conveying negative feelings and general rejection) traditionally used to refer to these suffixes are not always helpful when we wish to examine how these suffixes function within interaction. Indeed Gooch (1970: 4) notes the inherent ambivalence of these suffixes which take their meaning(s) from the context in which they are uttered, and where, for example, a diminutive, rather than express diminution can express a whole range of emotions from affection to pejorative irony. Bajo Pérez (1997: 71) notes that in some contexts the use of a diminutive, such as *Doña Manuelita* might connote respect in Latin America, while connoting affection or irony in a Peninsular Spanish speech community.

Emotive suffixation is, as Lang (1990: 207) concludes, a particularly distinctive feature of Spanish and one where its extensive and vigorous use distinguishes the language from other Romance languages such as Italian and Portuguese which also share this feature. Indeed, Lang further notes that in addition to the extremely widespread *-ito*, *-illo* and *-azo*, other suffixes such as *-ico*, *-ete* and *-ín* are showing clear signs of revival, and others still, such as *-azo* and *-ón*, appear to be developing new uses in the twentieth century.

We shall also see that there is some overlap with the previous section, as it is not always possible to make a clear distinction between what is an emotive and a non-emotive use of a particular suffix. In the following example the distinction is clear: the suffix *-ón* when attached to the root lexeme *tel-* (cloth) becomes *telón* (curtain) fundamentally changing the sense of the base and is therefore classed as a non-emotive use; the same suffix attached to *cincuenta* provides an adjective with potentially pejorative connotations as in *cincuentón* (on the wrong side of fifty) and is consequently an emotive suffix. Another distinctive feature of emotive suffixation is the fact that suffixes can be accumulated on the same base, for example *ahora* may become *ahorita* or *ahoritita*. While there are some dominant sequences, for example *-ete* + *-ón* (*guapetón* a good-looking hunk) and *-ón* + *-azo* (*cabronazo*, blow beneath the belt), the individual speaker has tremendous liberty to create sequences from the wide variety of suffixes which we shall examine below and to use, where necessary, variants (e.g. *-ecillo* for *-illo*) to insert extra phonemes to create new forms (e.g. 't' in *cafetucho* derived from *café*). We will also see that there is an element of regional and social variation, particularly in the use of diminutives with different suffixes favoured by different groups.

The most commonly used emotive suffixes are the following:

Diminutives

-ito/cito/ico/cico

-ito/cito is the most common diminutive and co-varies regionally with *-ico/cico*, used in Spain, principally in Aragon, Navarre, Murcia and Granada, and in parts of Latin America, e.g. Venezuela, Costa Rica, Cuba, Colombia. Contrary to what is the case in Spain, in Latin America *-ico* occurs when the final syllable of the root ends in 't' or 'd', e.g. *pelota* (ball), *pelotica*. In fact it is associated to such an extent with Costa Rica that its inhabitants are commonly known as *los ticos*. The use of *-ito* can be lexicalized, e.g. in parts of Latin America, *Espera un cachito* and *un cachito de café*, in Spain *una tortita* (a pancake) from *una torta* (a cake). In parts of Bolivia, the variant *-ingo* may be used in popular speech. Bajo Pérez (1997: 71) notes the euphemistic/respectful use of this suffix in Latin America, e.g. *el difuntito* to refer to the dearly departed.

While in Peninsular Spanish the use of the diminutive is generally confined to nouns (*la casita*) and adjectives (*estaba solito*) with very few adverbial forms (e.g. *ahorita*, from *ahora*), in Latin America its applicability can be much wider (e.g. *apenitas*, *nomasito* (from *no más*) and reduplication may be more frequent, as in *ahoritita*, *cerquitica*. It is also frequently used to provide affectionate diminutives of proper names, for example *Luisito*, *Carmencita*.

This diminutive can be used simply to express diminution, for example *un chico/un chiquito*, 'en aquella época no, era **guapita** pero no guapa' (Briz 1995: 216). It can also be used as a superlative for emphasis *ahoritita* (right this very minute) or to express the attitude of the speaker. For example, 'esta cinta nos está costando más **trabajito** rellenarla' (Lamíquiz 1987: 126) shows the diminutive used ironically insofar as the speaker is finding the recorded interview to which he refers more rather than less work.

As we shall see when we look at politeness strategies in Chapter 8, emotive suffixes, and particularly diminutives have a major role to play. For example, they allow speakers to pay attention to the face of their interlocutor and themselves in a variety of ways. In the following extract (Gooch 1970: 7) they allow the speaker, a customer in a shop, to mitigate the force of a request, expressed by an imperative, to the shop assistant:

Assistant: *¿Qué desea?*
Customer: *Crema Nivea, por favor.*
A: *¿En caja o en tubo?*
C: *Deme un **tubito**.*
A: *¿Grande o pequeño?*

In the following extract (Briz 1995: 223), they let a speaker reduce the threat to her own face. In the extract below from eastern Spain note how the speaker (C), who is on a diet, uses an abundance of diminutives (DIM.) to try self-mockingly to play down her (fairly substantial) calorie consumption to her cousin (P), and how P uses one diminutive (*sabrosito*) ambivalently, either to show affection to or to gently mock her cousin:

C: *¡Pobre de mí! si sólo he comido una **bocatita** de tres **bacaladitos** con un **poquitito** de ajoaceite en el pan y - y una*
P: *pues el ajoaceite (no te debías)*
    (. . .)
C: *unos **pimientitos** o algo pero el **bacaladito** ese así a palo seco, sin calentar ni nada tampoco si (bate) un **poquito** de **pistito***
P: *Sí, claro, está más **sabrosito***
C: *pone un **poquito** de **pistito** y el **caldosito** del tomate pero es que había nada más que, todo era a base de carnes y cosas, no me podía poner nada, ¡ay mi **primita**! me he alegrao mucho de verte*[4]

Other diminutives which are commonly used but which are much less productive than the variants examined above are:

-ete more common in Spain than in Latin America, may express endearment, but frequently has slightly pejorative connotations. For example, a mother refers to her daughter's boyfriend of whom she does not entirely approve as *el noviete* (Briz 1995: 140).
-in/ina is generally approbatory and found quite widely (and is particularly common in Asturias and Granada), e.g. '*hay que poner (. . .) unas hombreritas pequeñinas*' (Briz 1995: 144).
-illo/a is associated with Andalusia but can be found throughout the Spanish-speaking world. This suffix lends itself more to lexicalization than those we have looked at previously, e.g. *colilla* (cigarette butt) from *cola* (tail) and may change the gender of the base, e.g. *zapatilla* (slipper) from *zapato* (shoe). In the following extract it is used by an Andalusian woman talking about her husband being an emigrant worker in Germany: '*porque el hombre se va a Alemania, va a trabajar ¿no? entonces él lo que quiere es ahorrar unos **dinerillos***' (own data). In areas where *-illo* co-varies with *-ito/-cito*, it may have slightly pejorative connotations, as in the following example where the speaker is being somewhat derogatory about her daughter and the daughter's boyfriend: '*y son muy **gastadorcillos**, siempre van de cena por ahí y todo*' (Briz 1995: 140); '*ahí*

tienen cosas así **modernillas** *no una sección de música pues de hace diez años por ejemplo'* (Briz 1995: 161).

-uelo/a like *-ete*, may express endearment and has slightly pejorative connotations, e.g. *plazuela* tends to connote a meaner square than *plaza*.

Augmentatives

Augmentatives, while not in any way as productive as the diminutives we have examined above, play an important role in spontaneous informal speech and also in the type of journalese which seeks impact on the reader. Lang (1990: 111) states that 'regional distinctions are less critical with augmentatives than with diminutives, although particular areas may favour one augmentative form at the expense of another.' The principal augmentatives we shall deal with here are *-azo*, *-ón/ona*, *-ote* and *-udo*.

-azo/a

We have already examined the lexicalized use of *-azo* used to denote impact or a particularly salient action as in *tejerazo* (the attempted coup d'état in Spain by General Tejero). Similarly, it can indicate an action or result of an action, frequently in informal Spanish. For example, *le das un telefonazo* would be expressed in more formal Spanish as *le llamas por teléfono*. However, it can also be used with hyperbolic effect and its connotations are firmly rooted in context. For example, in the following extract the word *madraza* (from *madre*, a mother) is not used positively. Rather the speaker implies that she mollycoddles her daughter: '*y luego yo soy demasiado* **madraza** *¡ojo! mi marido ya me reñía porque soy demasiado* **madraza**, *incluso a veces les he llevado el desayuno a la cama*' (Briz 1995: 140). The daughter could show her appreciation (or disrespect) by referring to her mother as *¡qué madraza!*

-ón/ona is an extremely widespread suffix which is an augmentative, e.g. *cuatro* **intentonas** *de rebelión*, and can also have a wide variety of connotations, depending on context, ranging from approbatory through ironic to condemnatory, e.g. ' . . . *Jagger y Richards, una pareja de* **cincuentones**' (*Cambio 16*, 11.7.94) (with the implication that they are too old to be getting up to what they are doing), '*nadie ha criticado con tanto denuedo como él sus pecaminosa conductas, sus elevados gastos, sus muchos puros, sus* **comilonas** . . . ' (*Cambio 16*, 11.7.94). Diarmuid Bradley (personal communication) notes that the new suffix *-añero/a* is competing with *-ón/ona* in some number samples and gives the following example: ' . . . *parece inevitable que los formatos tradicionalmente infantiles se carguen de contenidos maduros, satíricos,* **treintañeros** *o* **cuarentones**.'

-ote/a is an augmentative which also takes its connotations from context. However, while in Spain these connotations are generally negative, elsewhere (e.g. in Central America (Quesada Pacheco in Alvar, 1996a: 109)) it may be used affectionately, e.g. *desvergonzadote* (shameless hussy). In some cases it has been lexicalized, e.g. *una palabrota* from *una palabra*. *-ote/a* can also be affixed to a verb to connote substandard performance of the action in

question, e.g. *bailotear* from *bailar*. Lang (1990: 115) notes that, while it is in general recession in the Spanish-speaking world, it does survive strongly in Central Spain and in the Spanish of the Mexican state of Jalisco.

Pejoratives

Compared to the two groups examined above, there is a wide variety of pejorative suffixes, principally *-aco, -acho, -ajo, -ales, -ango/engo/ingo/ongo/ ungo, -arro/urro, -astro, -ejo/-cejo, -eta, -oide, -orro, -uco, -ucho, -udo, -ute, -uzco, -uzo*. These suffixes cannot be used as freely as diminutives and augmentatives; rather, nouns and adjectives will tend to be associated with one particular suffix. Lang (1990: 122) notes that, while these suffixes may not be particularly productive when taken individually, they do, collectively, provide speakers and writers with a rich resource, particularly in informal tenor.

In the following example, the speaker uses the pejorative suffix *-aja* in a very informal set of directions he is giving to a friend: '*es un c- donde está la iglesia de san no sé cuántos pequeñaja pasao la vía*' (Briz 1995: 178).

Pejorative suffixes may frequently be used jocularly. In the following example, a man is arguing with a woman who is not sure whether to wear a bikini or a swimsuit at a particular public swimming baths: '*depende de lo buenorra que estás, si no estás muy buena no hace falta que lleves nada*' (Briz 1995: 158).

The augmentative **udo/a** is used most frequently with pejorative connotations and, unlike the emotive suffixes examined above, tends to change the noun to which it affixes to an adjective, for example, *panzudo* (pot-bellied) from *la panza*. Indeed, it displays a tendency to be affixed to parts of the body.

(ii) Compounding

Compound nouns have always been a feature of Spanish; however, in recent decades they have become, undoubtedly under the influence of English, an extremely powerful source of neologisms and, while some may be calques of English compound nouns, e.g. **hombre rana**, many are entirely indigenous, for example, '*los ochenta y los noventa dejan un legado de* **construcciones insignia**' (*El País*, 7.7.96). Compounding involves the creation of new words from independent words already existing in a language and may draw on a variety of combinations of these.

In Spanish, compounds may be be formed by the following combinations:

a verb followed by a noun, for example, *limpiahornos, elevalunas, cazatalentos, salvapantallas, apoyabrazos, guardaespaldas*;
a noun followed by an adjective, e.g. *pirata informático, espalda mojada, dirección asistida*;
a noun qualified by a noun followed by an adjective, under the influence

of English syntax, for example *estafilococos metacílin-resistentes* (methicillin-resistant staphylococci), *prueba ureasa-positiva* (urea-positive test);
an adjective followed by a noun, e.g. *todoterreno, largometraje*;
a noun followed by a preposition and then a noun, e.g. *olla a presión, ranura de expansión*. As a compound of this kind becomes lexicalized it may lose the prepositional element, e.g. *efecto de invernadero* is now commonly *efecto invernadero*.

Nouns can also be used attributively as the in case of *niño probeta, ciencia ficción, ciudad dormitorio, página Web, un buque ferry, una compañía líder, efectos calendario, una bomba lapa*. When nouns are used attributively, there are often doubts over whether to hyphenate both elements in the written language, e.g. *coche-bomba* or *coche bomba*. In the case of an adjective followed by a noun, where the neologisms are commonly calques of English, doubts may arise over whether to write them as one word (*librecambio*) or two (*libre cambio*). Similarly there is a lack of agreement over the pluralization of nominal compounds allowing for either the first or both nouns to be pluralized, e.g. *palabras claves* and *palabras clave* (DB).

There is evident overlap between the use of affixes and compounding, especially in the case of prefixes such as *auto-* (here in the sense of automobile rather than 'self'), *cine-, foto-* and *tele-*, and more recently *narco-, drogo-, inmuno-*, and so on which are derived from nouns or occasionally adjectives (*automóvil, cinematográfico, fotografía, televisión, nárcotico, inmune*) and which have proved a vigorous source of compounds, e.g. *autoescuela, fotoperiodismo, telenovela, teleconferencia, videojuego, narcotráfico, narcodólar, inmunodeficiencia, insulinodependiente, logopedia, pentacampeón*. It should be noted that two processes are involved here in the production of these prefixes: abbreviation in the case of, say, *narco-* and *tele-*, and the creation of special combining forms *drogo-* (from *droga*), *inmuno-* (from *inmune*) similar in nature to the traditional combining forms *italo-* (from *italiano*) or *indo-* (from *indio*).

Along with compounds we can also consider blends. Blends occur where two words merge into each other, for example, *informática* (*información* + *automática*) which has subsequently given rise to a host of similar forms, such as *ofimática* (*oficina* + *automática*), *docudrama* (*documental* + *drama*), *publirreportaje* (*publicidad* + *reportaje*) and are often used to humorous effect in the press and advertising.

(iii) Conversion

In conversion a word changes its class without any change of form. For example, an adjective can become detached from the noun it qualifies to stand as the noun itself, for example, *un coche deportivo* becomes *un* **deportivo**, *la* **cementera** stands for *una fábrica cementera*, *la* **autonómica** for *cadena de televisión de un gobierno general autonómico*, *la* **disquera** for *la compañía disquera* (DB). Conversely, a noun may fulfil an adjectival role as in *un viaje relámpago*, an example also of compounding. A feature of colloquial and advertising speech has been an increased use of certain adjectives as adverbs as in *se portó* **genial** *conmigo* or the use of nouns as adverbs *se pasó* **cantidad**.

(iv) Acronyms

The use of acronyms in the process of lexical creation in Spanish has been relatively recent, dating principally from the 1970s. Nonetheless, combined with the processes of derivation and compounding, acronyms have been the source of a significant number of new words.[5] Acronyms are generally derived from the initial letters of the words that make up a name, for example *OTAN* (*Organización del Tratado del Atlántico Norte*), and while they generally have their base in Spanish, may derive from the English (in the case of international organizations, for example) as in *GATT, UNICEF, ecu.* They may be pronounced as they are written, *otán*, or, in the case of alphabetisms, the different letters may be pronounced *egebé* (*EGB, Educación General Básica*, formerly the Spanish school-leaving certificate). In some instances a combination approach is adopted to facilitate pronunciation, for example *pesóe*, (*PSOE, Partido Socialista Obrero Español*). Acronyms, in the process of being fully lexicalized, may be condensed. *PNN* (*Profesores No Numerarios*) progressed from *pé éne éne* to *penene* while others may be expanded. *FLP* (*Frente de Liberación Popular*) has progressed from *éfe éle pé* to *felipe*.

Graphically, acronyms may start life as capital letters punctuated by full stops (*O.T.A.N.*), later losing the full stops (*OTAN*), subsequently only retaining upper case for the initial letter (*Otan*) and finally losing all capitalization. Examples of fully lexicalized acronyms are *ovni* (*objeto volante no identificado*), *láser* borrowed from the English 'Light Amplification by Stimulated Emission of Radiation', *sida* (*síndrome de inmuno-deficiencia adquirida*), *ecu* (European currency unit) now replaced by the coinage *euro*, *pyme* (*pequeña y mediana empresa*). Frequently, as elsewhere, there is a tendency to coin acronyms which are not only easy to pronounce but which also coincide with apposite words in the language; this is the case, for example, of *AVE* (*Alta Velocidad Española*) (*ave* = bird). The gender of acronyms generally accords with the principal noun contained in the name, for example, *el PP* (*Partido Popular*) or *la UEFA* (*Unión de Asociaciones Europeas de Fútbol*), although there may be doubt, *el/la FBI*. There may also be a lack of agreement on pluralization; for example, the following forms can all be found for the plural of LP (Long Playing): *los LP, los LPs, los LP's, los LPS, los elepes*. Alphabetisms relating to plural nouns, such as *Estados Unidos, Comisiones Obreras* are represented graphically by the duplication of the initial capital letters, *EE.UU., CC.OO.*, although when this proves too unwieldy, alternatives are sought. For example the DEU recommends that *Organizaciones No Gubernamentales* should be written as *las ONG* and not *las OO.NN.GG.* Nonetheless, abbreviations such as SS.AA.RR. (*Sus Altezas Reales*) are frequently in evidence (DB).

Derivation, compounding and blends, then, allow, where needed, a proliferation of related forms such as *pepero* (member of the *Partido Popular*), *peneuvista*, (member of the *Partido Nacionalista Vasco*), *priísta* (member of the *Partido Revolucionario Institucional Mexicano*), *pesocracia*, *sidoso*, *uefo* (a member of UEFA), *ufólogo* (UFO watcher) (DB), *yugre* (*yuppie* + *progre*) and *veteuveada* (*vetada en TVE*) (Rodríguez González, 1993a: 16). These are particularly in evidence in post-Franco Spain, which has seen a proliferation of political groupings capable of generating acronymic reference. They also occur frequently in business and advertising where, for example, the adjective *rumasiano*, for example, *rumasiano proceder*, derived from the acronym Rumasa (Ruiz Mateos, S.A., a company accused of serious financial irregularities), now connotes a particular style of business corruption (Rodríguez González 1993a: 20).

(v) Abbreviation

Traditionally, and generally in colloquial language, a number of words have been abbreviated to two syllables. There are the long-established examples of *profe* (*profesor*), *bici* (*bicicleta*), *la contra* (*los contrarrevolucionarios*). In some instances the abbreviated form has entered the standard language as in the case of *taxi* (*taxímetro*) and *cine* (*cinematográfico*), *foto* (*fotografía*). In many cases it is recognized by the population but only used in certain less formal registers of speech and writing, (e.g. *la mili* for *el servicio militar*, *llamar a los polis* (*policía*)).

In Spain, abbreviation has been a particular feature of the speech of young people and students as well as the anti-language of certain subcultures with, in addition to the traditional two-syllable abbreviations (e.g. *depre* – *depresión*, *ampli* – *amplificador*, abbreviations where there are often three syllables (e.g. *analfa* – *analfabeto*, *anfeta* – *anfetamina* and where the final vowel is frequently modified most commonly to *-a* (e.g. *estupa* – *estupefacientes*, *forasta* – *forastero*).[6]

(vi) Metaphor

While in many cases the metaphors used to describe new phenomena are coined abroad and are calqued by Spanish, as we shall see in 4.0.1, Spanish also creates its own metaphors. Such is the case of *canguro* which has displaced the borrowing *baby-sitter*, of *manguero* which is beginning to substitute the English borrowing *finger* used to refer to a covered aircraft access corridor, of *búho* (literally 'owl', a bus which runs at night) and *corbata* (literally 'necktie', used, in golf, to refer to a ball which goes round the edge of the hole without going in). More commonly, metaphor is used by speakers and writers in an ad hoc fashion. However, even here there are patterns of use. For example, Rodríguez González (1993a) identifies amongst others the following lexical fields as being rich in metaphor used to refer to politics, war, sport, games, spectaculars (e.g. bullfighting), religion and health. Díaz Rojo (1994: 55-66) gives the following metaphors taken respectively from religion, war and bullfighting:

*No nos toca jugar ni a la **canonización** ni a la **crucifixión** de González (ABC, 10.5.94)*

*¿Qué discurso hubiera hecho Aznar (. . .) si ABC no hubiese proporcionado **munición ideológica**? (El Mundo, 21.4.94)*

*La verdad es que viendo el otro día a Mariano Rubio yéndose con un **bajonazo** a la **querencia** del Banco de España (. . .), **aculándose en las tablas** y **echando sangre por la boca** (. . .) Blasco Ibañez **la fiera** está en los tendidos. (El Mundo, 21.4.94)[7]*

We have briefly described above the mechanisms which enable speakers and writers of Spanish a wide margin for creative use of their language and which ensure that most neologisms created in this way are immediately comprehensible to users of Spanish throughout the world. In the next section we shall look at borrowing and revisit these mechanisms, as they provide the means by which new lexis can be rapidly assimilated into Spanish and even prove a basis for the creation of further neologisms.

4.0.1 Creation of neologisms through borrowing

(i) Borrowing

Borrowing, without any concessions to the phonology, morphology and syntax of Spanish, is the process which comes in for the greatest amount of criticism from prescriptivist quarters. It is particularly evident in the media, which is constantly required to deal with new concepts which are not yet lexicalized in Spanish or when it wishes to revitalize old concepts by borrowing new foreign terms. Examples can easily be culled from articles dealing, for example, with new technology such as '*un buddy-film*', '*los mass media*', '*el vactor*' (virtual actor) '*los storyboards*' '*los shaders*' (a computer shading application), (*una película de cine*) *snuff* (*Cambio 16*, 1.4.96: 67, 83, 89). Indeed, in the domains of media and the arts, science and technology (information technology) and business and economics, readers are frequently called on to assume a knowledge of English, although the same journals may provide paraphrases and mini-dictionaries as linguistic support. Bookless (1994) shows that there is a wide gap between what is recognized by speakers and what is used in everyday communication.

In advertising, borrowing can clearly fulfil the need of revitalizing a concept already lexicalized in the host language; such is the case of *backup a domicilio* which already exists in Spanish as *asistencia a domicilio*. Advertisers targeting specific markets, in this case the home computer purchaser, can draw on the positive connotations of English jargon in this context, to appeal to their market.

In sport, borrowing occurs particularly frequently in live broadcasting where presenters may be reluctant to waste time by using long circumlocutions to refer to concepts not yet standardly lexicalized in Spanish, for example, or alternatively may wish to appeal to in-group knowledge shared by fans of a particular sport. The latter is particularly true in the case of written sports reports where borrowings from English or French are especially evident. For example, in one paragraph of an article about a Spanish tennis player's performance at Wimbledon, the borrowings *smash* and *break* appear:

> *El más flagrante (error) fue un fácil* **smash** *frente a la red, en el que la bola pasó por el lado de la raqueta de Steffi. Fue el único momento en que Arantxa pudo meterse en el partido. Y lo aprovechó. Logró sus únicos dos* **breaks** *del encuentro e igualó a cinco juegos.* (El País, 7.7.96)[8]

Borrowed lexis which becomes well known in one particular field, for example, sport, may subsequently be used figuratively in other fields. For instance, the English 'pole position' commonly used in motor and motor cycle racing, as in '*Lograron respectivamente, las* **pole position** *de 500cc y 125cc en los entrenamientos para el Gran Premio de Alemania*' (El País, 7.7.96) is also to be found, used figuratively, in the Economics section of the same newspaper, '*Salvador Barberà, (. . .) toma el relevo en la* **pole position** *española en materia de investigación.*' It is obvious that compared with the Spanish equivalent '*primera posición en la parrilla de salida*', the borrowing *pole position* has the advantage of economy of expression. Diarmuid Bradley (personal communication) notes that even further economies have been made with *pole position* being reduced to the manageable *pole* as in the following example: '*Patrese no es un piloto que haya conseguido muchas* **poles** *en su dilatada carrera deportiva . . . .*' (El Mundo, 22.9.91).

Borrowed lexis can also serve as a point of departure for lexical creation using the mechanisms decribed above but drawing on either purely imported stock or mixing Spanish and foreign elements. Such is the case of the suffix -*ing*, arguably a borrowing from French which in turn had been borrowed from English. This suffix has given rise to *footing* (jogging) and even *puenting* (bungy jumping, also referred to as *el benji* (DB)), for example '**Puenting, rafting**, *saltos de caída libre son vocablos que desde hace algún tiempo están en la boca de muchos jóvenes aficionados a las emociones fuertes*' (ABC, 31.7.93) (DB). El País recommends the use of the term *puentismo* (El País, 90. 343) (DB). In Spain there are what are called *reality shows* (television shows focusing on real-life problems and dilemmas of its participants), a concept lexicalized in Spanish although not yet in British English, where the constituent genres are lexicalized, for example, 'docusoap', 'confessional television'. The English genitive suffix apostrophe 's' can be found in Spanish commercial establishments such as *Pepe's*, adding a touch of exoticism. Diarmuid Bradley (personal communication) notes that the growth in popularity in keeping pets (*animales de compañía*) has led to an influx of exotic dogs presenting real challenges to Spanish dog lovers. The West Highland white terrier becomes *un westi(e)* and a compromise is reached with the Irish wolfhound, *un wolfhound irlandés*.

While borrowings are likely to be more frequent in certain fields of discourse (e.g. sport, computing, business and economics), their use also depends on the mode (speaking or writing) and the tenor (level of formality) of the discourse. For example, while the borrowing *el staff* might be used in informal discussion of staffing problems by lecturers, the university administration would not use this term in official documentation, opting for the indigenous *personal docente*.

Lexis which meets more than the ephemeral needs of Spanish speakers and writers is frequently integrated into the host language whether by **assimilation** (at the levels of orthography, phonology/prosody, morphology), **semantic extension** or through **loan translation/calquing**.

(ii) Assimilation

Assimilation takes place when a borrowed lexical item is not replaced by an indigenous term but rather is adapted in whole or part to the phonology/prosody, orthography and morphology of the host language. Given that Spanish speakers appear unlikely to accept the indigenous compound *mercadotecnia* recommended by the RAE as the equivalent of the English 'marketing', what phonology, orthography, and accentuation of the borrowed term are to be adopted to assimilate the word into Spanish? While 'marketing', in fact, poses little challenge to Spanish phonology, at the level of orthography writers are faced with three options – total assimilation (*márquetin*), which does not appear to have met with favour either, or retention of the borrowed orthography with or without accentuation to mark the deviant, in terms of Spanish, first syllable stress (*marketing* or *márketing*). In this instance, it is the latter variant which appears to be being adopted as standard.

Phonologically, English has had little effect on the pronunciation of borrowings and although it is generally accepted that the vast majority of borrowings enter the language through the written medium, those which enter the spoken language, often initially through the media, tend to be pronounced in accordance with Spanish phonology. For example, typically there is avoidance of initial 's', of complex consonantal clusters and of the phoneme /d/. Some may therefore become virtually unrecognizable in the spoken language, for example *pub* [pu] [paf]. If these borrowings fill a genuine lexical need and are adopted by the speech community, their pronunciation may subsequently affect their orthography. Such is the case, for example, of *slogan*, now frequently written as *eslogan*, *thriller*, which appears to have variants ranging from *triler* to *trailer*, and *junkie*, which has also spawned a number of variants including *yonki*. As regards stress patterns, the borrowed terms tend to reflect the stress patterns of the donor language and this is marked, as in the case of *márketing* above, by accentuation, as in *estrés, estándar, bumerán*.

At a morphological level, the processes outlined above of affixation and compounding are used to generate a host of derived forms. For example, in an article (*Cambio 16*, 8.7.96) about the TV serial *Star Trek*, it is possible to find the nouns, *los trekkers*, *los trekkies*, *la startrekmanía*, the verb form *startrekizarse* and the nominal compound *la cocina trek*.

Once a term has been assimilated into Spanish, problems may arise concerning derived forms. For example, what is to be the plural form of *fax*, *los fax* or *los faxes*? Should the verbal form be *faxear*, or *faxar*? Should the verbal form of *zapping* (i.e. browsing through different (TV) channels) be *zapear* or *hacer zapping*? Should a windsurfer be a *windsurfero* or a *windsurfista*? Commonly a number of variants coexist in the language and only when one finds common favour do the others fall into disuse. For example, in the case of to 'click' (with a mouse (comp.)), initially the derived forms *cliquear*, *hacer clic(k)* and the indigenous *pulsar* could be found; now *hacer clic* appears to be becoming the standard term. Once a borrowing has been commonly accepted into the language, it is easier for related forms to be accepted also; for example, *software* and *hardware* have subsequently been followed by *shareware*. This is even the case for borrowed elements such as the English suffix *-ing* which allows other forms to be created by analogy which do not exist in the donor language, for example, as we saw above, *el footing* (jogging).

(iii) Loan translations or calques

A loan translation or calque occurs when a host language takes a lexical item, commonly a metaphor, which has been coined in a donor language and translates it directly, as in *ratón* ('mouse' in computing), *rascacielos* (skyscraper). Such items are extremely common and frequently not recognized by speakers as loans in any sense as they are created from indigenous language stock. In time they may draw on the derivational mechanisms of Spanish to create lexical clusters, for example, *disco duro* now has the derived form *disquetera* (disk drive) which appears set to displace the earlier *unidad de disco* and the borrowing *disk drive*. Bookless (1994) points to the extreme creativity of writers and speakers of the English language in forging these metaphors and the way in which, once they have gained recognition, they are translated into practically all the languages which need to express that particular concept. Examples of calques of this kind are *el síndrome de las vacas locas* (mad cow disease), *comida basura*, *Europa fortaleza*, *en versión beta*, *grandes superficies* (*grandes surfaces* (French)).

Loan translations are often considered by purists to be 'better' or more in accordance with the host language than borrowings; for such reasons, for many years, there was an attempt to promote the calque *balompié* for 'football'; in the event, the largely assimilated borrowing *fútbol* was adopted as standard and has generated a number of derived forms, for example, *futbolista*, *futbolístico/ero*, *futbolín*, *futbito*. However, the calques *balonmano*, *baloncesto* and *balonvolea* have been adopted as standard in Spain (although *el básquet* is still alive), while the borrowings *voley-ball* and *voleibol* remain more common in Latin America.

(iv) Semantic extension and shift

Semantic extension occurs where a word in the host language acquires an additional meaning through contact with a donor language; in extreme cases this new meaning can replace the previous one (semantic shift). Also referred to as paronymic borrowing or popularly 'false friend syndrome', it is an extremely prolific source for change through contact in Spanish. Given that English, French and Spanish share a large number of of Latin roots it is very easy for the meaning attached to an English or French word to be transferred to its Spanish paronym; Bookless (1994) mentions the case of *versátil*, a little-used, erudite adjective generally used in Spanish to refer to people of an inconstant nature and now used, often by advertisers, in the current English sense of 'adaptable' as in *el microordenador versátil de escritorio*.

As we have already seen, this largely invisible form of borrowing was a primary motivation for the creation of the original news agency style guides. Indeed, this type of borrowing is most widespread in those parts of Spanish-speaking America, particularly Mexico, Puerto Rico and amongst Spanish-speaking communities in the United States, where contact with English permeates life to a far greater extent. Here, loans frequently enter the Spanish language directly, rather than being indirectly channelled through the media as we shall see in Chapter 9.

However, the media too, particularly in Spain, are a primary source of paronymic borrowing. The DEU (February 1995) singles out the case of the Spanish noun *evidencia* (something which is evident) as one of semantic extension through contact with English. There appears to be a marked increase in its use in contexts where English would use 'evidence', for example:

> there is no **evidence** against him (*no hay (evidencia)* **pruebas** *en su contra*)
> to call somebody in **evidence** (*llamar a uno (en evidencia) como* **testigo**).

They adduce as a possible cause for this semantic extension the poor quality of translation of American courtroom dramas for Spanish television. Of the multitude of common borrowings which the DEU is continuing to discourage we find:

> *esas* **especulaciones** *comenzaron hace dos años* (the DEU recommends *rumores*)
> *una reunión* **informal** (*oficiosa*)
> *ese documento no sólo* **ignora** *los intereses* (*se prescinde de*)
> *que revise su* **posición** (*postura*)
> *la alta* **moda** (*costura*)
> **abordar** *un autobús* (*subir a*)

While semantic extension and shift appears to be, in the majority of cases, a result of languages in contact, there are also instances where the users of

Spanish prefer to fill a newly created lexical gap by extending the meaning of an item already in the lexicon but unrelated to any foreign source. Such is the case of *soportar*, the meaning of which has extended from 'supporting' or 'bearing' to 'being compatible with' (computers), for example, a piece of software which *soporta más de 10 modelos de Mac*.

As we have already observed, when a borrowed term is seen to meet more than an ephemeral need it will normally be adapted to the phonology and morphology of the host language or even relexicalized from indigenous language stock. Furthermore, socio-cultural factors may hasten this process as we shall see in the case of football terminology below.

A significant area where there has been a relexicalization of borrowed terms illustrating the mechanisms described above is that of football. Latorre (1991: 769) charts a shift from the Anglicisms (adapted to the phonology of Spanish) prevalent in Chile prior to 1950 (the sport was introduced into the country in the late nineteenth century) and the Hispanicized forms used today. He also notes that where a borrowed term has proved to be particularly productive it is less likely to be replaced by a native one and cites the contrasting pair, the Hispanicized calque *balompié*, which has generated no derived forms, and the borrowing *fútbol*, which has many derivatives, as we have seen. 1950 is a significant date insofar as Spanish had been declared an official language of FIFA in 1946 (Castañón Rodríguez 1991). In the years which followed Latin American football dominated world class football. Latorre (1991: 769) provides the following table charting this change:

Terms used until approximately 1950:	Terms used at the current time:
1 *goalkeeper*	*arquero, potero, golero, guardameta, guardapalos, guardavallas, meta, guardián*
2 *backs*	*zagueros, defensa, marcadores, laterales, centrales*
3 *insiders*	*mediocampistas*
4 *wing*	*puntero, alero*
5 *centre forward*	*centrodelantero, ariete, punta de lanza, atacante*
6 *referee*	*árbitro, colegiado* (Spain), *juez, pito*
7 *scorer*	*marcador, tanteador*

Latorre (1991: 770) notes the productivity of the compound element *guarda* and of the borrowing *golero* (e.g. *golear, golazo, goleador, goleada* compared with the indigenous *tanto* which has generated *tanteador* (DB)). He also notes that this relexification has, in the case of football, taken place through the actions of language users rather than as a result of the efforts of lexicographers but notes that the latter are playing a significant role in the field of information technology. Diarmuid Bradley (personal communication) provides considerable evidence for the current use of the assimilated borrowing *linier* (pl. *linieres*) for linesman and notes the use of *lateral* as a standard term for 'winger', with *coletilla* as an alternative for 'referee' and *guardaredes* as 'goalkeeper'.

Castañón Rodríguez (1991) gives an interesting social history of football terminology. In Spain, during the initial stages of Francoism there was an ideologically-driven Hispanicization of football terms usually by means of direct translations, calques or, if necessary, adaptations of borrowings to the phonology of Spanish. However, after 1973, when players and trainers from Latin America were permitted to work for Spanish teams and with the recognized prestige of Latin American football, Latin American terms started to oust Castilian ones despite the best efforts of the authorities on style of the time. Later, as we have seen, the 1980s were characterized by the rise of the style guide with its attempts to unify usage, attempts which are regularly flouted by sports reporters, whose style has changed over the decades to incorporate increasingly 'youth' terminology (Castañón Rodríguez 1991).

As we saw in Chapter 2, one of the primary functions of the style guides is to suggest and promote the dissemination of preferred forms for borrowings whether these be in the form of indigenous equivalents or suitably assimilated forms. In many cases, however, they appear to be waging a rearguard action, especially when it comes to coining and attempting to impose indigenous terminology. Indeed, a comparison between different editions of the same style guide will show the weight of usage against prescriptive advice. For example, the indigenous acronym *UCE* (*Unidad de Cambio Europeo*) ceded place entirely to the *ecu*. Set against this, is the intensely creative process of assimilation and derivation which we have witnessed which testifies to the current vigour of the language and the ability of its speakers to use borrowings on their own terms.

4.1 Lexical variation

Given that Spanish is the mother tongue of speakers of both sexes, all ages, from all socio-economic groups, from a wide variety of ethnic communities spanning the five continents and that, as a world language, it is used by speakers and writers for multiple uses, all that we can do here is to give some small indication of the range of lexical variation within the Spanish language.

In considering variation it is useful to make a distinction between **user** variation and **use** variation. Users will select their codes from a range which may be marked for variables such as sex, age, socio-economic group, level of education, rural or urban provenance, geographic provenance and ethnic group. They will also select them according to the **field** of use, for example, political speech, sermon, informal conversation, according to **mode**, essentially speech or writing[9], and according to **tenor**, whether interpersonal (ranging from formal to informal) or functional (for example, exposition, argumentation, instruction).

In this section we shall briefly look at user variation and how this can affect lexical choice. We shall look at geographical and age variation focusing principally, but not exclusively, on lexis and referring as necessary to other relevant features, such as morpho-syntax, of these varieties. In Chapters 7 and 8 we shall deal with the issue of use-related variation when we examine issues such as discourse and genre, pragmatics and politeness.

4.1.0 User variation: geography

In the perception of speakers, the most salient differences are those related to the different geographical varieties of Spanish. The same word may have a completely different referent or sense depending on the country or the region in which it is used, for example, *un tinto* (used in Colombia to refer to a cup of coffee and in Spain to a glass of red wine) or *luego* to mean 'right now' in Latin America and 'later on' in Spain. Alternatively, different zones may have different terms for the same concept, for example:

zone	a flat	a bus	a pavement	a ballpoint pen
Peninsular Spain	*piso*	*autobús*	*acera*	*bolígrafo*
Canary Islands	*piso*	*guagua*	*acera*	*bolígrafo*
Mexico	*departmento*	*camión*	*banqueta*	*lapicero*
Argentina	*departamento*	*colectivo*	*vereda*	*plumera*
Puerto Rico	*apartamento*	*guagua*	*acera*	

Lexis used in some countries may have become archaic in others, for example, *una recámera*, 'a bedroom' in modern Mexican Spanish, is used to mean 'a dressing room' in Peninsular Spanish, while the more modern term *dormitorio* is used to refer to a 'bedroom'. Alvar (1996a: 96–7) gives a very interesting insight into how speakers of different varieties have chosen to lexify what is a relatively modern lexical area, terms relating to the car, and he contrasts these with what he terms 'panhispanic Spanish'. He notes how Spanish-speakers in Texas, who do not receive an education in the Spanish language, tend to rely on transferring agricultural archaisms where some correspondence can be found between the field of agriculture and automobiles and adopting English borrowings when no such correspondence can be made.

Panhispanic	Puerto Rico	Mexico	Texas	
automóvil	*carro*	*carro*	*mueble*	(car)
rueda	*goma*	*llanta*	*rueda*	(tyre)
conducir	*guiar*	*manejar*	*arrear*	(to drive)
freno	*freno*	*freno*	*manea*	(brake)
volante	*guía*	*manijera*	*rueda*	(steering wheel)
portaequipajes	*baúl*	*cajuela*	*petaca*	(boot)
parabrisas	*cristal*	*parabrisas*	*windshield*	(windscreen)

escobilla	*wiper*	*limpiaparabrisas wiper*		(windscreen wiper)
cinturón de seguridad	*cinturón*	*cinturón*	*seat belt*	(seat belt)
amortiguadores	*resortes*	*amortiguadores*	*springs*	(springs)

(Alvar 1996a: 96-7)

In certain lexical domains, for example the language of drug users, it is hardly surpising that there is little standardization between geographical varieties, given its nature as an in-group language in constant evolution, a primary purpose of which is to establish membership identity of a proscribed social group. Flores Farfán (1990: 26) provides the following examples:

zone	**to inject**	**marijuana**	**heroin**	**cold turkey**
Spain	*chutarse* *pincharse*	*María*	*caballo*	*andar con el mono*
Mexico City	*atizarse* *atacarse*	*material* *grifa*		*andar erizo*
Los Angeles	*picarse* *chivearse*	*mota* *yesca*	*chiva*	

Within countries too, there may be considerable variation in the lexis used in certain domains such as fishing and agriculture with, for example, in Spain, *carlota* is a variant of *zanahoria* in Valencia and *habichuelas* are a variant of *judías verdes* in the Alpujarras.

This has been one of the prime areas of interest for traditional dialectologists interested in charting, for example, the rich and varied seam of agricultural vocabulary in Spain. However, it is also an area where dialect levelling is most clearly at work, with the flight from the land, technologization, modern communications and the decrease in the relative importance of agriculture all contributing to the loss, over a few generations, of an area of clear lexical variation.

Items which form part of the standard lexicon in one country may have taboo connotations in another. Indeed, Telenoticias's style guide for Spanish language broadcasting (*El País*, 17.3.95) contains a list of 120 items of vocabulary which should be avoided so as not to give offence to listeners in other parts of the Spanish-speaking world. For example, *barro* and *cuchara* mean excrement and vagina respectively in Venezuela and *bollo* means clitoris in Cuba.

4.1.1 User variation: age

It is a commonplace that an individual's use of language, whether it be pitch, pronunciation, vocabulary or grammar, varies with age. However, perhaps the most interesting variety to examine in this context is that of youth language, not merely because up-to-date slang is the prerogative of young people but also because it shows considerable variation between different subgroups, for example, between *pijos* (a pejorative term for the sons and daughters of the wealthy middle classes in Spain) and *pasotas* (anti-establishment dropouts in Spain) and between countries, such as the *Bandas* argot in Mexico and *lunfardo* in Buenos Aires. It also demonstrates considerable creativity in ensuring a constant renewal of an in-group language primarily through relexicalization. We are dealing with language which by its very nature is ephemeral, and consequently we shall focus on the sources of one particular variety of youth language and the mechanisms its speakers use to ensure its constant updating. *Cheli* is what Halliday (1978) calls an anti-language and it originated in major cities of Spain in the 1970s within marginalized and primarily criminal subgroups, spread to a sector of the cultural elite and then was diffused into the wider youth community, principally to the *pasotas* but in some instances to Spanish youth in general. It is useful to note that the dissemination of this variety has not been confined to face-to-face contact between individual users, as is frequently the case of covert argots used, say, in prisons or between drug users, but has been achieved also through a flourishing publishing world of underground magazines and fanzines (e.g. *Kallejero*) as well as through graffiti and posters and the creative arts (such as pop groups like *Gabinete Caligari*), films (*Deprisa deprisa* by Carlos Saura, *Bajarse al moro* by Fernando Colomo and the films of Pedro Almodóvar and Alex de las Iglesias), literature (*Historias del Kronen*, 1994, José Angel Mañas). Also the audiovisual media have played a significant role in its dissemination and standardization with advertising seeing in it a useful tool with which to target a youth market.

All the developed world has witnessed a generational gulf opening up between young people and their parents' generation in the postwar period and Spain has not escaped this trend.[10] After a period characterized both by economic boom and by increasing protest against Franco, the immediate post-Franco period was one of economic recession and political disillusionment, and in this context a counterculture grew up in the jails and shanty towns of Seville and Barcelona, creating and using in-group slang where alternative vocabulary for criminal activity, notably drug using, was prominent. The language of these marginal groups proved attractive to a new dynamic countercultural movement known as the *movida madrileña* which sprang up in Madrid in the 1970s and which included film directors such as Pedro Almodóvar, photographers such as Ouka Lele, pop groups such as Gabinete Caligari and Kaka de Luxe and singers such as Alaska and Ramoncín.

The main linguistic sources for *cheli* were in-group language of criminals and petty delinquents, loans from *caló*, the language of another marginal group, the gypsies, and borrowings from the language of the lumpenproletariat. One significant element of this is the argot of drug users. According to Flores Farfán (1990: 23) this is highly developed in Spanish on account of two main factors. First there is the coming together of different ethnic groups involved in the trade which, in the case of Europe, mainly comprises

Moroccans, other Africans and gypsies. Second, there is the need for users to have a code through which to identify themselves as bona fide users when it comes to making drug deals. We shall look first at an extract from prison *caló* taken from a recording made in prison of two petty delinquents simulating the planning, in a public place, of a burglary (Martín Rojo 1994: 258–9). Here Martín Rojo provides a translation into standard colloquial Spanish as well as into English enabling the reader to appreciate how impenetrable this particular jargon is to those outside its user group.

> *locorro que aquí nos diñan la bronca y nos ostilan*
> *chaval que aquí nos van a descubrir y a cogernos*
> Kid here they're going to find out and catch us.
> *que no nos ostilan hombre ay ¡qué cango que tiene este, oye!*
> *que no nos cogen hombre ¡qué miedo tiene este, oye!*
> They're not going to catch us, man. Hey! This guy's really scared!
> (. . .)
>
> *lacorro, mira, ligueramos a la rachí y asina mucho mejor . . . entrifamos por la*
> *perlacha aquella y si no, esparrábamos la burda*
> *Chaval, mira, venimos de noche y es mucho mejor, entramos por la ventana*
> *aquella y si no, forzamos la puerta*
> Look kid, we'll come here at night and it'll be much better, we get in through that window there, or if not we'll break the door down.

What is interesting about this particular jargon, and what is the case in many jargons where users are able to present a coherent public image and exclude the uninitiated (e.g. the jargons of professional groups, of computer buffs), is that deviation from standard Spanish is achieved virtually through lexical choice alone (e.g. *burda* = *puerta*), the syntax and morphology remaining largely standard.[11]

In *cheli*, which is partly derived from *caló*, variation from the standard occurs not only at lexical level (although this is its most salient feature) but also structurally and phonetically. The following illustrative extract is taken from an early Almodóvar film, *¿Qué he hecho yo para merecer esto?* (1984), where the humour stems from the fact that the grandmother is talking to her grandson Tony in a variety grossly unsuited to her age and social status, i.e. *cheli*.

Abuela: *¡Ay! Cómo flipo con las burbujas ¿A ti no te enrollan?*
[. . .]
Abuela: *Estoy enrollada con el punto. Me aburrís.*
Tony: *Abuela, podemos montar un rancho en el pueblo ¿no?*
Abuela: *¡De abuti, tío!*[12]

The main features of this variety are:

- loans (especially from English but adapted to Spanish morphology and phonology) such as *flipar*, meaning 'to like/enjoy' and more recently rejuvenated by the use of the clitic *lo* (*fliparlo*), *grogui* from the English 'groggy', *un díler/dealer*, *plis*, *bróder* and loan translations, e.g. *un viaje*.
- semantic extension of standard lexical terms, for example, *enrollar*, which in standard Spanish means 'to roll (up)' and which now also means 'to like', *trabajar* which means 'to engage in criminal activity' with *currar* now used to mean 'to work'.
- new syntactic structures, for example, the use of the adjective *total* in adverbial position (*totalmente*).
- neologisms, such as *de abuti, dabuten, dabute, de buten* meaning 'wonderful'.
- lexical reduction which is unlike standard lexical reduction such as *mili, moto*, which are bisyllabic and where there is no phonological modification (except possible dislocation of stress). Rather words are segmented, e.g. *anarco* (*anarquista*), *anfeta* (*anfetamina*), *estupa* (from *estupefaciente*) to refer to the drug squad, *manifa* (*manifestación*), *masoca* (*masoquista*); they are trisyllabic and there is frequent modification of the final vowel.[13]
- frequent use of the suffixes *-ata, -ota* and *-eta* (e.g. *privata* (a drink), *drogata/ota* (a drug addict), *grifota* (pot smoker), *pinchota* (individual who regularly injects a drug), *coloqueta* (being drunk), *estar trompa* (to be drunk);
- frequent use of swearing and taboo expressions ¿*Qué coños/leches/ cojones/mierda/carajo, etc., es?, a mí no me pasa ni un **puto** duro, eres un **jodido** curita, ¡vaya ayudantes de **mierda**!*, and not euphemistic substitutes such as *diantres, porras*, very few of which are recorded in dictionaries of Spanish (Daniel in León (1994: 8–13)).[14]
- certain syntactic constructions, e.g. *ir de* (*va de moderno*) (he's dressed up as a trendy), *pasar de* (*paso de política*) (I'm not into politics), *quedarse con* (*se está quedando con nosotros*) (he's looking at us), redundant use of the pronouns *que* and *como*, e.g. '*Lo tuyo es **que** es demasiado/lo tuyo es que es **como** demasiado*' (What you're into is too much).[15]
- extensive lexicalization of certain lexical fields, for example, 'money' *guita* (lit. twine, or a taboo Southern cone expression for money), *lata* (tin), *manteca* (animal fat), *parné* (from *caló*), *pasta* (dough), *pastoja, tela* (cloth), drug culture, bodily needs (e.g. *pribar, trincar* (to drink), *chascar, jamar, jalar, manducar, papear, tragar* (to eat), *planchar la oreja, sobar* (to sleep)), drug-taking, e.g. *un viaje, ácido* (LSD), *chocolate* (hashish), *caballo* (heroin). Daniel (in León (1994: 17)) identifies the following lexical fields: parts of the human body, sex, women, prostitution, homosexuality, bodily functions, defects, qualities, money, entertainment, eating, drinking, drinks, drunkenness, drugs, theft, police, blows, fights, arms, bravery, death, dying, killing, blasphemy, insult, disdain, anger and surprise.
- in writing, use of non-standard orthography, for example the use of the grapheme 'k' as in *Kaka de luxe, okupa* (squatter) and 'x' in *un cómix* (an underground magazine).

- use of non-standard frequently stigmatized pronunciation, including for example sibilant [s], for example, *passo de vosotros*, elimination of intervocalic [d] in noun forms e.g. *el Estao*; use of contractions e.g. *ná* (*nada*).
- use of fillers, e.g. *o así, y tal, tío*.
- use of reflexive rather than standard active verb forms (Flores Farfán 1990: 26).

Casado Velarde argues (1988: 109) that one of the attractions of this variety to disaffected youth is its directness, which contrasts with the hypocrisy they perceive in the language of those in power – as evidenced, for example, by the level of euphemism employed, such as *reajuste de tarifas* for *subida de precios*, *interrupción voluntaria de embarazo* for *aborto* or *profesional del amor* for *prostituta*. The use of this variety cuts across socio-economic groups to become the language of protest of disaffected youth or those who aspire to this category as can be seen in the following extract taken from a novel, *Historias del Kronen*, where the protagonist and narrator is from a wealthy upper-middle-class Madrid family, with a friend Roberto, is talking to a shanty-town drug pusher:

> *El maki comienza a contar historias de tripis, de Gorvachofs, frambuesas y supermanes. Dice que su mejor tripi fue con los colegas de la mili, unos plátanos verdes, creo.*
> *¿Has hecho ya la mili? –pregunta Roberto.*
> *Hombre, ya te digo. Pero la mili ya no es ná. A mí me tocó hacerla en Madriz, como a casi tó quisqui ahora, y ná, se salía cada uno cada viernes al mediodía y a las cuatro ya en casita, como si fuera un curro cualquiera. La mili está ahora tirá, una tontería.*
> *El maki se pone a hablar con su novia mientras que yo rulo un porro.*[16]

Some features of note in this extract are the use of non-standard spelling and abbreviation in *maki* (pejorative contraction of *macarra* (thug, scum)), use of Anglicisms, for example, **rular** *un porro*, to 'roll' a joint, *tripi*, *supermán* (a dose of LSD), overlexicalization and metaphor, such as the use of four distinct terms for LSD, *tripi*, *Gorvachof* (probably taken from the time when the Russian president Gorbachov was at the peak of his popularity in Europe), *frambuesa* ('raspberry') and *superman* (the latter two being possibly similar in derivation to the English 'strawberry dip' and 'batman'[17], non-standard pronunciation and contraction, such as *Madriz*, *tirá* (for *tirada*), use of slang vocabulary, for example, *curro* for *trabajo*, *colega* for *amigo*, *tó quisqui* for *todo el mundo*.

It should be remembered that varieties such as the types of youth language described above merely provide alternative stylistic choices to those able to use them. Indeed, in a video-recorded group discussion organized in Valladolid (Spain) with a group of teenage delinquents at a remand school, the participants all approximated to standard Spanish for the benefit of the camera, with the only 'youth-related' language being used by the social worker

leading the discussion in an attempt to get them to relax. For example, he jok-
ingly sets two boys from different parts of Burgos against each other by telling
one not to mix with the 'scum' from the other boy's *barrio* –'*no te mezcles con
esa chusma*' (Videotaped corpus of spoken Spanish from Valladolid (Val.)).

4.2 Conclusion

Clearly the potential of the Spanish language for creating neologisms through
the mechanisms described above is enormous and its speakers exploit them
creatively, lexicalizing with ease new concepts and relexicalizing old tired ones.
We have seen how quickly 'useful' borrowings are not only assimilated but go
on to generate their own derived forms. Judged on this evidence, Green's
(1990a) argument that Spanish is becoming more not less Romance in nature
is a strong one. It would appear that the voices which proclaim the end of the
Spanish language is nigh, on the basis of the English interference they detect
in some of the 'CyberSpanglish' appearing on the Internet, are misjudging the
current resilience of the language.

We have also seen the vast scope emotive suffixation in Spanish affords for
lending attitudinal nuance and for negotiating interpersonal relationships.
This, in a sense, is a defining feature of the language.

The opposing forces towards unification and fragmentation are clearly at
work in the area of lexis, as elsewhere. On the one hand, individual groups of
speakers, for example drug dealers, are able to create varieties of the language
impenetrable to the uninitiated and speakers of regional and national varieties
are able to use lexical variants as symbols of identity. On the other, there are
clear attempts to agree on a supraregional and supranational standard in the
face of competing neological forms, a process, which, as we saw in Chapter 2,
is aided, in the case of the media which are responsible for much of dissemination of new forms, by the *libro de estilo*.

5   Spanish morpho-syntax

At the level of syntax, variation is much less marked and change takes place at a considerably slower pace, than in the areas of phonetics and lexis which we have examined previously. Variation and change, as we have seen, are closely intertwined; indeed, for change to take place, there need to be two or more variants used within a speech community. Over time speech communities will adopt one variant, generally seen as having greater prestige socially, rather than another. It is interesting that, in some cases, similar developments are taking place independently on both sides of the Atlantic. We already saw that that this was the case with the phonetic variants [ʎ] and [j]; it is also the case with what is called in Spanish *queísmo*, which generally involves the elimination of the preposition *de* in certain contexts, for example *tengo la impresión [] que* rather than *tengo la impresión de que*. In this chapter we shall look at those elements of variation and change which appear to be primarily internal to Spanish, dealing in turn with the verbal group, the noun group and the clause, and in Chapter 9 we shall examine areas of variation and change which are more directly attributable to a situation of languages in contact, such as Spanish with English in the south of the United States where, for example, some Spanish speakers are beginning to adopt English word order. Thus Spanish-language supporters of George Bush in his 1992 election campaign could be seen with banners calling for *cuatro más años* rather than the standard *cuatro años más*. Nonetheless, in many cases change may be attributable to both internal and external factors working in conjunction.

5.0 The verbal group

There is a remarkable degree of uniformity in the forms which make up the verb system throughout the Spanish-speaking world.[1] Indeed, when non-standard, often stigmatized, forms do occur, they also are relatively standard across the many geographical varieties, for example the regularization of the second-person preterite singular *¿Vinistes ayer?* (cf. *¿Viniste ayer?*). However, in addition to and more significant than the formal differences is the degree of variation in how these forms are actually used.

5.0.0 *Impersonal verbs (haber, hacer)*

Of the two uses of *haber*, as an auxiliary used to form compound tenses (e.g. *Ha venido pronto*) and as a verb used to mean 'there is/are', it is the latter which gives rise to variation. In standard Peninsular Spanish and in normative written Spanish throughout the Spanish-speaking world, *haber*, used to mean 'there is' or 'there are', occurs only in the third-person singular (e.g. *habrá*, *había*, *hubo*, *ha habido*, with the special form *hay* replacing the standard present indicative *ha* (e.g. *Hay pan*)). Pluralization of the verb is stigmatized as being uneducated.

However, in the Catalan-speaking parts of Spain as well as the Canaries and large parts of Latin America, it is common to find the impersonal verb *haber* 'regularized' so that it agrees in the plural with its noun complement, e.g. *Habían tres chicas* (standard: *Había tres chicas*). It is a feature which has been studied in the context of the *Proyecto Coordinado de Estudio de la Norma Lingüística Culta* as, while its use is more widespread amongst less educated speakers, it is also frequent amongst educated ones in certain capital cities, such as Caracas, Santiago de Chile and Buenos Aires. Interestingly it did not occur in the data from Mexico (Bentivoglio and Sedano in Fontanella de Weinberg 1995: 153) although Lope Blanch (in Alvar 1996b: 83) attests to its use in Mexico by all strata of society along with the tendency also to pluralize auxiliaries used with *haber*, for example, *Debían haber más de cien personas*. Fontanella de Weinberg (1995: 152–3) attests to its use in the quality press of Buenos Aires. In the areas of Latin America mentioned above its use is far less stigmatized than in parts of Spain such as Navarre and Aragón where it rarely occurs and when it does it is seen as a sign of lack of education. Similarly, the verb *hacer* used impersonally may also agree in the speech of some individuals, for example, *Hicieron (hizo) unos días estupendos*. Nevertheless, these usages remain stigmatized. There is also evidence in some varieties of Spanish of personalization of impersonal verbs, for example, '*aquí habemos (hay) mucha gente*' (Rodríguez Izquierdo 1982), a form also found in parts of Latin America. In the spoken language it is also frequent to find semantic rather than grammatical agreement of the verb, such as *La gente van (va)*, *El gobierno han (ha) decidido*.

5.0.1 *The passive*

In addition to the active voice (e.g. *El ejército mató al payaso*), which highlights the agent of an action, and the passive voice formed by *ser* and the past participle (e.g. *Ha sido matado el payaso*), which highlights the patient, Spanish can be said to have a 'middle voice' constructed with *se* + singular or plural verb (e.g. *Al payaso se mató*).[2] In Spanish the passive with *ser* is little used by speakers and writers, who show a distinct preference for a variety of other constructions. Indeed, Diego Quesada (1997: 41) notes its virtual demise in spoken Spanish although it is still found in written texts. Research by Hidalgo (in Diego Quesada 1997: 46) on its use in one written medium, the quality Madrid daily *El País*, showed that while the passive was indeed used in approximately 10 per cent of the contexts in which it was possible (e.g. '*Civiles desarmados huidos de Srebrenica* **fueron ejecutados** *con tiros en la cabeza*' (*El País*, 14.7.96), in over half of these the agent was also expressed (e.g. *fue enviado* **por** *los Estados Unidos*). Seco (1993: 94) notes *Agencia EFE*'s view that its use in writing may be due to the translation of English passives by Spanish ones and its recommendation that, if the passive is retained, Spanish rather than English word order should be respected, i.e. *Ha sido votado por el Congreso un crédito para los damnificados* and not *Un crédito para los damnificados ha sido votado por el Congreso*. Butt and Benjamin (1994: 364) note that while the passive with *ser* is less common with verbs of imperfective aspect (i.e. in imperfect, present and continuous tenses), its use is on the increase in writing and non-spontaneous speech, especially in Latin America (e.g. '*Las llamadas a casa del escritor* **eran respondidas** *por un contestador automático*', (*El País Internacional*, 20.2.89; in De Bruyne 1995b: 463, my emphasis)).

According to Diego Quesada (1997) the principal competing constructions which are used in place of the passive in spoken Spanish are as follows:

> *se mató al payaso*
> *mataron al payaso*
> *al payaso lo mató el ejército*
> *al payaso lo mataron*

Pragmatic reasons, essentially the extent to which the speaker wishes to highlight the patient (here *el payaso*) and to deflect attention from the agent (here *el ejército*) contribute to determining choice. However, in Diego Quesada's study it is the middle voice which accounts for the greatest proportion of alternatives to the passive. Amongst the reasons he gives for this move away from the use of the passive voice is the increase in clitic doubling (see 5.0.7) which has the effect of foregrounding the patient without recourse to passivization. For example, in *Lo vi a Memo* the use of the 'redundant' object pronoun *lo* enables the speaker to highlight Memo, rather than him or herself as encoded in *vi*.

5.0.2 Pronominal verbs

While most pronominal verbs are the same in both Spain and Latin America, there is, as Vaquero de Ramírez (1996: 37) notes, greater tendency to pronominalize in Latin America, for example, *amanecerse* (cf *amanecer*), *tardarse* (cf *tardar*). Butt and Benjamin (1994: 355) comment that some of these forms appear 'quaint, rustic or simply wrong to Spaniards'. There is also at present the tendency for intransitive forms, which in standard Spanish are pronominal, to lose the pronoun. This trend is particularly evident in the field of sport where *entrenar* (cf. *entrenarse*) and *calentar* (cf. *calentarse*) are used increasingly.

5.0.3 Ser/estar

The existence of two verbs 'to be' in Spanish, *ser* essentially used to denote inherent qualities and *estar* to denote resultant states, involves speakers in complex choices which are often difficult to explain.[3] Over the centuries *estar* has competed with *ser* and gradually taken over some of its functions. What is of interest here, is that this process is not complete as *estar* continues to take over functions hitherto the domain of its rival *ser*. Let us look at *ser* and *estar* in the context of noun + *ser/estar* + adjective. In standard Spanish the use of *ser* relates to the attribution of a quality shared by a group, for example, *María es grande* (María is tall, an inherent quality) and the use of *estar* to a quality that pertains to the individual alone, such as *María está grande* (María is (has grown) tall, a resultant state). In the following example, the meaning of *estar* has been extended to denote an inherent or group quality, a domain traditionally reserved for *ser*:

> G: . . . *la que me gustó mucho fue ésta . . . la de Rambo.*
> M: ¿*Rambo*?
> G: *Sí,* **está** *muy buena esta película.*

(Gutiérrez 1992: 112)

Most of the work done on *ser* and *estar* has been done within the context of languages in contact, in this case Spanish with the English of the United States, and therefore the varieties most affected are to be found in the southern United States and Mexico. Silva-Corvalán (1986) describes this innovative use of *estar* as a change in progress insofar as it is most frequent amongst younger generations of bilingual speakers. One factor affecting this change may be contact with the English language, which only has one verb 'to be'. Nonetheless, Silva-Corvalán (1986) argues that the language contact situation is not a trigger for change in itself but is merely accelerating a change which is already underway. Indeed, there is evidence that this change is also taking place in monolingual situations, as Gutiérrez's study of the speech community of Morelia, Mexico shows. De Jonge (1993) argues that the extension of the use of *estar* to replace *ser* in expressions of age in Mexico and Venezuela (e.g. *Juan está viejo/joven, cuando estaba niño . . .*) not used in the traditional sense to mean 'to look' or 'to become' initially reflects a new way of conceptualizing age, but, with increased use, gradually becomes the standard verb for this context.

5.0.4 Tense

Preterite versus perfect[4]

The difference between the perfect (*He cantado*) and the preterite (*Canté*) is temporal in standard Peninsular Spanish, with the perfect being used to refer to events which have some connection with the present while the preterite is used to refer to past events. Thus, while *le/lo vi ayer* is acceptable *le/lo he visto ayer* is not, although, as Butt and Benjamin note (1994: 223), it is sometimes used in popular Madrid speech and can be stigmatized as uneducated. In written Peninsular Spanish there is some evidence that the preterite tense, at least in the domain of news agency reports, is beginning to oust the perfect tense when referring to the recent continuing past, for example *Dijo hoy* rather than the Peninsular standard *Ha dicho hoy*. There is some evidence that the preterite is currently displacing the perfect in Spain and this departure from the Castilian norm is being actively combated by the DEU (October 95, 51).

In most varieties of Latin American Spanish there is already a strong preference for the preterite in present-related contexts and in Spain in the minority language regions of Galicia and Asturias where the contact language makes no distinction between prefect and preterite, there is also a similar preference, for example *No llegó todavía* rather than *No ha llegado todavía*.

In some varieties of Latin American Spanish, such as Mexican Spanish, the difference between the two tenses is not temporal but aspectual, with the preterite being used to refer to completed events and the perfect to events not yet completed.[5]

According to quantitative research carried out by De Kock (1991: 489), differences in usage are slightest in the press, somewhat greater in spoken Spanish and considerable between literary genres from both continents.

Present versus perfect

In Mexico the present indicative is standardly used with the adverbs *aún/todavía*, for example, *Todavía no abren las puertas* while Peninsular Spanish employs the perfect tense in this context (*Todavía no ha abierto las puertas*) (Lope Blanch 1995).

Continuous versus non-continuous forms

Continuous forms appear to be more frequent in Latin American than in European Spanish[6] and indeed more frequent now than fifty years ago. Their use is particularly prominent when Spanish is in contact with English which makes much greater use of this type of construction. In Spanish *Estoy leyendo* means 'I am (actually) reading (at this very moment)' and not 'I am reading (this book)' in the sense that I am part of the way through it. Thus, in the Spanish of the United States, bilinguals frequently use constructions such as *Cuando iba caminando a casa* (cf. *cuando caminaba a casa*) which mirror those preferred in English.[7] In Mexico the continuous form is frequently conjugated in colloquial speech with the verb *andar*, for example, *Ando caminando a casa*. Vaquero de Ramírez (1996: 32) notes that in Puerto Rico, where contact with English is intense, the use of the continuous form, frequently with the noun intercalated between the verb and the auxiliary, is common. She gives the following example, *Está su corazón latiendo bien* (cf. *Su corazón late bien*).

Future versus periphrastic future

In most of Latin America the future tense is no longer used to refer to future time; there is a strong preference for the periphrastic future formed with the auxiliary *ir a* + infinitive, for example *Voy a cantar* and not *Cantaré*. However, the future tense is retained as a modal of supposition or doubt with *Cantará* meaning (S/he will (surely) sing), *¿Qué le pasará a Juan?* (What can be the matter with Juan?), *Estará enfermo* (He must be ill), *No sé si vendrá Alicia hoy* (I don't know whether Alicia will come today). It should be added that the present tense is used extensively to refer to future time such as *Mañana voy de vacaciones*. In some areas, Peru, for example, the present continuous can also be used to refer to future time, e.g. *Estoy llegando mañana a las seis*.

5.0.5 Modality

The term **modality** refers to the expression of the speaker's attitude towards a proposition. For example, a speaker might qualify the proposition *Vendrá mañana* with the modal adverb *quizás*. Depending on how probable the speaker feels this proposition to be, he or she will choose either the indicative mood (*Quizás vendrá mañana*, more probable) or the subjunctive mood (*Quizás venga mañana*, less probable). Mood is central to the expression of modality in all varieties of Spanish although there are a variety of other mechanisms which can express speaker attitude (e.g. modal verbs such as *poder* and *querer*), modal adverbs (e.g. *tal vez, ojalá*), use of the future tense (*Llegarán sobre las once*). In this section we shall assume a knowledge of standard expression of modality and concentrate on areas of salient variation and change.[8]

Modal verbs

Standard Spanish makes a distinction between the use of *deber* + infinitive and *deber de* + infinitive. The former expresses deontic modality or external obligation as in *Debe estudiar* (He must study) and the latter epistemic modality or implied belief *Debe de estudiar* (He must be studying). In Spanish today *deber* + infinitive is increasingly coming to express both notions with a consequent loss of this particular modal distinction, for example '*es porque debían saber que iban a ver algo espectacular . . .* ' (Fontanillo y Riesco 1994: 65).

The subjunctive

Although there are still three forms of the subjunctive mood, the present, the imperfect and the future, in reality the future subjunctive has long ceased to be used by speakers and writers and tends in Spain only to be found as retained usage in administrative or legal texts. It has been replaced mainly by the present subjunctive, for example *Sea lo que sea* rather than *Sea lo que fuere*. Butt and Benjamin note (1994: 272) that it is quite common in newspaper style in some regions of Latin America.

The imperfect subjunctive has two competing forms (*-ra* and *-se*) which are interchangeable in virtually all contexts. Language change has consistently favoured the *-ra* form, which predominates in spoken and written Spanish, although the *-se* form is used in the written language for stylistic effect. Most Andalusian and Latin American varieties of Spanish have tended to favour 'raísmo' with the *-se* being more commonly associated with varieties of Spanish spoken in the rest of the Peninsula. Nonetheless, both varieties alternate to a greater or lesser extent in most areas, as can be seen in the following example where the speakers, two young male reporters from Valladolid (Spain) use alternate forms when speaking about the disadvantages of not having another local paper with which to compete:

> JB: *No, eso es . . . eso es evidente, que como en esta ciudad, que tiene, con la provincia, medio millón de habitantes, hay sólo un periódico, y claro, si **hubiera** dos, pues espabilaríamos más, estaríamos . . .*
> FF: *Sí, pero yo creo que no, eso no . . . bajaría, o sea, no baja la calidad, yo creo, vamos, y aunque **hubiese** otro periódico, hombre pues sí, como dice Julián, te obligaría a estar un poco más despierto. (Val.)*[9]

Indeed, both forms may alternate in the speech of an individual speaker, as we can see in the following example:

> *estos amigos empezaron a apoyarme un poco, a buscarme para que no me **quedase** encerrada y . . . **saliese** con la gente y . . . **siguiera** la vida de antes*
> (Carbonero Cano 1982: 52)

One use of the *-ra* form (where the *-se* form is also found but much less frequently) is as a stylistic variant of certain indicative past tenses, for example 'La sesión, que **comenzara** a las cuatro de la tarde, se prolongó hasta la madrugada' (Agencia EFE 1989a: 57–8). While this usage is decried by the Academy and the style guides for being a pedantic affectation, it is very frequently found in journalistic texts. Lunn and Cravens in Fleischmann and Waugh (1991: 150) argue that the *-ra* form can be used to mark information that readers can be expected to know, whether from previous paragraphs in the newspaper or from world knowledge, and therefore it is useful in information-rich journalistic prose to mark low-priority information or to credit the reader with 'insider knowledge'. They give (1991: 150) the following example of the *-se* variant:

> *Al día siguiente de que Isabel Preysler . . . **iniciase** en un chalet de Marbella su verano, según informamos en la página 44 de este número . . . (¡Hola!, 17 August 1985)*

We have already noted the virtual disappearance of the future subjunctive; indeed, there is a tendency internal to Spanish, and common to other Romance languages, for the subjunctive to lose ground to the indicative mood. In standard Spanish, the use of the subjunctive is either obligatory (e.g. after the subordinator *para que*) or optional (e.g. after the expressions of doubt *quizá* and *no saber*). Where it is optional, there is a difference in meaning between the two forms, the indicative expressing greater certainty (e.g. *Quizá viene mañana* expressing more confidence in a person's arrival the next day than *Quizá venga mañana*). Silva-Corvalán (1994: 269) notes that the subjunctive, and its meanings, are being lost most rapidly in optional contexts. While this is particularly the case where Spanish comes into close contact with English, it is a process which affects the Spanish spoken in Spain and Latin America and is not confined to rural, uneducated speakers.

Conditional utterances

In standard Spanish, the most common patterns, amongst a wide variety, are:

> *si* + present + present/future
> *Si como mucho me engordo/engordaré.*
> *si* + past subjunctive + conditional
> *Si comiera/iese mucho me engordaría.*
> *Si hubiera comido mucho me habría/hubiera engordado.*

However, in spontaneous speech a number of alternatives occur, some of which are considered more accpetable than others.

> *No . . . directamente no se ha llegado a plantear nunca . . . supongo que si algún día me lo **plantearán** pues me **marchaba** o no **haría** el programa . . .*
> (Stewart *et al.* 1991)

The example above is taken from an interview with a journalist who is speculating on what her reaction would be if the radio station for which she worked wanted to censor the content of her programme. As we can see from this example alone, spoken Spanish provides considerable variation from the standard conditional utterances, *Si me lo plantearan/asen no lo haría*, that is a protasis (or *si* clause) in the imperfect subjunctive and the apodosis (or consequence) in the conditional tense and *Si me lo hubieran/esen planteado no lo habría/hubiera hecho* with the protasis in the past anterior subjunctive and the apodosis in the conditional perfect (or the past anterior subjunctive in the case of a restricted number of verbs, e.g. *haber, poder*). Most grammars accept as standard, although with reservations, the use of the imperfect indicative in both the protasis and the apodosis, as this is a widespread feature of colloquial and non-standard speech, *Si me lo plantearan/aban no lo haría/hacía*. What is interesting in the example above is that the speaker uses both forms of apodosis, the imperfect and the conditional, which may be an example of free variation or may imply a difference in the perception of how likely she perceives each course of action (the use of the indicative may indicate greater probability, i.e. she may feel that she is more likely to walk out than to refuse to do the programme).

Beatriz Lavandera and Carmen Silva-Corvalán[10] have both studied variation in conditional utterances and possible stylistic variation, the former in Buenos Aires and the latter in northern Spain. In both these communities a further variant is possible, that is the conditional in the protasis (*Si me lo plantearían . . .*) of conditionals referring to the present or the future, a variant which in Spain is particularly frequent in the Basque country and the surrounding provinces of Burgos, Palencia and Logroño. In the case of conditional referring to the past, the standard past anterior subjunctive is used (*Si me lo hubieran planteado*). Lavandera argued, in the case of Buenos Aires, that the use of the conditional indicates greater probability, for example:

> Si **tendría** que hacer una cosa como esa, me gustaría.
> Si **consiguiera** trabajo, me voy a dar una vida de reyes.
>
> (Silva-Corvalán 1989: 129)

Thus, in the first example, the speaker considers it more probable that he or she will have to 'do something like that' while in the second example the speaker finds it less probable that he or she is going to get a job.

She also shows that, the greater the educational level of the speaker, the less the conditional is used in the protasis and that the use of the conditional in the apodosis is socially stigmatized.

In the community of Covarrubias in northern Spain, Silva-Corvalán does not detect any semantic distinction between the imperfect subjunctive and the conditional, although she does argue, as we have with the example which introduces this section, that the use of the imperfect appears to indicate greater probability. In the following example (1989: 133), the conditional and the imperfect subjunctive appear to be free variants:

> Y decíamos, 'Si ahora despertaría y se viese con su trajecito del Corazón de Jesús'

Silva-Corvalán (1989: 136) has also described variation in subordinate clauses where in standard Spanish the standard form would be the imperfect subjunctive, for example in hypothetical utterances such as the following:

> Digamos que yo estoy, como se dice, como si estaría (estuviera/iese) reprimido todo el día.
>
> (Silva-Corvalán 1989: 136)

Another similar context of variation is in speech acts of requesting, demanding, and so on where the use of the imperfect subjunctive would be the standard norm, for example:

Entonces yo le decía que me compraría novelas del oeste y tal.

5.0.6 Proforms and clitics

The proforms and clitics which we shall consider in this section include subject clitics, direct and indirect object clitics and reflexive clitics. There is considerable variation in the use of proforms and clitics throughout the Spanish-speaking world both in standard and non-standard varieties.[11] The main areas of concern to us here are variation in the choice of object pronoun (*leísmo, laísmo, loísmo*), clitic doubling (*Le di el libro a María*), the presence or absence of personal pronouns (*(Yo) creo*), the position of clitic *No lo puedo comprar/No puedo comprarlo*, word order *Se me cayó/Me se cayó* and the non-standard marking of plural forms (*Se los di* for *Se lo di*).

For reference, the clitics which concern us here are detailed below. We have not included the disjunctive pronouns which, with the exception of the first- and second-persons singular (*mí, ti*) are identical to the subject pronouns.

Subject	Direct object	Indirect object	Reflexive	Possessive pronoun	Possessive adjective
you	*me*	*me*	*me*	*mío*	*mi*
tú/vos	*te*	*te*	*te*	*tuyo*	*tu*
él	*lo /le*	*le*	*se*	*suyo*	*su*
ella	*la/le*	*le*	*se*	*suyo*	*su*
ello	*lo*	*le*	*se*	*suyo*	*su*
Vd.	*le/la*	*le*	*se*	*suyo*	*su*
nosotros/as	*nos*	*nos*	*nos*	*nuestro*	*nuestro*
vosotros/as	*os*	*os*	*os*	*vuestro*	*vuestro*
ellos	*los/les*	*les*	*se*	*suyo*	*su*
ellas	*las/les*	*les*	*se*	*suyo*	*su*

Leísmo, laísmo, loísmo

Leísmo/loísmo

This is an area where there are two clearly defined standard norms *leísmo* and *loísmo* and a great deal of non-standard variation in the choice of direct and indirect object pronouns. Originally *lo/los* were the direct object pronouns used to refer to male persons, for example, *Lo/los vi* (I saw him/them) and *le/les* were the indirect object pronouns *Le/les di el anillo*. In Spanish today, in certain areas, principally Spain, the indirect object pronouns *le/les* have ousted the direct object pronouns *lo/los* to become standard usage as referring to persons. Vaquero de Ramírez (1996: 38) notes the expansion of *leísmo* through Spanish-speaking America as a more courteous variant. For example, it has penetrated administrative letters in the Caribbean, where the standard closure is now *Le saluda*.

The most widespread use of *leísmo* involves the use of *le(s)* rather than the standard *lo(s)* for the direct object when referring to male persons, for example **Le(s)** *llamé por teléfono para decirle(s)* rather than **Lo(s)** *llamé por teléfono para decirle(s)* and has penetrated Peninsular Spanish usage to such an extent that it has become the standard prestige and indeed the only usage in most of the country and is the accepted form in standard grammars. However, most of Latin America retains the more conservative form *lo* (*loísmo*) in these contexts, although there are some areas where *leísmo* prevails (e.g. Paraguay, although here *le* substitutes all singular and plural third-person forms and is stigmatized as uneducated usage). Kany (in Fontanella de Weinberg (1995: 155) notes that some Latin American authors adopt in their writing the Castilian *le* as the direct object for persons as they find it lends it a note of distinction. The use of *le* to refer to female persons is also widespread in Spain although less accepted at the level of language prescription. For example the *Manual de español urgente* advises against its use, finding examples such as the following unacceptable (*Comunicó a la diputada que no podía recibirle(la)*). The use of *leísmo* in other contexts is socially stigmatized. Nevertheless, it is found, either referring to inanimate objects (or to animals), *Se le perdió el reloj y no pudo encontrarle (lo)* or substituting the neutral object pronoun *Lo* (*propuso eso pero no le aprobaron*) (Agencia EFE 1989a: 58).

Laísmo/loísmo

Laísmo refers to the use of the direct object pronoun *la* in contexts where the indirect object pronoun *le* is standard usage, for example, *La (le) di el regalo*, and, while being a stigmatized form throughout most of Spain, is the predominant form in parts of Castile (e.g. Valladolid) and indeed is much more widely used by all social classes than the stigmatized forms of *leísmo* (Klein 1979: 45–64). Here, *loísmo* refers to the use of *lo* in place of the indirect object pronoun *le*, for example, '*el ayuntamiento los (les) ha dado unas copitas*' (Fontanillo and Riesco 1994: 87). It is worth commenting in this connection that although Valladolid is often cited as as the home of the prestige standard where the 'best' Spanish is spoken, this standard is located amongst an educated elite and not amongst a significant proportion of the local population.

Clitic doubling

Clitic doubling occurs when there is what might be called a 'redundant' use of the direct or indirect object clitic, given that the (in)direct object itself is also expressed. In certain contexts this has become obligatory, for example, *Le gusta a María ir al cine* and in others, where the referent is human, it may be preferred usage, as in *Le di el libro a María* (indirect object clitic). Green (1990a: 107) notes that doubling in such contexts is clearly gaining ground.

Indeed, in most varieties of Latin American Spanish (e.g. that of Santiago de Chile) the 'redundant' indirect object clitic is always used.

There is also a form of doubling which is non-standard usage in Spain but generalized throughout Latin America, that is the doubling of the clitic where the referent is not human, for example *Lo cogió el libro* (direct object clitic). In the case of the direct object clitic in Santiago de Chile, Silva-Corvalán (1989: 109–15) argues that this use is not redundant but rather marks emphasis (*topicalidad*) and that its use does not appear to be socially stigmatized in that particular community.

In conversational Spanish the object clitic follows and is bound to the verb with the infinitive (*comerlo*), the gerund (*comiéndolo*) and the imperative (*cómelo*) and in all other cases precedes the verb (e.g. *Lo como*). Thus, where there is more than one verb, the position of the clitic is variable and depends on the emphasis which the speaker wishes to attribute to the utterance, for example:

> *Quiero ir a darle una sorpresa.*
> *Quiero irle a dar una sorpresa.*
> *Le quiero ir a dar una sorpresa.*
>
> (Silva-Corvalán 1989: 101)

However, this area of semantic distinction is perhaps in danger. For there is a further (and possibly growing) non-standard type of clitic doubling mainly involving utterances which allow for the repetition of the subject or object, for example:

> *Yo me tenía que vacunarme.*
> *El la fue a dejarla.*
>
> (Silva-Corvalán 1989: 105)

This usage is redundant and according to Silva-Corvalán (1989: 105), if indeed it is becoming more widespread, it will spell the end of the rich semantic distinction described above.

Pluralization

Also widespread in Latin America is the tendency to mark the plural in sequences such as *Se lo/se la di (a ellos/a ellas)*. As the plural is ambiguous in the indirect object pronoun *se* there is a tendency to add the plural to the direct object pronoun (*se los/se las*) even when it is logically singular. Kany in Fontanella de Weinberg (1995: 156) provides the following authentic examples:

> *Si no se los dijera me iría a acostar molesto.* (Argentina)
> *Hacía frío pero no lo sentían; el trabajo y el mezcal se los quitaba.* (Mexico)

De Mello (1992a: 165–79) has studied this phenomenon in eleven major cities and notes that this pluralization does not only occur in popular varieties of Spanish but also in cultured speech. While it is not found at all in La Paz, Lima, Madrid and Seville, it is particularly common in Mexico (where cultured and uncultured speakers show a similar frequency of 76 per cent) and in Bogotá and is also found in Buenos Aires, Caracas, Havana and Santiago de Chile.

Order of clitics

The prescribed order for clitics, regardless of their position in relation to the verb (enclitics or proclitics) is the following:

1 *Se*   2 *te, me, os, nos*   3 *le, lo, la, les, los, las*

For example:

> *Me lo perdí.* (I (went and) lost it.)

In a number of non-standard (principally rural stigmatized) varieties of Spanish the first two categories of clitic may be reversed, for example:

> *Me se cayó.* (*Se me cayó.*) (I dropped it.)

The presence or absence of the subject personal pronoun

In Spanish as in a number of other Romance languages (e.g. Italian, Catalan) person is generally encoded by means of inflection of the verb, for example, *Hablo, Hablas.* There are cases where the same inflection can be used to refer to more than one person, such as *Habla* (he, she, it, you (singular, formal) speak(s) or *Hablaría* (I, he, she, it, you (singular, formal) would speak. For example:

(Yo)	hablo	nosotros/as	hablamos.
(Tú)	hablas	vosotros/as	habláis.
(Él/ella/Vd.)	habla	ellos/as	hablan.

Thus the use or omission of the personal pronoun responds to a choice on the part of the speaker or writer. In the following example, the second speaker does not use the personal pronoun to refer to himself:

> (E): *¿Cuántos años has estado haciendo esto tú Roberto?*
> (R): *Pues, empecé de diez, hice ayer setenta, así que total, sesenta.*
>
> (Val.)

Spanish, like a number of other Romance languages, for example, Italian, Portuguese, does not require the presence of the subject pronoun which, when it occurs, may precede or succeed the verb. Indeed, in the majority of cases, the *tú* pronoun is absent, the familiar form being present in the conjugation of the verb. Of all the personal subject pronouns it is *usted(es)* which most frequently accompanies the verbal form. Additionally, there is variation in the frequency of pronominal use between different Spanish-speaking regions. For example, Carbonero Cano (1982: 55) argues that there is a particularly high frequency of use in the Spanish of Seville and attributes it to a need for disambiguation given that speakers do not pronounce the verb ending in the case of (*Tú*) *comeø*, and that therefore this could be confused with (*Él/ella/Vd.*) *come*. Lipski (1994: 335) points to a much higher retention of subject pronouns in Puerto Rican Spanish. One explanation here is that of close contact with English with its obligatory use of pronouns.

The presence or absence of the subject personal pronoun in Spanish has long attracted the attention of linguists.[12] While some earlier studies investigated pronominal use in written data and concentrated more on its function as disambiguator (mainly in the case of third-person pronouns), more recently there has been a recognition of the fact that terms used for speaker/hearer reference may function very differently in face-to-face interaction. Indeed, the high frequency of the use of personal pronouns in the first-person singular with verbs of cognition (*Yo creo que, Yo pienso que*) and at the beginning of utterances may be more closely related to issues of the presentation of self and to conversational style (there appears to be a higher use of the personal pronouns in some areas, such as Andalusia, than others) than to the traditional explanations given above. Similarly, the inclusion or omission of the second-person pronouns (*tú, vos, vosotros, Vd., Vds.*) may depend more on the negotiation of a relationship. For example, the use or omission of *Vd.* can encode the relationship between speaker and hearer as, amongst others, one of respect, of distance, of solidarity depending on the context.[13]

In the following extract (Stewart *et al.* 1991), the speaker, a university lecturer, is contrasting his opinion, with that of his interlocutor (another lecturer):

> *fíjate que es que . . . ahí se plantea una cuestión que a mí me parece importante... la que dices **tú** . . . la de la inercia . . . yo no sé si **tú** habrás apreciado . . . **yo** al menos sí lo . . . lo he visto que en general dentro de los estudiantes la mujer es bastante más consciente que el hombre . . .*[14]

Here, the lecturer is making a (possible) contrast between his experience of students and that of the other lecturer he is talking to. At the same time he is also using the T (*tú*) pronoun as positive politeness[15] to place on record his respect for the other lecturer's opinion '(*la (cuestión) que dices tú*', i.e. his identification of inertia as an important issue) and, rather than making a general statement of fact, he uses self-reference (*yo al menos lo he visto*) to protect his own self-esteem in the eventuality that the other speaker should disagree with his interpretation of events.

In ways such as these, the use of the T/V pronouns can serve a pragmatic function (Rodríguez Izquierdo 1982), in particular as a politeness device to pay attention to the face of the other speaker (Stewart 1992). Thus the use of *tú* can place on record and appeal to solidarity with the hearer (or, through the power semantic, express disdain and rejection) while the use of *usted* can express deference and respect, or alternatively social distance. Thus speakers can choose to what extent they place on record their perception, at a given point in time, of their relationship with their interlocutor. Hence, an appreciation of the social values attributed to one or another pronoun as well as the importance of their inclusion in the conversation can allow speakers to negotiate a relationship with others.

Vos, *tú* and *usted* can all be used for generic reference although the grammatically indefinite pronouns *uno* and *se* are preferred in written language.[16] Enríquez (1984) notes a particularly low occurrence of the subject pronoun with generic reference. Factors which may influence the choice of the T form for generalizing reference are a desire for involvement on the part of the speaker or because the speaker is generalizing from personal experience (Bobes Naves 1971: 33; Llorente Maldonado 1977: 114 in Enríquez 1984) or in order to establish solidarity with one's hearer (Haverkate 1984).

In the following extracts (Stewart *et al.* 1991) both speakers, a journalist and a lecturer in law, are clearly speaking from personal experience:

> *entonces cuando por la mañana* **sabes** *que se convoca una manifestación de estudiantes o . . . vamos una cosa similar pues* **te informas** *un poco del tema . . .* **miras**, *vamos, yo por lo menos pues miro . . .*

> *tú llegas a clase . . . entonces en la clase hay de los trescientos alumnos que tienes inscritos . . . pues normalmente vienen ciento cincuenta ciento sesenta . . .* **tú** *llegas a clase,* **das** *tu clase y* **te vas**[17]

The first speaker is aware that she is talking from personal experience and that what she is saying could be interpreted both as that and as a statement of a general rule. Therefore she self-corrects to make it clear that what she is talking about relates to her personal experience and should not be interpreted as a generic. Similarly, the second speaker's inclusion of the pronoun *tú* marks out as personal experience what could easily be taken as a general rule.

Possessive adjectives and pronouns

These should normally be covered under the noun group (5.1) but for convenience will be examined here. Possession is standardly denoted by the possessive adjectives *mi(s)*, *tu(s)*, *su(s)*, *nuestro/a(s)*, *vuestro/a(s)*, by, primarily in the case of ambiguous uses of the third person, *de* + personal pronoun (e.g. *de él*) and by the possessive adjectives/pronouns *mío/a(s)*, *tuyo/a(s)*, *suyo/a(s)*, *nuestro/a(s)*, *vuestro/a(s)*, for example, *¿Es tu coche? No es mío, es de ellos, es un hijo mío.*

In parts of Latin America, particularly those where there is contact with the indigenous languages it is common to find duplication of possession, for example, *Dicen que la iglesia la vendieron **sus** antepasados **de esa***, and ***Su** hijo **de ella** ha crecido mucho*. In areas where there is contact with English, the possessive adjective may occur in contexts where it is standard in English but not Spanish such as *Le duele **su** pierna izquierda* (cf. *Le duele **la** pierna izquierda*).

5.1 The noun group

5.1.0 *The noun*

Nouns in Spanish are either masculine or feminine in gender, and the vast majority are easily recognizable as such by their final morpheme, *-a* (feminine) or *-o* or absence of *-a* or *-o* (masculine), although there may be exceptions (*la mano, el día*). Some nouns (homonyms) change their meaning according to which gender is used for example, *el cólera* (cholera), *la cólera* (anger). Others may be used in either the masculine or the feminine in the singular, for example, *el/la mar, el azúcar moreno/la azúcar blanca* although only one gender is used in the plural (e.g. *los mares*).[18] Fontanella de Weinberg (1995: 157) notes that throughout Latin America there is considerable variation and change in progress and the same can be said about Spain.

One salient area of variation and change concerns nouns where the etymological gender does not correspond to that which is expected. This may result in a change either in the noun or in the gender of the article in order rectify the perceived anomaly. For example, given that words ending in *-a* tend to be feminine and those ending in *-o* masculine, the use of the feminine article with a noun ending in *-o* as in the case of *la radio* (an abbreviation of *radiotelegrafía*) runs counter to speakers' expectations and in many areas (parts of Andalusia and Latin America) the masculine form is preferred (*el radio*). In some areas hypercorrection has generated the stigmatized hybrid form *el arradio*, or *el amoto* as in the following extract from the speech of a middle-aged Valencian (Spain) woman: '*y claro tenían los **amotos** ahí y como van buscando si están robás*' (Briz 1995: 250). Also nouns which end in a consonant or *-e* may be subject to variation as gender is not clearly signalled by the morphology of the noun, for example, *el casete/la casete, el calor/la calor, el sartén/la sartén*. Nouns which end in *-a* but standardly take the masculine article because of etymological reasons, such as *el reuma, el poema* may also be 'standardized' to *la reuma, la poema*.

Another area of interest concerns nouns which begin with a stressed *a* (e.g. *área, águila*). For reasons of stress and pronunciation these attract the masculine article in the singular (*el área, el águila*). Fontanella de Weinberg (1995: 159) gives the following examples of how, in Argentinian (Buenos Aires) and Chilean Spanish, there has been a reassignation of gender to these nouns in line with the masculine singular article demonstrated by the agreement of the adjectives which accompany them:

> *...disparándose en la cabeza con **el mismo arma*** (*La Nueva Provincia*, 14.6.1990)
> *permite cubrir **todo el área** dental* (*Televisión Nacional Chilena*)

We have already examined (2.1.4) the pressure to provide feminine forms of professions previously exercised predominantly by men and the confusions that change in progress has given rise to. In some Latin American countries, for example in Buenos Aires in Argentina, feminine forms (*la jueza, la jefa, la concejala*) are standard usage amongst all groups in society (Fontanella de Weinberg 1995: 158). On occasion, when a neutral noun ending in the feminine morpheme *-a* refers to an individual of masculine gender (e.g. *el modista*) pressure is brought on the noun to conform with the gender of the article with now *el modisto* being the preferred form used by many journalists despite injunctions from the style guides which point out that the *-a* ending of the noun is etymologically neutral. Fontanella de Weinberg notes (1995: 159) that in the speech of the Colombian working class and peasantry there is a tendency to use analogy to create masculine forms by using the *-o* ending as in *criatura/criaturo, pareja/parejo, nuera/nuero* (normally *yerno*).

5.1.1 *The adjective*

In some varieties of Latin American Spanish (e.g. Mexican) there is a tendency to adjectivize certain nouns and adverbs and consequently make them agree in gender and number with the noun that they qualify. For example, *Para bailar la bamba se necesita una poquita (un poquito) de gracia, Están medios locos.*

Another development in progress in the educated speech of both Spain and Latin America is the adverbialization of adjectives (which we have already examined as a feature of non-standard youth speech in 4.1.2), for example, *Allá me adapté más **fácil**, lo pasaron **regio**, ellos hablan **distinto*** (De Mello 1992a: 225, 231, 235). This has traditionally been considered to be a feature of uneducated speech. Yet De Mello, in a study of this phenomenon in the Spanish of educated speakers of ten cities from Spain and Latin America, shows how it has also permeated the speech of this group, although to a lesser extent than that of the less educated. His study shows that this tendency is most frequent in Caracas, Bogotá, Buenos Aires and Havana, of average frequency in San Juan, Madrid and Santiago de Chile and least frequent in Lima, Mexico and Sevilla. The adjectives most frequently used in this way are *rápido*, followed by *distinto, tranquilo* and *duro*.

Adjectives can also be used as adverbs as a conversational resource for expressing agreement, for example:

A: *No debe ser motivo para que lo descuidemos.*
B: ***Evidente**. Estoy de acuerdo.*

(De Mello 1992a: 232)

5.2 The clause

5.2.0 *Queísmo/dequeísmo*

Both *dequeísmo* and *queísmo* are long-standing features of Spanish on both sides of the Atlantic which have attracted a great deal of scholarly attention. In standard Spanish, verbs may or may not be followed by a preposition in the subordinate clause, for example, *Creo que va a venir*, *Pienso que sí* and *Tengo miedo de que va a llover*, *Me he acordado de que no va a venir*. In brief, *dequeísmo* refers to the addition of a preposition where none exists in standard Spanish and *queísmo* refers to the elimination of one standardly included.

Thus *dequeísmo* refers to the inclusion of the preposition *de* in a subordinate phrase normally introduced by the conjunctive pronoun *que* alone, for example, *Creo de que*, (cf. *Creo que*), *Resultó de que* (cf. *Resultó que*). It can also refer to the substitution of the prepositions *a*, *en* and *con* by *de*, for example, *No hay derecho de (a) que...*, *Se empeña de (en) que...*, *Está de acuerdo de (con) que ....* One reason put forward for *dequeísmo*, at least in the case of verbs of perception, is the existence of broadly equivalent pairs, such as *temer que ...* and *tener miedo de que ...*; here *dequeísmo* would be a consequence of the migration of the preposition *de* from the latter to the former.

In Spain, *dequeísmo* is stigmatized (see, for example, the style guides) and mainly on these grounds it has been argued (Gómez Molina 1995) that *dequeísmo* is an example of variation rather than change in progress, given that change most frequently involves a shift towards using a prestige variant. Indeed, according to his study based on a speech community in Valencia, the younger generations, the middle classes and women speakers use *dequeísmo* significantly less frequently than, for example older males from lower sociocultural groups. Vaquero de Ramírez (1996: 38), however, observes that it appears to be a change in progress in Latin America. Fontanella de Weinberg (1995: 162) notes that in Chile and in Buenos Aires in Argentina *dequeísmo* is also stigmatized to the extent that while it frequently occurs in speech, it rarely does in journalism. García (1986), who has worked on the educated speech of the capital cities of Colombia, Chile and Argentina observes a stylistic difference between the two forms; where *de* is used the subordinate phrase is seen as less immediate, less binding, less categorical. According to her view, the use of *Creo de que* rather than *Creo que* would indicate a lesser commitment of the speaker to the opinion expressed.

Queísmo refers to the elimination by a speaker of a preposition (generally but not exclusively *de*) which in standard Spanish would accompany *que*. For example, *Me he acordado que* (cf. *Me he acordado de que*), *Insiste que venga* (cf. *Insiste en que venga*). Although in some cases *queísmo* may be due to hypercorrection where a speaker is anxious to avoid *dequeísmo* and consquently omits the preposition *de* even when its use is standard, the phenomenon is too widespread for this to explain the majority of use. *Queísmo* can be responsible for certain losses of semantic distinction when the inclusion or omission of a pronoun modifies the meaning of the verb. For example, the loss of the pronoun *a* removes the semantic distinction between, *esperar que pase el autobús* (to hope (and wait) that the bus will come by) and *esperar a que pase el autobús* (to *wait* until the bus comes by).

In the Community of Valencia in Spain, Gómez Molina argues that *queísmo* is a case of language change in progress given that it is used most frequently by the youngest sectors of the population by women and by the middle classes.

5.2.1 Prepositions

An area where change appears to be in progress is where there is the loss of the prepositional phrase in relative clauses such as *La casa que vivo* (cf. *La casa en la que vivo*).

In Spain, and particularly in Galician and Catalan-speaking areas, there is an increase in the use of the possessive rather than the prepositional phrase after an adverb of location, for example, *detrás mío/a* (*detrás de mí*), *delante tuyo/a* (*delante de ti*), *enfrente nuestro/a* (*enfrente de nosotros*). It is possible that this development is a result of language in contact as constructions such as these are permissible in Catalan; alternatively it could be the result of analogy, following the model of constructions such as *al lado mío*. In any case, Llorente (in Almela Pérez 1991: 436) notes the spread of this construction throughout Spain and through all social groups. Almela has studied the frequency of occurrence of the different adverbs which are used in these constructions; going from the most to the least frequent they are: *delante, encima, detrás/enfrente, cerca debajo lejos, arriba, abajo, dentro, atrás adelante, fuera, afuera, adentro.*

In large parts of Latin America, mainly from Mexico as far as Colombia and Venezuela, the preposition *hasta* is used to denote the beginning of an action, for example, *¿Hasta cuándo viene María?* (When will María arrive?) whereas elsewhere in the Spanish-speaking world it denotes the end of an action or process, such as *Cantan hasta las diez* (They'll sing until ten). Similarly *desde* is used to denote the end of an action often with an emphatic function, for example, *Regresé desde el domingo* (I got back *desde* Sunday (but I wasn't expected until Monday). In the case of *hasta* such diametrically opposed usages can give rise to confusion between speakers of different varieties. Kany (in Fontanella de Weinberg 1995: 166) gives an example of cross-cultural miscommunication in the following dialogue between himself and a doctor's receptionist (X):

Kany: *—¿Está el doctor?*
        (Is the doctor in?)
X: *—El doctor no está. Al rato regresa.*
        (The doctor isn't in. He'll be back shortly.)
Kany: *—¿Estará hasta las ocho?*
        (Will he be there until eight?/Will he arrive at eight?)

(Kany wants to know if the doctor will stay until eight.)

X: *–No, llegará mucho antes.*

(No, he'll arrive long before then.)

(The receptionist thinks that Kany wants to know whether he'll arrive at eight.)

In Spanish the preposition *a* is commonly used before certain kinds of direct object, in particular before particularized humans, for example *Vi a Miguel Angel* but not *Vi un doctor* or *Vi el horario*. Consequently it is frequently known as 'personal *a*' although it appears in a wider range of contexts than this might suggest. It can be used to refer to humanized animals for example.[19] However, the rules which govern its use appear to be unstable. In some contexts, it appears to be omitted as in *Yo conozco ø un ingeniero que gana*, although this may be a result of *queísmo* (5.2.0) as in *de un personaje ø que no le interesaba en nada* or a performance error as in *ø los norteamericanos, les daban vacaciones* (data from Santo Domingo in Whitehead (1998)). Vaquero de Ramírez (1996: 35) notes its omission in Puerto Rico, Bolivia and Venezuela. In other contexts, speakers and writers increasingly use the personal *a* to personify all kinds of nouns. Butt and Benjamin (1994: 314) give the following example of a personified noun: '*Los cazas llevan bengalas de magnesio para confundir a un misil dirigido*' (*Cambio 16*).

5.2.2 Relative pronouns

Spanish offers a choice of three relative pronouns to refer to a human antecedent, *el/la que*, *el/la cual* and *quien*. While Butt and Benjamin (1994: 48) note that in the case of Peninsular Spanish *el/la cual* belongs to a more formal register, this is not the case in Latin America, and indeed, as De Mello notes (1993: 87), *el/la cual* is the preferred form in the major cities of Bogotá, Buenos Aires, Caracas, Lima, San Juan and Santiago, for example:

> *tuve una maestra, tú sabes, yo te conté, la señora Natalia,* **la cual** *abrió para mí todo un universo*
>
> (De Mello 1993: 84)

In Mexico City, Havana, Madrid and Seville the preferred form is *el/la que* and in La Paz both forms enjoy equal currency.

5.2.3 Word order

As Butt and Benjamin note (1994: 464),[20] word order in Spanish is free compared with English and French, although it is less free now in the twentieth century than it had been in previous centuries. De Bruyne (1995a) gives eleven alternative word orders for the clause *El criado trajo para mí una carta*. Hickey

(1983/84: 30) notes that in Spanish the subject-verb-object (SVO) word order has become unmarked and far commoner than others, possibly under the influence of English word order, although VS is not infrequent. Thus SVO (e.g. *Alicia lee el libro*) is now the unmarked order and departures from this are typically marked. Hickey (following Contreras (1976)) argues that word order does not appear to be used in Spanish for primarily grammatical reasons (e.g. it is intonation not word order which distinguishes between question and statement in *Viene María* and *¿Viene María?*). Nor is it used for semantic reasons (for example, *Viene María* has the same meaning as *María viene*). However, in the case of this last example there are clear pragmatic differences in that the first phrase may constitute an answer to a question such as *¿Quién viene?* while the second answers a question such as *¿Qué hace María?* This distinction can be conveyed in different ways in different languages with English, for example, using stress.

Hickey (1994) argues that word order is affected either entirely or mainly by pragmatic, stylistic and discoursal considerations and he discusses these under the following headings: theme and rheme, given and new, the end-weight rule and the presentative principle. The first two of these are pragmatic; normally what is already known to the speaker or listener, either made available in the preceding text or recoverable from world knowledge, is presented first (the given) and is followed by information which is considered not yet known to the listener and reader. It is interesting to note how the Latin American headlines we examine in Chapter 8, while adhering to expected word order do not make the subject explicit. The effect of this is to present as given information probably not available to readers who are thereby incited to read on to fulfil their 'need to know'. In the example below, taken from *Reformas – Novedades de Yucatán* (22.5.97),

> *Descubren 'pruebas' contra PRI*

the pragmatic effect is to raise the question in the reader's mind of who precisely has discovered the evidence.

The 'end-weight' rule is essentially stylistic and involves placing the longest element at the end of the clause as can be seen in the following example taken from *El País*, 24.5.97:

> *Pero detrás de ese buen ambiente general se escudó (V) una lucha a cara de perro por los intereses nacionales (S).*

Finally, the presentative principle involves placing in sentence-final position, elements which are to be developed in the succeeding clause. Hickey (1994: 12) provides the following examples:

(a) *Al evolucionismo, que ya hemos tratado, se opone el fijismo. El fijismo es la teoría de que las especies son invariables, fijas.*

(b) *El fijismo se opone al evolucionismo, que ya hemos tratado. El fijismo es la teoría de que las especies son invariables, fijas.*

From the results of a questionnaire administered to native speakers of Spanish he argues that the (a) form is judged to be more logical, natural and acceptable than the (b) form.

In the spoken language too, word order is a crucial element of cohesion. Enríquez (1984: 157–8) notes the frequent occurrence of what she calls '*partículas anunciativas*' (presentative particles) such as *entonces, también, igualmente, en fin, en realidad, así, así pues, es decir (que), es que, es más, además, luego, desde luego* and *efectivamente* at the beginning of an utterance expressing, or even merely implying, continuity with what has been said previously. She cites the following example,

> . . . *creo que se . . . perciben los extraterrestres por otro sentido que no es ninguno de los cinco nuestros. Entonces, nosotros no los podríamos percibir;* **entonces**, *ellos tienen que hacerse perceptibles, porque ellos también tienen vista y oído . . .*

Stewart (1992: 312) argues that one explanation for the frequent occurrence of the first-person personal pronoun as the initial element of a turn could be its cohesive function in establishing relevance for the utterances as well as, on occasion, its function in attention-getting and actually winning the turn as in *Yo, yo, yo creo que . . .* (I, I, I think that . . .) (Val.).

Certainly it is true to say that word order in the spoken language is freer than in the written language and, with intonation, contributes greatly to achieving cohesion.

Word order in Spanish may be under some pressure from contact with English. Butt and Benjamin note the strictures issued by the *El País* style guide admonishing writers for inserting adverbs into verbal phrases, e.g. *El presidente está dispuesto claramente a dimitir* and observe that nonetheless this is a very common order in Spanish. Certainly, in the Spanish spoken in the southern states of the United States there is clear evidence of contact with English as we shall see in Chapter 9.

In parts of Latin America (particularly Cuba) subject pronouns may be used before the verb in questions, for example:

> *¿Qué tú quieres?*
>
> (Kany in De Bruyne 1995a: 619)

5.3 Conclusion

The language system, certainly at the level of formal educated speech and writing, is remarkably standard in terms of its grammar, syntax and orthography. While variation in the lexis available to speakers and in the ways of pronouncing is indubitably greater, there are supranational norms which facilitate

communication. Language change may be prompted by contact with a powerful neighbour such as English and is most evident in the lexis; however, effects
can also be noted in the very morpho-syntax of the language. Moreover, it is
interesting to note that some of the changes affecting Spanish are occurring in
areas where there is little direct contact with this language as well as those
where contact is immediate. In this chapter we have examined the language
system as such and have only briefly reflected on how it is used by speakers for
particular purposes. In Chapters 6 to 8 we shall examine some of the very different uses which can be made of the same language system.

Part III

The Spanish language in use

So far we have concentrated our attention on the more traditional areas of phonology and phonetics, orthography, lexis and morpho-syntax while at the same time focusing on areas where variation or change or both are in evidence. In the preceding chapters we examined the forces at work shaping the evolution of the Spanish language, driving at times towards greater unification and at others towards greater fragmentation and variety. In the following three chapters, the focus will fall on how different speakers and writers of Spanish use an inherently variable language system for a number of different purposes. For not only do speakers tailor the language they use in order to negotiate and maintain social relationships but they also draw on its resources to be able to persuade, request, issue instructions, or pay compliments, to name but a few language functions. Here we are dealing not merely with the different levels of formality adopted by different speakers in different circumstances but also with how individual speakers use the same language system differently to achieve their interactional goals. In Part III, the focus will fall on variation according to use (often called **register**), broadly within the Hallidayan (Halliday and Hasan 1985: 24) discourse framework introduced in 3.2.2, of **field** (what is going on in the discourse), **mode** (the medium selected for communication, either written or spoken) and **tenor** (the relationship between the speaker/writer and the hearer/reader, including such variables as formality, deference).

Chapter 6 will deal with the area of interpersonal relationships encoded by the choice of **personal pronoun** and **address form**. One area where variation in the use of both the spoken and written language is particularly salient is in the choice of forms of address, whether in face-to-face spoken interaction or in written correspondence. For example, a Mexican speaker may introduce a colleague on one occasion by saying *Le presento al señor licenciado Morales* while on another he or she may use the informal *Te presento a Juan Alberto*. In writing to the same individual he or she may address him as *Estimado señor Morales* or *Querido amigo*. Obviously, the use of *tú*, *Vd*. and *vos* can be viewed from two angles, that of the user and that of use. The variants available depend primarily on the region of the speaker and to a lesser extent on factors such as socio-economic group. The rules governing their use may be radically different from one speech community to another. For example, in Madrid *tú* can be used in a very wide range of circumstances whereas, say, in Mexico City its use is more limited. Change in the conventions of use has been significant across the Spanish-speaking world and variation is such that incomers to any Spanish-speaking community must rapidly acquire the 'local' rules for use to enable them to negotiate their relationships successfully with other speakers. Consequently, we have chosen to deal with T/V in the part of the book dedicated to language in use, rather than in Part II where the focus would have fallen on what is for us the less interesting area of which variants are used in which community.

Chapter 7 will concern itself with the conventions of different **discourses** and **genres**. Are the conventions for newspaper headlines the same in Mexico as they are in Spain? Are the conventions for a parliamentary address the same either side of the Atlantic and to what extent are they constantly evolving? Are 'political correctness' and euphemism used similarly in different speech communities? In this chapter we shall examine a sample of genres of Spanish (e.g. administrative, legal, political, journalistic) to see to what extent modernization is evident, to see how new genres arise to meet new social circumstances, to see changes in patterns of discourse and to examine differences and similarities between the same genre in different parts of the Spanish-speaking world.

Another related area is that of **cross-cultural pragmatics** or 'how to do things with words' (Austin 1962). Are the linguistic strategies for making a request the same, for example, in Mexico as in Peninsular Spain? Are the conventions **for linguistic politeness** (Brown and Levinson 1987) the same for Ecuador as they are in Peninsular Spain? In **Chapter 8** we shall investigate pragmatics and politeness, that is how speakers use the language to achieve certain objectives, whether these be requesting, apologizing, or complimenting, and how they establish and maintain relationships with other speakers as they do so. We shall also look at some of the rules governing **conversation**. The ability to understand 'local rules' for communication affects the ability of speakers from one part of the Spanish-speaking world to communicate with those from another. These rules are deeply grounded in society and may colour the attitudes of some Spanish-speaking communities towards others, for example, northern Spaniards may appear brusque to, say, Colombians.

Our aim, in these chapters, is not to deal with these issues exhaustively but rather to focus on some of the research which has been carried out in the area and to raise questions about conventions of use which can thereafter be applied to the variety or varieties of Spanish with which the reader is most closely acquainted. We shall pay particular attention to the use of *tú* and *usted* because it is here that many of the issues underlying style-shifting (or variation of usage within the individual speaker) are thrown into sharp relief, notably the importance of the relationship between speakers in terms of the notions of power and solidarity and equally the importance of the domain or setting in which language is used. These notions will provide a grounding for the issues dealt with in Chapters 7 and 8.

6   *Tú, Vd.* and forms of address

Address systems[1] and the conventions which govern their use provide a window into how a particular society conceives of the social relationships which make it up at a given moment in its history. Certainly, as we shall see, it is no coincidence that the unparalleled shift towards the use of the familiar second-person pronoun *tú* in post-Franco Spain has gone hand in hand with increased democratization and a move away from enforced deference to individuals and institutions. According to Juan Arias (*El País*, 14.8.91) the prevalent use of *tú* is symbolic of the new Spain. '*Tutearse es muy español. Es casi un distintivo de la nueva España. ¿Será un pecado? Hay quienes ven esta riada de tuteo como el inicio de un derrumbamiento de autoridad y de respeto.*'[2]

Brown and Gilman's (1960) influential investigation of second-person pronoun usage in French, German and Italian examined the interrelationship between society and language. Perhaps their most important contribution was their claim that usage was governed by two semantics, both located within society: that of **power** and that of **solidarity**. According to the power semantic, the more powerful person uses the familiar pronoun (known as T) and receives, in return, the deferential V form. Power is derived from a variety of sources: age, social class, sex, wealth, physical strength, institutional role (family, army, State, Church). Thus older people are assumed to have power over younger people, parents over children, teachers over pupils, employers over employees and address between them is non-reciprocal. If, however, both interlocutors are perceived as equal, then reciprocal address can be adopted, the more powerful sectors of society tending to use mutual V and the less powerful, mutual T. To this original semantic was added the dimension of solidarity or perceived social distance. Solidarity has its base in family, religion, profession, sex, birthplace, ideology, and so on. Under this semantic, power equals can choose, regardless of how powerful they are, between showing that they are solidary with their interlocutor (because, say, they both come from the same place) by use of T, or, alternatively, can choose to mark social distance by use of V. Brown and Gilman argue that in modern societies the solidarity semantic dominates choice of pronoun, with a consequent reduction in non-reciprocal address and this is certainly the case in Spain where non-reciprocal address is relatively rare.

However, before moving the discussion on to consider patterns of use in different societies it is useful to consider the different pronominal paradigms, or sets of pronouns and their related verb endings, which have evolved in the Spanish-speaking world.

6.0 Pronominal Paradigms

6.0.0 *Spain*

In Peninsular Spain the form *tú* emerged as the familiar second-person pronoun with *vosotros/as* as the plural form. *Usted* and *ustedes* (abbreviated to *Vd./Vds.* , *V./Vs.* or *Ud./Uds.*), contractions of the third-person honorific *Vuestra Merced* and *Vuestras Mercedes* were adopted as the formal pronouns of address accompanied by the third-person form of the verb.[3] Thus the standard Peninsular paradigm is currently as follows:

Standard peninsular paradigm

	Singular	**Plural**
Familiar	Tú eres, comes, etc.	Vosotros/as sois, coméis, etc.
Formal	Vd. es, come, etc.	Vds. son, comen, etc.

While this is the prestige usage in Spain, two other main patterns of usage can be found.

There is the standard usage of the Canary Islands, also found in parts of southwestern Spain, where the plural familiar pronoun *vosotros/as* has fallen into disuse and has been replaced by *Vds.* for both the formal and the familiar accompanied by the standard third-person plural verb ending. This usage is more closely aligned with that of Latin America.

There is also the much less widespread stigmatized use of the formal plural pronoun conjugated with the familiar form of the verb, which occurs in parts of western Andalusia and the Canary Islands (Green 1990a: 97). For example,

> Ustedes queréis muchas cosas.
> Ustedes diréis donde vamos.

> (Criado Costa and Criado Costa 1992)

6.0.1 *Latin America*

In Latin America there are two main patterns, *tuteo* (the use of *tú*) and *voseo* (the use of *vos*), although there are areas where *Vd.*, *tú* and *vos* are all used. In the plural, the pronoun used is *ustedes* conjugated with the third-person plural of the verb regardless of whether the relationship is familiar or formal, the plural familiar pronoun *vosotros/as* having fallen into disuse.

Tuteo

The singular familiar pronoun *tú* is widely used (e.g. in Mexico and most of the Caribbean). Thus the pronominal paradigm for a country where *tú* is used is as follows:

Standard Latin American (tuteo) paradigm

	Singular	**Plural**
Familiar	*Tú eres, comes,* etc.	*Vds son, comen,* etc.
Formal	*Vd. es, come,* etc.	*Vds. son, comen,* etc.

Voseo

There is also the competing form *vos* which is the familiar second-person pronoun in a large number of countries. *Vos* was originally used in Golden Age Spain as a polite second-person singular pronoun but was finally ousted from the polite slot by *Vd.* and from the familiar slot by *tú* in Peninsular Spanish. *Vos* is principally used in the southern cone and most of Central America, and is also found in parts of Ecuador, Colombia, and so on. According to Canfield (1981, in Penny (1991: 20–1)), these were principally the regions which were most remote from the main lines of communication with Spain.

Thus *vos* was retained either as part of a two-way (*vos/usted*) or three-way (*vos/tú/usted*) system.[4] According to Lipski, while the use of *vos* in place of *tú* is widespread and virtually the norm in spontaneous speech in certain countries, particularly in Central America, Argentina, Uruguay and Paraguay, the co-existence of the prestige norm (*tú*) and its predominance in all but regional literature leads to a certain amount of linguistic insecurity. The degree to which the use of *vos* is stigmatized or is accepted as the regional standard is in constant flux as societies evolve. Caterina Weinerman (in Carricaburo 1997: 25) tells of visiting a boutique in Buenos Aires in the late 1960s and being horrified to be addressed by the shop assistant in, what was for her at the time, the vulgar *vos* form. Less than ten years later she says that she would feel insulted if the *vos* form were not used as *Vd.* had acquired, in the interim, connotations of respect for old age. The semiotic value of *vos* and its association with the people, as opposed to the elite, led to the adoption of this form for official purposes by the Revolutionary Sandinista government of 1979 in Nicaragua. Lipski describes how not only billboard slogans addressing the population used the *vos* form, as in *Nicaragüense, cumplí con tu deber* (where *cumplí* is the imperative form used with *vos*), but also official correspondence within the military used this form in addition to the solidary address form *compañero*.

More generally, in Central America (Costa Rica, Guatemala, El Salvador, Honduras, Nicaragua, and parts of Panama) as well as the countries of the River Plate (Argentina, Uruguay and Paraguay) the use of *vos* (*voseo*) as opposed to the use of *tú* (*tuteo*) predominates. While *vos* is used in the subject

Figure 6.1 Map of *tú/vos* in Latin America (based on Mar-Molinero (1997))

position and as the disjunctive pronoun *Voy con vos, ¿A vos te parece?* all other realizations of this pronoun are derived from the *tú* paradigm (i.e. the direct and indirect object pronoun *te*, the determiners *tu, tus*, and the possessive pronouns *(el) tuyo, (la) tuya, (los) tuyos, (las) tuyas*).

Conjugation of vos

There is considerable variation in the verbal form conjugated with *vos*, not all of which can be covered here.

The pronoun *vos* was originally conjugated with the familiar second-person plural verb endings, *-áis, -éis, -ís*, and this usage has survived (occasionally with the loss of the final *s*) in parts of Latin America such as southern Bolivia, Costa Rica, rural Panama, parts of Venezuela and Chile.

In Argentina (where the use of *vos* is most thoroughly accepted) and in Paraguay, Uruguay and Central America (where use is widespread if, on occasion, stigmatized), the principal verb endings for the three conjugations (*hablar, comer, vivir*) are *-ás, -és* and *-ís* although *-ís* may also occur in second-conjugation verbs, for example, *Vos comís* (You eat).

In the Andean countries of Chile, Ecuador and Bolivia it is not uncommon for *vos* to be conjugated with the second-person singular familiar (*tú*) verbal ending, for example, *Vos eres, Vos tienes*.

Principal conjugations of vos

	-ar paradigm	**-er** paradigm	**-ir** paradigm
Vos	*hablá(s)*	*comé(s)*	*viví(s)*
		comí(s)	
	hablái(s)	*coméi(s)*	*viví(s)*
	hablas	*comes*	*vives*

According to Lipski (1994) there are two areas where a new pronominal paradigm appears to be in the making.

In Chile, where the use of *vos* had been stigmatized since the nineteenth century, particularly in educated circles, where academicians of the language such the grammarian Andrés Bello proscribed its use, there is what Torrejón (1986, 1991, in Lipski 1994: 202) calls *el voseo culto de Chile*. This is the use of the *vos* verbal forms by young educated urban middle-class speakers who either use the *tú* pronoun or avoid personal pronominal use altogether. Further work by Torrejón (1991, in Carricaburo 1997: 35) suggest that as Chilean society is evolving, there is gradual simplification of what was an extremely complex system of address including two forms of *voseo, tuteo*, the use of *Vd.* and a variant *su merced* used to give deference to the elderly. This system was used not only to encode power and distance but also to express emotion. Thus a parent could use *Vd.* affectionately to a baby or in anger passing from *tú* to *usted* to remonstrate with a child.

In El Salvador a three-way system appears to be developing amongst the educated urban classes (Lipski 1994: 259), where *vos* and *Vd.* occupy the extremes of intimacy on the one hand and respect on the other, with *tú* occupying an intermediate position, signifying familiarity but not intimacy. Interestingly, there are places where there appears to be a reduction in the paradigm and where *usted* covers both familiar and formal use such as eastern and central Colombia and rural Panama.

It should be clear by now that not only are there significant differences in the paradigms available to speakers in different countries and regions of the Spanish-speaking world and within individual countries and regions, but that also different values attach to the use of one paradigm rather than another. For example, the use of *vos* is frequently stigmatized and certain verbal conjugations used with *vos* appear to mark out speakers as, say, rural rather than urban or uneducated rather than educated. Now the question arises: on what grounds does a speaker select one form rather than another in face-to-face interaction?

6.1 The use of *tú* and *Vd.* in face-to-face interaction

As we shall see, the conventions of use of T/V vary widely for each social grouping which develops its own rules governing the choice of the V or the T form, for example whether the V form is used systematically with representatives of administration, professionals, older family members, and with whom and in what circumstances the T form can be used. In highly stratified societies such as, say, Mexico these rules may be clear and widely accepted; this may also be the case in societies such as Nicaragua or Spain where a significant shift towards the use of the T form may mark out rejection of a previous society, be it under Somoza or Franco. Nonetheless, even within these societies, rules governing use are in constant flux. In this section, we shall review Lambert and Tucker's (1976) study of the use of T and V in Puerto Rico and Colombia, given that this was the first influential study to apply Brown and Gilman's theory to the Spanish language. We shall compare their findings with more up-to-date evidence gathered from Carricaburo (1997). Then we shall look at two other studies, one carried out in a rural village in central Spain (Moreno Fernández 1986) and the second amongst Spanish speakers in New Mexico (Jaramilla 1990), to see how change towards the T form is penetrating even the most conservative of speech communities.

Lambert and Tucker addressed the factors affecting patterns of address in Puerto Rico and Colombia amongst groups of young people. In particular, they investigated the age, sex, socio-economic status of the interlocutor and the setting (urban vs. rural) and administered to their respondents a lengthy questionnaire requiring informants to self-report on which pronoun they would use in addressing a wide selection of potential interlocutors, ranging from the nuclear and extended family to members of the professions, religious orders, and so on. Informants were also asked to report on religious affiliations and personal and family personality traits.

In their study of Puerto Rico, Lambert and Tucker reported (1976: 155) no 'stable, pervasive forms of address' with the exception of reciprocal *tú* amongst friends. Within the family they discovered at that time non-reciprocal forms of address, in particular with grandparents who received V and gave T and between some children and parents. They also discovered differences in norms between one community and another with rural Arecibo favouring non-reciprocal forms of address determined primarily by age, and urban Ponce favouring reciprocal forms. Carricaburo (1997: 22), in a more recent study, notes that *tú* has now permeated all social classes; however, older people may still use non-reciprocal T and expect to be addressed by V. In mixed-sex conversation it is the man who has the power to initiate the use of T; indeed men use this form the most and women receive it the most.

The study in Colombia was more limited, relating to a small group of middle-class, Catholic young people from urban Bogotá. They found relationships within the family more likely to be reciprocal, based mainly on reciprocal *tú* although a subgroup of girls addressed their mothers with reciprocal V d. Also rules governing the use of pronouns outside the family appeared more clear-cut, with reciprocal V d. being the pervasive norm between adults and children. Sex was also reported to be a major determining factor with boys using reciprocal V to certain other males (cousins, visitors, strangers, classmates and friends) and reciprocal T to an equivalent group of females; girls tended to use reciprocal T for male and female members of these groups. Carricaburo (1997: 40–3) notes that Colombia is a country which is *ustedeante* (where the pronoun V d. predominates) and where sometimes the impression is given (in Bogotá, for example) that this is the only singular pronoun. What is, in fact, interesting is that V d. is used both to mark deference and also to signal solidarity with T being used in a friendly but nonetheless distant relationship.

If we turn to the case of Spain, we can see that the use of *tú* was once for a very short period, under the Second Republic, the prescribed form of address and its use by previously servile sectors of the population functioned, in a sense, as an emblem of Republican affiliation and a commitment to a major change in the power structures of Spanish society, as is illustrated by George Orwell in his account of this time.

> Waiters and shop-walkers looked you in the face and treated you as equal. Servile and even ceremonial forms of speech had temporarily disappeared. Nobody said 'Señor' or 'Don' or even 'usted', everyone called everyone else 'Comrade' and 'Thou', and said 'Salud!' instead of 'Buenos días'.
>
> (George Orwell, *Homage to Catalonia*, 1966: 8–9)

Since then *tú* has been associated in post-Francoist Spain with the urban young and not-so-young of a progressive orientation, has become so widespread that the intimate connotations attaching to its use have been, in many instances, eroded, or as Josep Vicent Marqués puts it '*Ahora que quienes estamos entre los 35 y los 45 años nos tuteamos con el mismísmo Leviatán, o sea, con los ministros y consejeros autonómicos, hablarse de tú con alguien carece de toda emoción*'.[5] This author also records his impression, echoed elsewhere, that, in some settings such as, for example, between his university students and himself, Vd. is making a comeback. Certainly, it would be interesting to chart the use of T/V in educational environments where one suspects that changes have been the most extreme. Still in 1980, one study of Madrid youth (Alba de Diego and Sánchez Vidal) found that the vast majority of pupils used V with their teachers (only using T when the teacher was particularly young, where the class was very small or amongst the oldest pupils). More recently the use of T has become more widespread, but its systematic use depends on the ethos of the school. Carricaburo (1997: 11) notes that the main factor prompting the use of Vd. is age and that difficulties arise when there is a conflict between age and status; for example, one has to address someone the same age but of a higher status. In these circumstances, males tend to opt for T and females for V.

One thing that appears likely, in Spain, is that the constraints of domain (i.e. the nature of the communicative event in which T/V is used) rather than role relationship are more likely to determine the use of one or other pronoun. For example, a representative of a pharmaceutical company is more likely to use V in a formal meeting with a client than when mixing socially with the same client. The same representative may prefer to use T in a group discussion with a number of invited experts when he wishes to retain power as chair of the discussion, but use V in individual interviews with these same experts when it is important to defer to their expert status; obviously the pronoun used may need to be negotiated, but reciprocal use is the norm (Miguel Muñoz, personal communication). Unfortunately, there are few up-to-date surveys of the use of T/V in urban Spain, as reseachers appear to have preferred to investigate rural communities where there is often greater variation and where non-reciprocal forms of address still persist.

In such a study, Moreno Fernández (1986) investigates the use of T/V in the Spanish village of Quintanar de la Orden in Castilla-La Mancha in order to find out what differences existed between different groups of speakers (age, sex, class) and which groups tended to give and receive which form of address. He discovered that women speakers use T more than men and that this was particularly marked in the over-fifty age group (interesting insofar as women are generally argued to be those who are most active in promoting language change); unsurprisingly the younger speakers used T predominantly; and that men between the ages of twenty-one and fifty were more likely to use V than those younger or older. Men with a higher level of education, such as students and shopkeepers, were more likely to use T than the less-educated such as joiners or waiters. Indeed, Vd. was used predominantly amongst those who only had primary education, a fact which shows that the power dimension is still in operation. However, the overwhelming evidence of the study was that reciprocal address was the norm and that the factors influencing the choice of Vd. were, in descending order of importance: interlocutors older than the speaker, strangers, 'respected' professionals such as the doctor, parish priest, teacher, those who had a degree, elderly people. Potential for change was most evident amongst the middle classes where clear norms of interaction were least stable; linguistic conservatism resided in speakers who were older, had the least formal education and were of the lowest socio-economic groups. Indeed these were the speakers who still retained non-reciprocal forms of address in a number of circumstances.

A broadly comparable study was carried out in a small rural community, the village of Tomé, in the Río Grande Valley of New Mexico in the southwest of the United States. Here June Jaramilla interviewed fifty Spanish-speaking informants, all with strong links with the community, in order to investigate the use of T/V in a variety of role relationships (e.g. member of nuclear or extended family, service-oriented personnel, etc.) and a variety of formal and informal domains (e.g. nuclear and ceremonial family, low status and high status professional). While she found that personal address in Tomé was generally consistent with norms of standard usage (use of T for informal domains and V for formal ones), she also found that particular norms of interaction were more conservative than reported elsewhere. For example, non-reciprocal use of T/V is standard between parents and children although there are signs of change which are greeted with dismay by some older members of the community. In the words of one fifty-seven–year-old woman, 'No hay respeto. Más antes había muncho amor en la familia.' (Jaramilla 1990: 19). Vd. predominates in godparenthood, kinship and close friendship (*compadrazgo*) relationships. Furthermore, in this particular community, non-reciprocal address, based on the power semantic, persists in some relationships and domains outside the family. For example, employees address their employers more than 90 per cent of the time with V but receive it in return considerably less.

Indeed, communities with strong family links and highly developed family ceremonies such as the mountain villages of the Alpujarras in Andalusian Spain are likely to have clearly defined conventions governing the use of T/V. For example, in these villages (Navarro Alcalá-Zamora 1979) the establishment of a *compadrazgo* relationship implies, by definition, a move from T to V unless there is a 'blood' relationship between the families thus united.

6.2 Naming

A related area of language use and one which varies considerably across the Spanish-speaking world is that of naming, whether it be the use of titles such as *señor* or of diminutives such as Marisé (a diminutive of María José). It is an area which has been addressed by the *Ministerio de Asuntos Sociales'* (1989) guidelines for non-sexist language use (see 2.1.4) where speakers and writers are urged to avoid the term *señorita* in favour of using *señora* for married and unmarried women alike in order to avoid defining women in terms of their relationship with a man. It is also an area of great interest to social anthropologists investigating kinship patterns and social relationships.[6]

Alba de Diego and Sánchez Vidal (1980) suggest that it is probably most useful to look at the terms used for naming along the axes of power and solidarity outlined above with the use of titles, kinship terms, and so on in relationships dominated by the power dimension and the use of proper names, diminutives (*hipocorísticos*) and nicknames (*apodos*) in relationships governed by solidarity.

For example, they suggest that in non-reciprocal relationships an employer may use the employee's surname, or title plus surname (*Martínez, Sr(a) Martínez*) while the employee may use in return the title (*señor/a*) or the deferential *don/doña* plus first name (e.g. *Don Miguel*). In Spain, individuals receive two last names, their father's first surname followed by their mother's first surname. Thus, the son or daughter of *Juan Herrera Fernández* and *Carmen García Martín* would receive the surnames *Herrera García*. Normally, only the first of these is used in address unless this surname is so common as to make it difficult to distinguish its holder, in which case both surnames are used. Both surnames can be employed either to heighten respect or create distance. In Mexico, respect towards high-status individuals can also be encoded by reference to their profession or professional qualifications, for example, *el señor licenciado Navarro*. Berk-Seligson (1990: 137–40), in her study of the bilingual courtroom, refers to the widespread expectation of use in Spanish-speaking America of *señor*, *señora* and *señorita* in 'assymetrical social relationships whenever a person of lower social standing addresses a person of higher standing'. For example:

Interpreter: *¿En algún momento durante el transcurso del vuelo se asustó usted,* **señora***?*

Witness: *Sí,* **señorita***. Yo venía nerviosa porque como eso no es como el avión, eso da como vueltas y yo traía nervios.*

(Berk-Seligson 1990: 138–9).

She goes on to state that this is a basic rule for children addressing adults unless they use specific kinship terms such as *papá, mamá, tío, abuelo*. While this was once the case in Spain[7] Alba de Diego and Sánchez Vidal's 1980 study of Madrid youth shows that only 10 per cent of informants stated that they would use *señor/señorita/señora* with unknown adults. Indeed, in this study, the preferred forms of address for one category of known adults, that is teachers, was:

first name	20 %
don + first name	40 %
señor + first name	2 %

last name   4 %
no response   34 %

The conventions governing the use of *don/doña* + first name, which allows speakers to play simultaneously on the dimensions of intimacy and respect, and which is found both in Spain and Spanish-speaking America, vary from community to community. In village communities in Andalusian Spain, to receive *don* confers a particular kind of prestige: its recipient is either an older and respected member of the community or a degree holder with a 'career' (Pitt-Rivers 1971: 72). In certain countries of Latin America, the use of *don/doña* in face-to-face interaction merely connotes respect due to older members of the community (e.g. The River Plate area and Chile). In Ecuador it is used to address members of the indigenous population, in Guatemala it is used in rural areas and in Venezuela it is used only in popular speech (Carricaburo 1997: 60). As we mentioned earlier, the generalized use of *compañero* was promoted in Sandinista Nicaragua and also in Allende's Chile and Castro's Cuba to connote equality and solidarity.

In Spanish, as in many other languages, there is a wide range of diminutives available for first names. Given the religious connotations and general unwieldiness of many of these names *María del Carmen* (*Maricarmen*, *Carmen*), *Purificación* (*Puri*), *Juan José* (*Juanjo*), many speakers may opt to be systematically called by the diminutive; with others, the use of the diminutive will depend on role relationships and domain. For while the economist *José Villaverde Santos* will be called *Pepe* by his colleagues in the bar, they may prefer to address him by *José* in more formal settings (Val.). However, *Marisé López* may more rarely be called by her given name of *María José*. Accepted diminutives may vary from country to country, with *Fede* being an accepted diminutive of *Federico* in Spain and *Lico* being a standard Chicano diminutive of the same name (Galván and Teschner 1991).

Apodos or nicknames are not generally used to address a speaker to their face; in rural communities in Spain they can function to distinguish between individuals who share the same name (a feature of endogamous communities) or, on occasions, to express moral opprobrium (see Pitt-Rivers 1971) although, given that these *apodos* often run in families, this only really applies to the first to receive the nickname. In Mecina, in southern Spain, (Navarro Alcalá-Zamora 1979), for example, nicknames can be derived from pronounced physical features (e.g. *Roncos, Labios, Hocicos, Pelo Rizao*, etc.), speech defects and tics (e.g. *Sequeseque, Miracielos*, etc.), profession (e.g. *Forestal, Enterrador*, etc.) although the vast majority are derived from first or last names or place names (e.g. '*Fernandicos*', '*Bautistas*', '*los de Narila*', etc.). In addition to these family *apodos*, individuals can receive their own nickname on the basis of some personal characteristic; for example, a woman who has suffered from polio as a child may be called, in her absence, *Paquita la cojilla*, a man whose job it is is to rear a kid goat may be known as *el (hombre) de la cabra*.

Use of kinship terms (which do not imply a family relationship) and pet names such as *hombre, mujer, hijo/a, chico/a, niño/a, mano/ito, cielo, mi vida, mi alma, compa(dre)/compita* varies widely from community to community. For example, while the word for a male child *niño* is preferred in Spanish Andalusia (and, in certain contexts, can be used with males of any age such as waiters), *hijo* is more prevalent in the north and *muchacho* has wider Latin American currency. Mexico has a particularly rich stock of terms to refer to children ranging from *socoyote* to refer to the youngest of a brood through *escuincle* (when the parent is angry) to the affectionate *papacito*.[8] *Mano* is a feature of non-prestige Mexican Spanish and can be used as much as a filler as a term of address (see Galván and Teschner), as can *hombre* in Peninsular Spanish. The widespread use of *tío* as a term of address amongst marginal youth in 1970s Spain appears to have permeated the colloquial usage of young people in Spain.

6.3 Illustrative texts

To illustrate some of the variables discussed above, we reproduce below two sample texts. The two texts are taken respectively from Spain and Mexico and the speakers are all middle-class, educated males aged between thirty-five and seventy-five years old.

The first text is taken from a discussion programme broadcast on the Spanish regional television channel *RTVE Castilla y León* in 1987 on the topic of *Semana Santa* (Holy Week). The male presenter (MA) is in his thirties and the three invited guests are older males, perhaps the best known of whom being the former (right-wing) mayor of Valladolid, Francisco Fernández Santamaría (FF).

MA: *Y en el estudio tenemos a tres invitados que pretendemos que sean los representantes de tres de las juntas de Semana Santa más importantes de la región, aunque en esto habría que tener cuidado porque de todos es sabido los celos, a veces, y las competencias que existen hasta en una manifestación como es de este tipo. Empiezo por mi derecha,* **Salvio Barrioluengo,** *¡Buenas tardes!*

SB: *¡Buenas tardes!*

MA: *Secretario de la Junta de Semana Santa de León.* **¿Qué tal?**

SB: *Muy bien, muy bien, me alegra mucho estar aquí con* **vosotros.**

MA: **Francisco Fernández Santamaría,** *que lo es de la Junta de Semana Santa de Valladolid, ¡Buenas tardes!*

FF: *¡Buenas tardes!*

MA: *Y Eduardo Pedrero, que es el único presidente, no secretario, de la Junta de Semana Santa de Zamora, ¿no?*

EP: *Sí, efectivamente.*

MA: *¿***Estáis** *de acuerdo en que son las tres más importantes o hay alguna más? ¿Me he dejado alguno en el tintero?*

SB: *Bueno, yo creo que eso sería . . .*

(Stewart *et al.* 1991)[9]

What is noticeable about this introduction is that the form of address adopted initially by one of the invited guests and later by the presenter is T, although at this point only the plural form of address *vosotros* (*con vosotros, estáis*) has been used. No titles have been used and all the guests have been addressed by first name + (first) surname. In the case of Francisco Fernández Santamaría both surnames have been adopted. This may be because Fernández is an extremely common surname; alternatively, it could reflect a desire to pay greater respect to the oldest guest who has the highest status. It is noticeable that the presenter has chosen the impersonal and informal greeting *¿Qué tal?* in addressing Salvio Barrioluengo, thus enabling him to avoid the individual use of *tú* with his guest. Equally interesting is Salvio Barrioluengo's reply where he uses the familiar and informal *vosotros* form along with the formal and impersonal *Me alegra mucho*. MA is similarly informal with Eduardo Pedrero where the interactional *¿no?* effectively replaces any formal greeting such as *buenas tardes*.

The second extract is taken from the Mexican soap opera *Luz y sombra* ('Light and shadow') (broadcast on the Spanish state channel, RTVE in January 1995). The speakers are A, a recently retired businessman, and B, a middle-aged practising businessman.

B: *Como no **don Gildo**, ahora **le** doy lo que me pidió por teléfono.*

A: *Muchas gracias **Carlos Alberto**. **Ten** la seguridad que este dinero tendrá un buen uso. **Puedes** estar absolutamente seguro.*

B: *Lo sé, don Gildo. Por eso se lo doy sin que tenga la necesidad de decirme para qué es.*

A: *No tengo por qué ocultártelo, **muchacho**. Este dinero va a ser para ayudar a una jovencita que después de mucho tiempo ha vuelto a estudiar. Ah, este, y si alguna vez allá en Tampico fui ofensivo contigo lo hice a nombre de que soy un viejo metiche que creía que estaba haciendo el bien, hombre. Perdóname, muchacho.*

B: *Ojalá que en la vida de todos los hombres siempre hubiera un viejo metiche que les llamara la atención como **Vd.** lo hizo conmigo, don Gildo.*

A: *Tu corazón siempre ha sido sano **Pineda**, **Pinedita** como diría el difunto Néstor, que Dios proteja de los corajes posmortem que le hemos hecho pasar todos, sin respetar su memoria. Bueno, **hijo**, este viejo carcamal ya se va. Tengo muchas cosas que hacer.*

B: *Espéreme, don Gildo. He pensado en Vd. mucho últimamente. Mire, aquí en la empresa siempre están surgiendo problemas técnicos. Creo que debo insistir en que trabaje con nosotros lo antes posible, **ingeniero don Gildo Soberanes**.*[10]

What is interesting about this extract which, being scripted, is not naturally-occurring and presents stereotypical rather than real discourse, is the assymetrical power relationship (based on age) which is reflected in non-reciprocal patterns of language use. The older man uses T to the younger and receives V in return. The older man is addressed by the deferential but solidary use of *don* + first name, respect is paid to his professional status in *ingeniero don Gildo Soberanes*, and he is in a later part of the extract addressed by the more distant and respectful *señor Soberanes*. The younger man is addressed by the solidary use of both first names, a practice common in Latin America if not in Spain, *Carlos Alberto*, by the use of the last name without title *Pineda* and indirectly by a diminutive of this *Pinedita* (diminutives being more likely to be attached to the first name rather than the second in Peninsular Spanish) and by the kinship terms *muchacho* and *hijo*. The younger man pays respect to the older by explicit use of *usted* while the older man never actually uses the solidary pronoun *tú* although he uses the T form (e.g. *puedes*). It should nevertheless be noted that Lastra de Suárez (Schwenter 1993: 11) suggests that assymetical use of T/V is on the way out in Mexico and is being replaced by reciprocal T.

6.4 Conclusion

While throughout Spain and Latin America the resources available to speakers to address each other are broadly the same, the use which is made of these may vary widely from community to community. At the same time, the whole area of address and naming is one where change is evidently in progress. For example, with the move away from an agricultural society in Spain in the twentieth century, the rich seam of *apodos* is being lost. On the other side of the Atlantic, speakers in El Salvador appear to be gaining a three-way pronominal paradigm, *tú/vos/usted*, allowing them to express ever more complex interpersonal relationships. We have seen the close relationship between pronominal use, naming and concepts of personal identity; similarly we have alluded to relationships between political ideology and personal reference. One area where further investigation is called for is that of the use of T/V and naming in professional domains where the interplay between the variables of power and solidarity is particularly complex.

7 Discourse and genre

For the purposes of this section we shall be using **genre** not to refer to literary genres such as poetry or the novel but to non-literary genres, that is conventionalized communicative events (written and spoken) recognized as such by the professional communities which adopt them, for example, the genre of a political speech. **Discourse** will relate to the ways in which certain social groups use language to convey their attitudes towards certain areas of socio-cultural activity, for example, racist discourse, officialese, sexist discourse. We shall again focus on the two principal dimensions of language use which have concerned us in previous chapters, variation (principally cross-cultural variation) and change over time. Given the scope of this book, this section can only seek to give an impression of the significance of these two dimensions of language use. The areas we shall concentrate on here are: change in administrative and legal genres, variation and change in genres of political discourse and the development of 'European' Spanish, cross-cultural variation in the written press with a special emphasis on the conventions governing newspaper headlines, and taboo, euphemism and political correctness.

7.0 Administrative Spanish

As we have already mentioned (2.1.3), there has been considerable pressure for change in administrative discourse in the latter half of the twentieth century, not only in Spain but throughout the developed world under the influence of movements such as the Plain English campaign.[1] However, given the particular circumstances of a prolonged, non-secular dictatorship in Spain until 1975, the distance that change has had to cover since the early days of Francoism is arguably greater than in other developed countries. It should also be pointed out that the pace of change is very uneven and what are considered archaic practices in one institution may remain unchanged in another. The two sample texts below are representative to a certain extent of change over a twenty-five-year period. They are degree parchments from a Spanish university from the years 1970 and 1995 respectively. The genre of the degree parchment, here and in other countries, demands a degree of solemnity, tradition and precision and provides an instance of powerful institutional discourse. Furthermore, administrative discourse tends in itself to be higly conventionalized leaving few margins for individual creativity. In such a context, the changes which we chart below acquire added significance. Nonetheless, as we shall see, the 1995 text remains largely conservative, and indeed has made no concessions to demands for non-sexist discourse. Significant language choices are highlighted in bold.

Sample text 1 (Degree parchment: 1970)

ILTRE. SR.:

D............................ natural de ...., provincia de ....
de .... años de edad, **domiciliado** en .... provincia de
......................., calle de ...., n° ...., D.N.I. n°
....
expedido en .... fecha .... de .... de 19............,
a V.S. expone:

Que ha terminado en la Escuela Universitaria de Idiomas (De Traductores y de Intérpretes) los estudios que integran la carrera de ....
.... y deseando abonar los derechos reglamentarios para la expedición del correspondiente Diploma, a **V.S.**

SUPLICA se digne dar curso a la adjunta instancia que eleva a la superioridad en súplica de que le sea expedido el referido Diploma de
....

Dios guarde a V.S. muchos años.

Bellaterra, ... de .... de 19.........

(firma **del interesado**)

ILUSTRE SR. DIRECTOR DE LA ESCUELA UNIVERSITARIA DE IDIOMAS (De Traductores y de Intérpretes) DE LA UNIVERSIDAD AUTONOMA DE BARCELONA[2]

Sample text 2 (Degree parchment: 1995)

Certificación Académica Oficial

Don..
Secretario de ....

CERTIFICO: Que de los antecedentes que obran en la Secretaría de este Centro resulta que .... natural de ....

provincia de .... **nacido** el día .... de .... de
................., de nacionalidad .... tiene cursadas y aprobadas
todas las asignaturas que constituyen la carrera de Diplomado de
Traducción e Interpretación (...................................), por el Plan
de Estudios de 21-7-86 (BOE 4-9-86).

Aprobó toda la carrera el día .... de .... de ....,
obteniendo la calificación de APTO.

Abonó los derechos de expedición de Diploma el .... de ....
de .... Cumplidos todos los requisitos establecidos por las dis-
posiciones vigentes, se expide esta certificación, con el visto bueno del
ilustrísimo señor Decano para que se le pueda otorgar el título correspondiente, en Bellaterra a .... de .... de ....

Vº Bº
El Decano,   **El funcionario,**   **El Secretario.**[3]

The principal changes which have taken place over this period are the
following:

- the absence of any ritual or formulaic reference to God in the more recent
  text (cf. *Dios guarde a V.S.* . . .);
- a significant reduction in the number of honorifics to refer those responsible for granting the degree award. In the 1970 text the majority of these
  are abbreviated (*D* (*Don*), *V.S.* (*Vuestro Señoría*), *ILTRE. SR.* (*Ilustre Señor*)),
  a consequence of their frequency of use in texts of the time. In the 1995
  text there are only two references: both of these, *Don* and . . . *el ilustrísimo
  señor Decano* are unabbreviated perhaps showing that their use is now so
  circumscribed to a limited number of extremely formal text types that
  readers may not be expected easily to access their referent.
- the use of the first person in the more recent text (*CERTIFICO*) to present
  a more personal public face to the university administration, contrasting
  starkly with the 1970 text where the graduand is presented as supplicant
  in the presence of a superior being (*SUPLICA se digne* . . . *que eleva a la
  Superioridad en súplica de* . . .). It should be added that the syntax of this
  last phrase would contravene most of the current recommendations for
  'plain Spanish' which we examined in 2.0.3: the legalistic use of *dar curso*,
  the redundancy of *adjunta*, the *muletilla* or empty formula *que eleva a la
  superioridad* and the excessively complex prepositional phrase *en súplica de*
  expressing a starkly assymetrical power relationship.

In short, the two texts project very different relationships between the
university and its graduand. Nonetheless, it is interesting to note that the more
recent text does not conform to the recommendations currently espoused by
a number of public institutions to avoid what might be interpreted as sexist
use of language (see 2.1.4). All reference to participants, whether the graduand

(*nacido el día*) or the administration (*Don, Secretario*), is masculine where alternative forms are equally possible (e.g. *nacido/a*).

Notwithstanding changes both recommended and actually effected in adminstrative genres in the last twenty-five years, the discourse of 'officialese' stills abounds in Spanish. Indeed, the following document, a post office form to be signed when sending an item abroad to be paid for by the addressee, in current use both in Spain and Mexico, amply demonstrates its tenacity.

Sample text 3: (Post Office form)

> *El que suscribe ('El remitente') reconoce por este documento que, no obstante el consentimiento dado por el DHL Internacional España, a petición nuestra de que los cargos que les sean adeudados por los servicios realizados al amparo del conocimiento aérea arriba mencionado sean abonados por el destinatario, nosotros seguimos siendo enteramente responsables de abonarles todos los cargos pagaderos por el Remitente por los servicios realizados al amparo de dicho conocimiento aéreo incluyendo gastos de flete, tasas, derechos arancelarios, costes administrativos, gastos de almacenamiento y de retorno del envío a nosotros, siendo ello de su exclusiva incumbencia la determinación de los mismos, comprometiéndonos a abonarles los cargos mencionados inmediatamente a requerimiento de ustedes.*[4]

Certainly, this document falls far short of the clarity and economy currently recommended by the Ministry and it does not make any concessions to non-sexist language (*el que suscribe, el Remitente*). The most striking features of the text are:

- repetition (for example, of the legalistic formula *al amparo de conocimiento aéreo*);
- subordination (the whole text comprises one sentence);
- use of gerund (*siendo todos ellos, comprometiéndonos a*);
- marked word order (*a petición nuestra*).

Nonetheless, it does succeed in creating a relationship of equality between the customer and the institution by the use of personal pronouns (*nosotros* and *ustedes*) and avoids the use of archaisms and *muletillas* (see Chapter 2).

Other Spanish institutions (for example, the Inland Revenue) continue to place the customer in the position of supplicant by the use of formulae unchanged since the times of Franco. The following extract is taken from a 1990 document (art. 32.1, R.D. 1684/1.990) enabling the taxpayer to apply for a receipt for tax paid:

Sample text 4: (Inland Revenue document)

> *En su virtud, a V.S.,*
> SUPLICA: *Se digne acordar la práctica de la certificación solicitada en los términos contenidos en el cuerpo de este escrito.*

It is precisely the relationship embodied in the archaic form of address V.S., the verbs *suplicar* and *dignarse* and the verbosity of the remainder of the sentence, which the Spanish Ministry's style guide is designed to combat.

Another genre where change is evidently in progress in Spain is that of the administrative letter, traditionally of extreme formality. The following letter concerning a twinning arrangement between a Spanish and a Scottish town shows this tension. It is a hybrid text where set formulae are used in conjunction with an attempt at interpersonal friendliness, informality and comprehensibility.

Sample text 5: (Town-twinning letter)

Querida (+ first name):

Siento tener que comunicarte que por circunstancias imprevistas, El Coordinador Deportivo de este Ayuntamiento no podrá asistir a la reunión del próximo sábado día 24 de octubre, referente a los Encuentros Deportivos que se van a celebrar en esa ciudad el año 1.993.

No obstante, me ha encargado que os comunique la intención de este Ayuntamiento de participar en los mencionados Encuentros acatando las bases que nos remitísteis, si bien nos será del todo imposible participar en la modalidad de GOLF, puesto que este deporte no se practica en nuestra localidad.

Aprovecho la ocasión para mandarte mi más cordial saludo.
(name of town), *21 de octubre de 1.992*
El ANIMADOR CULTURAL[5]

P.D. Te ruego me envíes un FAX para confirmarme que has recibido éste y comprendes lo que te quiero decir en él.

While this text contains elements of 'plain Spanish', it nonetheless displays a level of formality that the writer is aware may prove a barrier to communication with his English-language correspondent, hence the more informal postscript allowing for further communication. The text is interesting on account of the way it shifts between registers. It uses the informal address form *querida* (which is more likely to be used with a close friend) rather than the more formal *mi querida* or *estimada/distinguida*, the *tú* form and the first person singular (*siento, me ha encargado, aprovecho*, and so on) rather than the more formal *Vd.* and a relatively informal ending compared with the standard practice of adopting third-person reference, such as *le saluda atentamente* + name. However, these features co-occur with an essentially formal text typified by the hyper-formality of *acatando las bases que nos remitísteis*, the use of the formal *mencionados, referente a, la modalidad de* and the precision involved in presenting the year as 1.992.

7.1 Legal Spanish

While there are currently moves in Spain to apply the principles behind plain language campaigns to legal genres, the *Libro de estilo para juristas* (Millán Garrido), which appeared in 1997, is a conservative document, which, with the exception of a glossary of legal terms and abbreviations, deals primarily with general issues such as spelling and bibliographic referencing. As in other non-Spanish-speaking countries, legal discourse, in part for reasons pertaining to the status of documents in the eyes of the law, has been much slower to change than its administrative counterpart. It should be added that a primary feature of many documents from the legal field is to be legally binding and it is therefore to be expected that economy of expression will be sacrificed to explicitness. Furthermore, legal discourse by nature tends to be powerful, to express gravitas, employ set formulae and be maximally formal. Furthermore, its readership is restricted typically to those trained in its use and those compelled to use the legal system; it is not directed at a general audience. Alvarez (1995: 53), while noting that legal discourse shares many of the features of adminstrative discourse, identifies the following features as being particularly characteristic of this genre:

Morpho-syntax

- frequent use of abstract nouns, e.g. *la modificación, la inhabilitación lo establecido*
- frequent use of the gerund, e.g. *y no **habiéndose** probado . . .*
- frequent use of infinitives and past participles, e.g. ***transcurrido** el plazo*
- use of complex prepositional and adverbial phrases, e.g. *de conformidad con*
- extensive subordination and frequent absence of connectors
- the use of the archaic future subjunctive, e.g. *los que **utilizaren** o **prestaren** a menores . . .*
- the archaic postposition of the pronoun *se*, e.g. ***Líbrese** testimonio de esta sentencia (que se libre)* and non-standard use of the possessive pronoun, e.g. *el día 30 de octubre, a las once horas de **su** mañana*
- certain automatic collocations of adjectives with nouns and a tendency towards adjectives being placed before the noun, e.g. ***manifiesta** contradicción* and frequent use of adjectives relating to previous mention in the text, e.g. *aludido, mencionado, citado y precitado* and *dicho y antedicho.*

Lexis

- terms restricted to legal discourse such as *intestado, bastantear* (to officially accept the credentials of an attorney or proxy)
- terms from standard Spanish which acquire precise legal meanings, e.g. *actor* ('plaintiff' (normally 'actor'))

- terms clearly Latinate in origin (e.g. *usufructo*) and borrowings from Latin, e.g. *prima facie*
- frequently used terms which are clearly polysemic and take their meaning from context, e.g. *caso* (act, case, defence, action, etc.).

In this section we shall examine the Spanish used in two legal documents, an adoption order from a Peruvian court from 1993; and a Spanish legal document drawn up in 1997 on the occasion of a father bequeathing his estate solely to his wife, not equally dividing it between his wife and children as is standard practice in Spain. The children are required by law to consent to this departure from the norm and the document is to be signed by the eldest daughter. Thus both documents, while containing standard formulae, can be said to have been drawn up expressly for an individual purpose and are not standard documents which may have fossilized with time. In both cases, for obvious reasons, actual reference to the individuals concerned has been deleted.

Two extracts from the adoption order have been included: the introduction to the declaration by the birth father of the prospective adoptee, and the final ruling of the juvenile court.

Sample text 6: (Adoption order)

> En Lima a los nueve de febrero de mil novecientos noventitres, comparecen al local del Juzgado don (+ name), identificado con su libreta electoral número (+ number), sufragante, natural de Lima, de veinticinco años de edad, conviviente, segundo de secundaria, comerciante, y doña (+ name), identificada con su libreta militar número (+ number), de veintidos años de edad, natural de Lima, conviviente su casa, cuarto de secundaria, domiciliados en (+ address) presente en este acto la señorita Fiscal Provincial, Doctora (+ name), identificada con su carnet expedido por el Ministerio Público, todos reunidos para llevarse a cabo la diligencia de Consentimiento que deberán prestar los padres biológicos del menor materia de autos, la misma que se efectúa en los siguientes términos:

> En este acto al no contar con documento de identidad la señora, es decir a sus veintidos años manifiesta no tiene libreta electoral se le citará en nueva fecha para su manifestación, realizándose SOLO LA DECLARACION DEL PADRE BIOLOGICO quien se encuentra debidamente identificado, . . .

(. . .)

> RESOLUCION DE FOJAS DOSCIENTOS CUATRO. Lima, Veinticinco de Mayo de mil novecientos noventitres. Estando al mérito de la razón que antecede: Téngase por consentida la Sentencia de fecha de diecisiete de Mayo de mil novecientos noventitres, corriendo a fojas doscientos y doscientos uno y,

proveyendo el escrito de fojas doscientos tres, Ofíciese conforme está ordenado.
———————— *Es copia fiel de su original en referencia y a la que me remito en caso necesario. -Expido la presente en original debidamente corregida y confrontada de acuerdo a Ley. -Lima, a los veintiseis días del mes de Mayo de mil novecientos noventitres.*————————[6]

This is an example of a text which gives every sign of having been drawn up speedily to fulfil required formalities and which is readily accessible, for the most part, to the lay person, although the final ruling is couched in less accessible Spanish. While certain lexis (e.g. *sufragante, foja*) marks the text as coming from the southern cone of Latin America, it is nonetheless expressed broadly in supranational Spanish. It is characterized by particularly long sentence structure with subordination and frequent non-standard word order (for example, the fronting of the venue and date of the proceedings resulting in the postposing of the verb *comparecer*). If we take Alvarez's (1995) model of analysis, we can see that there is non-standard use of:

- abstract nouns (e.g. *para su manifestación*)
- the gerund (e.g. *realizándose sólo la declaración*)
- past participles (e.g. *identificado con, domicilados en, reunidos para, debidamente corregida y confrontada*).

Additional features are:

- complex prepositional phrases (e.g. *menor materia de autos, en mérito de*)
- archaic postposition of the preposition *se* (*téngase por consentida, Ofíciese conforme está ordenado*)
- terms restricted to legal discourse (e.g. *auto*)
- terms from standard discourse which acquire precise legal meanings such as *menor, sentencia, diligencia*
- polysemic terms which clearly take their meaning from context (e.g. *acto*).

It is interesting to note the use of the first-person singular in the final ruling (*me remito, expido*) which in other genres could be said to contrast with the maximally formal style of the remainder of this element of the text.

The extract below is taken from an oath of consent drawn up in Spain and, while sharing many of the features of the above text, is less accessible to the lay person.

Sample text 7: (Oath of consent)

III. - Que por este acto presta

CONSENTIMIENTO

que en derecho fuere necesario, en su caso, a tal voluntad testatoria, considerando que en tal sucesión nada debe recibir, y es conforme a derecho el llamamiento único en favor de la esposa del fallecido, madre de la compareciente.

En ello se ratifica, previa lectura que yo, el Notario, le hago de la escritura, que ella también lee, entendiendo el idioma español en que se redacta, firmando. La identifico por medio de la documentación exhibida. De lo cual y del contenido de la escritura que extiendo en dos folios de papel timbrado del Estado, exclusivos para documentos notariales, serie . . . , números........, yo, el Notario, DOY FE.

Firmado y rubricado:

Signo, firma y rúbrica:

Con el sello de la Notaría.[7]

In this document, to an even greater extent than in the administrative documents we examined previously (texts 1–5) and the adoption order from Peru which we have just studied, there is evidence of archaism. Consider, for example, the use of the future subjunctive (*fuere*) (see 2.1.3 and 3.4), and the impersonal pronoun *ello*. The syntax of the text is contorted, with extremely complex subordination (see, for example, the first sentence) and there is much stylistically marked non-standard word order (e.g. *En ello se ratifica, previa lectura que yo, el Notario, le hago de* . . . , *nada debe recibir* for *no debe recibir nada*). There is use of abstract nouns and noun phrases (e.g. *sucesión, voluntad testatoria*) and of gerunds (e.g. *considerando que, formando*). A proportion of the lexis relates almost exclusively to the field of law (e.g. *fallecido, sucesión, compareciente, extender* (in the sense of 'to draft'), there is use of empty formulae (e.g. the use of *rubricado* which simply repeats the sense of *firmado*) and circumlocutions such as *hacer lectura* for *leer, por medio de* for *por*.

Obviously the two documents above are narrowly representative of a tiny fraction of the text types associated with different legal genres. Nonetheless, linguistically they are characterized by many of the features associated with legal Spanish.

7.2 Political Spanish

In this section we shall examine the genre of political oratory and will look first at significant changes in styles of political oratory in Spain in the last forty years of the twentieth century by contrasting an extract of a speech made by General Franco to the Spanish Cortes (parliament) in 1967 with one made by the Spanish Prime Minister Felipe González to the Cortes a quarter of a century later. Obviously we shall be contrasting two very different speakers of different political ideologies and personal idiosyncracies. Nonetheless, there are elements in these speeches which can be related to discourse conventions of the time. Just as Franco's speeches no longer contained the rhetorical flourishes, the emotive imagery and the extensive paragraphs characteristic of the nineteenth and early twentieth centuries and are what Bühler (in Cillán Apalategui 1970: 22) called representative rather than expressive, González's speech is no longer characteristic of those of the middle years of the twentieth century. In order to examine whether local cultural constraints are evident in this genre, we shall then contrast the speech by Felipe González with one by his counterpart at the time, President Salinas of Mexico, addressing the Mexican parliament. Finally, we shall examine an intervention by Felipe González in the European Commission, a body where the French rather than English language dominates, to see whether the influence of other European languages (notably French), and the need to address a multilingual audience create discourse conventions different from those which operate within Spain.

It should be remembered that all these speeches have been written to be read and therefore, while they show few of the features of spontaneous spoken language such as hesitation and pausing, ellipsis and self-correction, they do incorporate more repetition than is typical for a written text and are less conceptually and syntactically dense.

Sample extract 1: Francisco Franco Bahamonde, Caudillo of Spain

(From Franco's speech of 17 November 1967 (Cillán Apaletegui 1970: 123–4) given at the opening of the new Cortes[8])

(. . .)

Hemos de demostrar también, con la misma nitidez, con la misma contundencia incontestable de los hechos, que un moderno Estado con autoridad no es un Estado arbitrario, ni un Estado brutal, ni un Estado policíaco, ni un Estado dictatorial. Un moderno Estado con autoridad puede ser, y España lo es, un Estado de Derecho, en el que los ciudadanos sientan garantizados sus derechos civiles, protegida su vida, su hacienda, su familia, su trabajo, su deseo de vivir como les acomode, dentro del respeto al bien común y al de cada uno de sus compatriotas. Un Estado con autoridad plena sobre los intereses individuales y de grupo, de los que no depende su existencia y da a cada uno lo que sea suyo; está en cada momento en condiciones de decir 'no', tanto a las irresponsables reclamaciones de la demagogía como a las solicitaciones de los grupos de presión de los poderosos. Todo esto es posible gracias a un poder ejecutivo, que ha sido y seguirá siendo vigoroso y eficaz, y a un poder judicial de una integridad e independencia absolutas, que castiga o absuelve al particular o al Estado, a la corporación o al individuo sin otro norte, ni sin otra mira que la recta aplicación de la ley.

Tenemos ahora estas Cortes renovadas y reverdecidas, emanación y representación del pueblo, que a través de ella, hace oír su voz y expresa sus ilusiones, sus deseos, sus ambiciones, sus temores o sus indignaciones. Cada uno de vosotros tiene contraído un sagrado compromiso de fidelidad al pueblo español, del que aquéllos que os eligieron son parte. Vuestro trabajo asiduo y diligente en las comisiones, vuestro contacto estrecho y constante con los que os eligieron, vuestro sentido del deber, de la responsabilidad y de la justicia son las únicas condiciones que podrán justificar ante vuestros compatriotas el cumplimiento del mandato que ejercéis por la voluntad del pueblo.[9]

What is noticeable about this speech is:

- the reiteration of abstract nouns which stand as political symbols (e.g. *Estado* (9 mentions), *pueblo* (3), *autoridad* (3), *compatriota* (2))
- the use of religious reference (*un sagrado compromiso de fidelidad*)
- the dense lexical networks (*Estado de Derecho, derechos civiles, poder judicial, la Ley, la justicia*)
- the literary preposing of the adjective in *un moderno Estado* creating a marked form (especially in the spoken language) and indeed a word order more consonant with the written (literary) language than the spoken (*en el que los ciudadanos sientan garantizados sus derechos civiles, protegida su vida*)
- the repetition (*protegida **su** vida, **su** hacienda, **su** familia, **su** trabajo, **su** deseo de vivir como les acomode*)
- the frequent **geminations** (*estas Cortes **renovadas** y **reverdecidas**, **emanación** y **representación** del pueblo*).

Cillán Apalategui (1970: 28–37) shows that this was the most personalized of the speeches of Franco he studied and while in this extract Franco does not use the first-person singular form or the pronoun *yo*, he does use the *nosotros* form (although not the pronoun) to refer to himself and his addressees (***Hemos** de demostrar también . . . , **Tenemos** ahora estas Cortes,*) and he makes especial use of *vosotros* forms in addressing the members of the Cortes (*cada uno de **vosotros**, **os** eligieron, **vuestro** trabajo, **ejercéis***) playing on solidarity and imbuing the speech with a religious dimension. According to Cillán's study, Franco's speeches are characterized by very low levels of personalization and conversely high levels of impersonalization. Cillán Apalategui also notes

(1970: 24) that Franco uses few comparatives or superlatives in his speeches and that he extremely rarely adopts terms from colloquial registers (in a speech from 1964 he unusually uses the word *tontos*). Consequently, his speeches are characterized by the use of standard Spanish, in a style more closely approximating to writing than to speech and characterized by a high number of abstract nouns acting as political symbols (e.g. *régimen, orden, autoridad, unidad, patria, ley, libertad, justicia, nación, democracia, derecho, pueblo, interés, responsabilidad*).

It is interesting to note how these same abstract nouns also act as political symbols to a government of a widely differing political complexion. The following short extract is taken from Felipe González's speech at his inauguration as Prime Minister on 30 November 1982.

Sample extract 2: Felipe González, Prime Minister of Spain

> *Todos debemos pensar en el presente y en el futuro de España, aunque sea de distinta manera. Hacer compatibles esas diversas maneras y conjugarlas al servicio del interés común es lo que nos exigen los ciudadanos con su rotunda votación.*

> *Nuestro horizonte como socialistas, con la responsabilidad de gobernar para todos los españoles, es profundizar constantemente en las libertades de las personas y los pueblos de España.*

> (Díaz Barrado 1989: 397)[10]

Here we encounter the same lexis that characterizes the speeches of Franco, (e.g. reference to *interés común, responsabilidad, libertad*), although here, evidently, the political beliefs to which they refer are somewhat different. Furthermore, the marked word order in the sentence beginning *Hacer compatibles...* and the gemination (e.g. *de las personas y los pueblos de España*) are also markers of the genre of political speech which, in this instance, González shares with Franco, and which are features widely attested in political speeches this century.

However, despite these apparent similarities, there are areas in which political discourse in Spain has changed to quite a considerable extent. Manuel Alvar (1993) has analysed the *Debate sobre el estado de la Nación* held in the Spanish Cortes in 1989, consisting of a prepared speech by the Prime Minister, Felipe González, and the spontaneous debate which followed it. He makes the point (1993: 74) that the Marxist terminology which had previously characterized socialist discourse such as *la dictadura del proletariado* or *la lucha de clases* had largely disappeared and further notes the presence of abstract nouns of the kind discussed above. However, more significantly, he notes presence of technical jargon and circumlocution with, for example, *estructura presupuestaria* replacing the less technical *presupuesto* or *velocidad de crecimiento de las expectativas* replacing *aumento esperado*, although it could be argued that the 'plain' alternatives he proposes do not express precisely the same meanings. In particular, he notes the use of affixes as can be seen in the following extract which Alvar uses to demonstrate the verbose obscurity of sections of the political debate:

Sample extract 3: Prime Minister Felipe González (Spain)

> *Entendemos que la cronificación del desempleo estructural del 7,5 (...) no es un argumento suficiente para no aceptar la consolidación por lo menos del concepto para debatir en ejercicios presupuestarios posteriores (. . .) No se puede abordar de forma capital, en definitiva, un problema que requiere soluciones integradas, soluciones globales, ya sean de naturaleza macroeconómica, microeconómica o promocional.*
>
> (Alvar (1993: 101) my emphasis)[11]

In this highly subordinated extract we can see complex affixation in the use of the suffix *-ificación* affixed to the adjective *crónico*, the suffixes *-al* and *-ario*, and the prefixes *micro-* and *macro-*, all representative of economic jargon. This adds up to a text which is extremely difficult for the listener to process, an intentional or unintentional result of the discourse chosen. However, it does send the signal that the speaker is partaking of the discourse of an in-group of economic experts.

Moving on to analyse the variety of Spanish spoken in official forums of the European Union, the status of Spanish within the EU should be taken into consideration. For while, as we saw in Chapter 1, Spanish is a working language of the EU, French and English are the two most widely used languages within EU bureaucracy, with French as the language most frequently taken as the model for translation into other languages (Clyne 1995: 15). Indeed Clyne notes that German, English and French are influencing the speech of officials both through transfers and what he calls 'Eurowords' (e.g. 'virement' in English). Another point to be taken into consideration is the fact that these speeches, unlike those given within a national context, require to be translated into up to eleven other languages, placing constraints of clarity and translatability on speakers.

The sample extract below is taken from a statement by the outgoing President of the Council of Europe, Felipe González, on the Spanish Presidency (16 January 1996).

Sample extract 4: President of the Council of Europe, Felipe González (Spain)

> *Ante la importancia de las pequeñas y medianas empresas como fuente de empleo, de crecimiento y de competitividad, se ha facilitado su mayor acceso a la información, a la formación y a la investigación, eliminando los obstáculos que afectan a su funcionamiento.*

En materia de energía, se ha avanzado de forma sustancial en la directiva sobre normas comunes en el sector de la electricidad.

En investigación y desarrollo, los esfuerzos se han centrado en la adaptación del IV programa marco a consecuencia de la ampliación.

En el área de medio ambiente, destaca la posición común alcanzada sobre la revisión del programa LIFE, así como el importante debate sobre la política de aguas.

En transportes, se ha conseguido, entre otros resultados, aprobar la posición común relativa a la directiva sobre dimensiones en el transporte por carretera y se ha adoptado la directiva sobre handling en el transporte aéreo.

En agricultura, los esfuerzos se han concentrado en las OCM pendientes de revisión, aprobando la del arroz y avanzando en la del vino. Está pendiente el dictamen de esta Asamblea sobre la reforma de la OCM de frutas y hortalizas para su adopción a la mayor brevedad posible.

En pesca finalmente, destaca por su importancia la plena integración de España y Portugal en la política común y, en la vertiente exterior, el acuerdo concluido con el reino de Marruecos.[12]

We can note here, that in contrast with sample text three, this text is extremely clear in its exposition. Its main distinguishing features are:

- lexical 'Eurospeak', for example, *directiva* (and the verbs which collocate with it e.g. *avanzar en, adoptar*), *IV programa marco, plena integración, normas comunes, posición común,* (and elsewhere in the text) *moneda única, mercado interior, reformas estructurales.* These are all samples of lexis readily associated with the EU.
- the use of acronyms. In this extract and elsewhere in this speech, certain recently coined acronyms are used with the assumption that they are immediately comprehensible to the other participants in the meeting, e.g. OCM, OSCW, SPG, *los países ACP* (none in MEU (Agencia EFE 1989a)).
- the use of borrowings: EU programmes are known by their original titles, principally coined in English or French. Here we have the example of *el programa LIFE*; elsewhere González refers to *el (programa) MEDIA*. There is evidence of direct borrowing from English in González's use of the term *handling*; yet in English the noun would require to be specified ('baggage handling'). There are also examples, elsewhere in the speech, of calquing in the nominal compound *estados miembros* and in the construction commonly proscribed by the style guides *los asuntos a tratar, la vía a seguir* (Agencia EFE (1989a: 133) recommends alternative structures such as *los asuntos que deben ser tratados, la vía que se ha de seguir*). The word order of the phrase *espacio socialmente integrado*, while possible in Spanish, is closer to that of French. Indeed, the choice of certain nouns and noun phrases, while belonging fully to the Spanish language, is arguably more frequent in the European domain given their proximity to French, for example the use of *vías, procedimiento de seguimiento, propiamente dicha.*

- affixation: while there are no significant examples in this extract of significant affixation, elsewhere in the speech González refers to *el proceso de preadhesión, nuestra coordinación interinstitucional, La Conferencia Euromediterránea, programas plurianuales, relanzamiento del proceso de negociación, Agenda transatlántica, La Conferencia Intergubernamental, contactos bilaterales.*

- the use of the passive with *se*, e.g. *se ha facilitado su mayor acceso, se ha avanzado de forma sustancial, se ha conseguido (. . .) aprobar,* which, according to Calzada (1997), is a distinctive feature of this type of speech where speakers are frequently scrupulous in their attribution of agency.

The sample extract below is taken from a speech by the Mexican President to the Congress of the Union in April 1995.

Sample extract 5: President Carlos Salinas de Gortari of Mexico

Honorable Congreso de la Unión, mexicanos:

Con el respeto que es propio entre los Poderes de la Unión, asisto a la apertura del primer periodo ordinario de sesiones del Congreso. Asimismo, entrego ahora el informe sobre el estado general que guarda la administración pública del país. He cumplido, así, con el mandato constitucional. Es particularmente grato que este deber se satisfaga en la sede reconstruida de la Cámara de Diputados, cuyo nuevo arreglo la hace, a la vez, un espacio más apropiado para el trabajo legislativo y un recinto más digno para la democracia.

Los propósitos y las realizaciones

En el pasado informe de Gobierno, expresé mi compromiso decidido de continuar con el cambio que los mexicanos han demandado: cambio para consolidar las nuevas vinculaciones con el exterior y, al interior, cambio para promover nuevas relaciones del Estado con la sociedad. De esta manera, buscamos mayor presencia de México en el mundo, más amplio y seguro ejercicio de las libertades de nuestra patria, mayor estabilidad en las condiciones de la vida productiva y más oportunidades de alcanzar el bienestar, especialmente para quienes más lo necesitan.[13]

It is noticeable that this speech is expressed in a supranational variety of Spanish which is not linked to a particular country and region. Like the other speeches we have examined, there is a high incidence of abstract terms (e.g. *libertades, bienestar, democracia, patria*) and the use of a formal register. The length of the sentences used by Salinas is typically longer than those of the speeches we have looked at previously; however, the syntax is relatively simple and he uses similar rhetorical devices to those discussed elsewhere, for example, repetition (*el cambio . . . cambio . . . cambio, mayor . . . más . . . mayor . . . más . . . más*). The speech is not marked by jargon (unlike González's speech to the EU) and appears direct as it is expressed in the first person singular (*asisto, entrego, expresé*) and the first person plural (*buscamos*).

Sample extract 6: President Fidel Castro of Cuba

This last sample is taken from the very end of speech made by Fidel Castro to the Union of Young Communists on 4 April 1997 whom he addresses as *Queridas compañeras y queridos compañeros.*

> (. . .) *Les haría una pregunta. Si la ley Helms-Burton, Torricelli y compañía, si los políticos cínicos que hoy dirigen a ese vecino del Norte siguieran haciéndolo como hasta hoy durante muchos años y siguieran con el bloqueo y su hostilidad 50 años ¿ustedes estarían dispuestos a rendirse? ¿Ustedes estarían dispuestos a entregar la patria? ¿La Revolución? ¿El socialismo? Ese no fuerte y vibrante es lo único que se puede esperar de ustedes, y es lo único que esperamos de ustedes.*
> *¡Socialismo o muerte!*
> *¡Patria o muerte!*
> *¡Venceremos!*[14]

This speech, given also in a supranational variety of Spanish, is characterized by a much more informal, interactive style and yet heavily draws on the same rhetorical device of repetition that we have seen elsewhere. Throughout the speech as a whole there is also heavy use of abstract nouns for example, *el socialismo, la revolución, la patria* and also of concrete nouns and noun phrases which relate to the discourse of communism, such as *el pueblo revolucionario, el lumpen.* Castro uses euphemism and irony in *ese vecino del Norte*, playing on the friendly connotations of *vecino* and uses the colloquial and ironic *y compañía* when referring to what he sees as punitive legal measures by the United States. It is interesting to note that in the Latin American variety of Spanish which Castro uses to address his young audience, he does not have the *vosotros* form of the verb with which to call for solidarity.

While the discourses of these different speeches may be very different with elements which clearly relate them to say, 'Eurospeak' or communism, the genre of the political speech remains largely the same throughout. Common threads are, for example, the use of abstract words as 'empty' symbols to be filled by a particular discourse and that of standard rhetorical devices such as repetition, gemination, parallelism and the manipulation of the interpersonal dimension.

7.3 Newspaper reporting

One of the interesting features about the quality press throughout the Spanish-speaking world, is that while it uses for the most part 'standard' supranational Spanish, the use it makes of it can be markedly different from one country to another. This occurs despite the fact that, as we have seen in 2.1.2, it draws much of its information from the same sources (principally Agencia EFE and English and, to a certain extent, French-language press agencies) and broadly espouses the same principles contained in the style guides. Thus different conventions may govern different subgenres of news reporting such as headlines, editorials, and so on. At the same time, it is obvious that there are detectable geographical differences between the different varieties of Spanish used in the different Spanish-speaking countries which, while attenuated in the quality press, are nonetheless easily detectable. For example, in a study comparing the press of Buenos Aires and that of Madrid (Carrera de la Red and Zamora 1991:1101–9) the following features, amongst others, are found to distinguish the Spanish of Argentina (EA) from that of Spain (EE):

Morphology

- preferences for certain affixes in different varieties, e.g. a greater preference in EA for the adjectival suffixes *-al* (*distrital*), *-ario/aria* (*eleccionario*), *-ico* (*monopólico*), *-ista* (*cortoplacista*) and *-orio/oria* (*civilizatorio*), of nominal suffixes *-ista* (*financista*) and *-ismo* (*cuentapropismo*), and of *-ar* verbs (*bancar*).

Syntax

- the use in EA of an adjectival form *grupo etario*, *conducción partidaria* compared with the use in EE of adjectival paraphrase, *grupo de edad*, *dirección de partido*.
- the preference in EA for the preposition *de*: *la lucha de*, *adhesión de* compared with the preference in EE for other prepositions: *la lucha por*, *adhesión a*.
- differences in preferences for prepositions in the case of prepositional verbs, e.g. *ingresar a* (EA), *ingresar en* (EE).
- preference for the use of pronominal verbs in EE, e.g. *clasificarse* (EE), *clasificar* (EA).

Lexis

- the use of the same words with different meanings, e.g. *bronca* ('anger' (EA), 'a row' (EE)).
- the greater frequency of collocation of one word rather than another in each variety, e.g. *ingreso* (EA), *entrada* (EE).
- different words for the same concept, e.g. *afiche* (EA) and *cartel* (EE).
- greater lexicalization in one variety than another, e.g. *bloquismo* (EA), *conjunto de partidos o asociaciones que forman un frente común* (EE).

The two short texts selected below from *Reforma* (*El Norte*) (2.9.97) from Mexico and *El País* (24.5.97) from Spain illustrate to what extent the quality press in Spain and Latin America share a supranational norm although, as Butt and Benjamin (1994: viii) note, at the level of the popular press, headlines such as *Choros chupan tres palos a Cristal* (Thieves steal three million *soles* from Crystal Brewery) are probably incomprehensible outside their country of origin. In addition to examining issues of genre and discourse, we shall also comment on salient differences between written Peninsular and Mexican Spanish, differences which have been partly the subject of Chapters 4 and 5.

Sample extract 1: Reforma (El Norte) (2.9.97)

> 'La democracia no es caos'
> MEXICO – *Ahora que hay un equilibrio de poderes también es obligatorio acreditar, frente al pueblo, que la democracia no es caos ni violencia y que México perdió el miedo a la democracia, señaló hoy el diputado federal Porfirio Muñoz Ledo.*
> *Muñoz Ledo, coordinador de la fracción parlamentaria del Partido de la Revolución Democrática (PRD) en la Cámara de los Diputados, en entrevista radial rechazó que la rebeldía sea violencia.*
> *El legislador perredista. . . .*[15]

Before moving on to considerations of genre and discourse, it might be useful to point out a few salient differences between Peninsular and Mexican Spanish, many of which have been commented on in Part II of this book.

In this text there are a number of features which are markers of American usage, for example the use of the preterite tense *perdió* to describe an action clearly linked to the present (*ahora que*) where Peninsular Spanish would have adopted a perfect tense (*ha perdido*), the use of the attributive adjective *radial* common to Latin America where Spain uses *radiofónico*, the use of *fracción* to refer to a party's representation in Parliament. While in Peninsular Spanish the term *el grupo* would be employed, *fracción* carrying somewhat negative and extraparliamentary connotations of splinter group and the use of *acreditar* where Peninsular usage might favour *admitir, reconocer*. Nonetheless, none of these variants prove in any sense a barrier to comprehension and similarities far outweigh these minor differences. By way of example, it is interesting to note how the Mexican text uses the same derivational mechanisms to create an adjective from the acronym PRD (*perredista*) as does Peninsular Spanish (e.g. *peneuvista* from PNV).

As regards the genre of news reporting, this text clearly exemplifies the use of direct speech (marked by *señaló hoy*) and indirect speech (marked by *rechazó que*, the ellipted form of *rechazó el hecho de que . . .*). A distinguishing feature of news reporting is the post-position of the verb relating to the source of the information as illustrated by the two verbs mentioned above. Equally of interest is another distinguishing feature of journalese, notably the variety of terms used to corefer to the article's source (*el diputado federal Porfirio Muñoz Ledo, Muñoz Ledo, coordinador de . . . , el legislador perredista*).

Sample extract 2: El País (24.5.97)

El delegado del Gobierno en Extremadura llama al PSOE 'compañero de viaje de terroristas'

El delegado del gobierno en Extremadura, Oscar Baselga, aseguró ayer que nadie le va a dar lecciones de demócrata y menos 'aquellos que durante tanto tiempo han sido compañeros de viaje de terroristas de Estado y salteadores de cuarteles', en alusión a los socialistas, informa EFE.

Baselga realizó estas declaraciones después de que el grupo parlamentario socialista pidiera su comparencia ante la Comisión de Justicia e Interior para informar sobre la actuación de las fuerzas de seguridad en la llamada Marcha de Madrid en defensa de la enseñanza pública, celebrada el sábado pasado. Los sindicatos denunciaron que miembros de la Guardia Civil se personaron en algunos centros escolares días antes para conocer quiénes iban a acudir a la marcha.[16]

Starting with matters relating purely to language variety, in this text we have a use of the perfect tense where Latin American Spanish would adopt the preterite (*han sido* rather than *fueron*) and the use of only one surname. As we saw in 6.2 there are a number of factors which determine whether or not both are used. Nonetheless, in a comparison between the two papers, *El País* appears to omit the second surname with greater frequency than the Mexican paper. The Mexican preference for both surnames would be in line with the greater requirements for linguistic deference in this country which are discussed in 6.3.

As regards genre, the similarities are notable particularly concerning the mix of direct and indirect speech and attribution to the source of the news item and also the conventions for signalling this (*informa EFE, aseguró ayer*). Indeed, the 'objective' conventions of reporting here contrast with the heated discourse of the right-wing source who is heaping invective on the socialist opposition using terms such as *terroristas de Estado* and *lecciones de demócrata* which take much of their meaning from a knowledge of who is using them and in which context. As we shall see below, this particular headline follows the conventions of standard Spanish whereby the expected word order is subject + verb of opinion + reported speech.

While the conventions of news reporting may appear broadly similar, there is a fairly striking difference between the quality press in both countries in the conventions which govern newspaper headlines. In the Mexican press (and in the press of much of Latin America, see Romero Gualda 1991: 544), there is a strong tendency to front the verb using a verb-subject-object (VSO) word order as in the following headlines taken from the domestic news page of *El Norte* (2.9.97).

(i) *Iniciará José Angel Gurría gira por Texas mañana*
(ii) *Apoyará el PRI llamado al combate de la corrupción*

(iii) *Considera periódico Expansión nueva era política en México*
(iv) *Destaca diario el País apertura de Zedillo hacia el Congreso*
 (v) *Acepta Oposición reto: Consensará economía*

In the Spanish quality press, this would be a much more marked word order, although it is not uncommon to find participles fronting a headline. The following examples are taken from El País (24.5.97):

 (vi) *Intervenidos 250 kilos de cocaína pura en una cala de Tenerife*
(vii) *Aprobado el reglamento de ayuda a víctimas de delitos violentos*

The principal word order in headlines of news reports adopted by the Spanish press is SVO or SV + complement:

(viii) *Los reclusos hacen una crítica política legítima según Floren Aoiz*
 (ix) *Aznar asegura que mantendrá el consenso con González en política europea y antiterrorista*

It is interesting to note that while the Mexican press adopts a word order very different from that of English, it employs the kind of 'telegraphese' favoured by sections of the English-language press. In the examples above, articles are systematically suppressed (e.g. *(una) gira*, *(el) llamado*, *(el) periódico*) and in (iii) a whole idea is ellipted ('*Considera periódico Expansión (que se inicia una) nueva era política en México*'). Romero Gualda (1991: 545) notes that while the same process affects the Spanish press, it does so to a much lesser extent.

Another feature of news reporting in the Mexican press, and that of other Latin American countries, is the use of the third-person plural. This form is normally used to avoid, for whatever reason, making reference to the agent or indeed making direct allegations. However, as Romero Gualda notes (1991: 544) the subject of the verb frequently appears in the first sentence of the article. Thus the function of this convention may be to create a 'need to know' in the reader. The following examples taken from the Mexican regional press *Reformas – Novedades de Yucatán* (22.5.97) function in much the same way as the use of the past participle in the Spanish press discussed above:

 (x) *Involucran en narco a otros dos Generales*
(xi) *Descubren 'pruebas' contra PRI*

The conventions of fronting the verb and using the third person are shared to a greater or lesser extent by other quality newspapers from major Latin American cities, such as *La Tercera* from Chile, *El Espectador* from Colombia.

Romero Gualdo (1991: 545) notes a non-standard usage of the impersonal *se* in headlines. Expected word order in standard Spanish is *se* + verb + subject. However, she observes fronting of the subject and cites the following example:

(xii) *Curso en área de retardo mental se iniciará el 29*

Word order in the press on both sides of the Atlantic may deviate from standard norms to achieve its communicative goals. For example, in the case of direct reported speech normal word order would be name of speaker + verb (of speech) + reported speech, for example:

(xiii) *Aznar asegura que mantendrá el consenso con González en política europea y antiterrorista* (El País, 24.5.97)

It was noted earlier that a feature of press reporting is the post-position of the source of the information. Romero Gualda (1991: 546) notes that expected word order can be broken for communicative effect, as in the following example that she cites:

(xiv) *En Williamsburg no habrá confrontación entre EE.UU. y sus aliados asegura Reagan* (El País, 29.5.83)

In this example, not only is the source of information given at the end, but the location 'Williamsburg' has been fronted with the 'new' information provided in the body of the sentence.

In the case of newspaper headlines and arguably in newspaper reporting more generally, then, two principal tendencies can be detected. On the one hand, certain conventions of standard Spanish can be and are violated for communicative effect, whether to foreground new information, to achieve maximum impact or to create a need to know in the reader. Second, these conventions may be characteristic of one side of the Atlantic or the other, of particular countries and of particular newspapers. Additionally, it is evident that there is a geographical dimension to variability with newspapers partaking to a greater or lesser extent in the use of a supernational norm.

7. 4 Taboo: euphemism and political correctness

Each society creates its own cultural taboos as well as rituals for their avoidance. Societies will have spoken, or largely unspoken, rules about what can be said, by whom and in what circumstances. Sex, death, religion and bodily functions are amongst the most traditional areas of cultural taboo and we shall examine these shortly. However, in the late twentieth century political correctness, or the replacement of terms deemed to be objectionable to certain minority groups (e.g. ethnic minorities, women, people with a disability), has been a feature of pluralistic societies. It reflects a concern that language should not reinforce latent racism, sexism or prejudice against distinct groups in society. It has given rise to considerable polemic and conservative groups in society feel moved to pillory those who are seen to 'politicize' language, usually citing aprocryphal examples such as the purported substitution of 'short' by 'vertically challenged'.[17] At the same time, there are discourses which for ideological reasons seek to mask what are harsh realities (unemployment, racism, torture, and so on), often using metaphors from other fields; the medical-related term in English 'surgical strike' elides what might be seen from another perspective as the deliberate taking, by means of bombing, of innocent lives (cp. Hodge and Kress (93: 162)).

In this section, we shall examine both traditional and more recent areas of taboo and the mechanisms available to speakers to represent them, albeit with varying degrees of avoidance.

One area which is taboo in most cultures is that of sex. Calero Fernández (1991) carried out a study into sexually-related terms in Spain and found that many more swearwords relate to the male genitals than to the female (according to her, only three relate to the clitoris *pipa*, *pepita* and *pepitilla*). Those relating to the female genitalia are more likely to be offensive (alternative to *coño* include *bacalao*, *chuminada*, *chupajornales*, *guajero*, *tonto*). However, the majority of those relating to male genitalia have highly positive connotations (e.g. *valer un huevo* (to be worth a testicle. i.e. to be great), *ser cojonudo* (from *cojón*, testicle/ball), *estar o ser de carajo* (from *carajo*), *tener cojones*, *con más huevos que nadie*, *salir o no salir de las pelotas* (from *pelotas*, balls). She compares these with a tendency to derogatory reference to the female genitalia, for example, *ser un coñazo*, *no valer un higo*. It should be pointed out that many derived terms such as these are inherently ambivalent; *huevón* for example can mean both cowardly and brave; the feminine derived form *huevona* has only derogatory connotations. Hence, it could be argued that society's views of men and women are encoded in this ambivalence. The Mexican author Octavio Paz (1959) has dedicated a major section of his influential work *El laberinto de la soledad* to the Latin American verb *chingar* (to fuck) in which he reflects on the myriad meanings the derived forms of the verb can take in different contexts. According to Paz, an understanding of how this verb functions in context can provide deep insights into the belief system of the Mexican (male). Indeed, each speech community can have a range of taboo terms which may be specific to it. We have already noted for example in 2.0.1 the case of what in Peninsular Spanish is a common verb *coger* (to take) acquiring obscene connotations in Latin American varieties and requiring replacement by other verbs, typically *agarrar* or *tomar* in collocations such as *agarrar un camión* (Mex.).

Calero Fernández (1991) also identifies a long list of euphemisms and insulting expressions used to refer to homosexuals. She lists forty-nine terms to refer to men, for example: *ser de la acera de enfrente*, *ser del bando contrario*, *ser de la cáscara amarga*, *marica/ón*, *sarasa*, *mariposón*, *loca*, *bujarra/ón*. However, she only identifies five expressions used to refer to homosexual women which are: *tortillera*, *bollera*, *marimacho*, *machorra* (both these expressions are derived from *macho*), *ser del sindicato de la harina*. She also investigates vocabulary relating to masturbation and finds that there is a lack of terms relating to women's experience.

She notes, in the words and expressions relating to the sexual act, a predominantly male perspective coupled with violence and aggression: *fusil*, *látigo, envainársela, ir (des) armada, clavársela, dar un escopetazo*, and so on. She compares this with the terms used from a female perspective: *pedir guerra, querer guerra, calientabraguetas, calientapollas*, and so on. As in the case of the parallel terms examined above which derogated the women but not necessarily the man, this data provides further evidence that society, in lexicalizing certain areas, has clearly encoded its implicit beliefs about the respective roles of men and women.

Alberto Miranda (1993: 98–100) provides examples of common euphemisms which are frequently used in place of these terms. For example, the interjection *carajo* (originally used to refer to the penis but now without semantic content), can be replaced by *caray, caramba, caracoles, canastos*. *Joder* (originally used to refer to the sexual act) generates *jolín(es), joroba(r)(se), jobar, jopé, jo*. Blas Arroyo (1995) notes that in bilingual areas, in this instance in Valencia, Spain, speakers may resort to the contact language in search of euphemistic forms. For example, they may prefer the Catalan *collins* to the force of the Spanish *cojones*.

As well as interjections with sexual connotations, Spanish has a whole range of terms which are derived from religious lexis and which also have euphemistic variants, for example, *hostia(s)* (from the holy host) generates *ostras, ostris, ostis, oscuis, órdiga*. The blasphemy implicit in taking the name of God (*Dios*) in vain is avoided by, for example, the use of *diez* (e.g. *me cago en diez/me cachis/mecacho en diez*). Azevedo (1992: 267) gives the following terms used for naming God: *el Señor, el Todopoderoso, el Creador* and for referring to the devil (*el diablo*): *el Maligno, el Malo, el Enemigo, el Feo, el Patas, el Colorado*. Certainly in interjections such as *¿Dónde diablos/demonios . . . ?* there are a number of euphemisms which can be substituted such as *diantre* and *demontre*. Finally, there is the area of bodily functions where there are hosts of euphemisms for defecating, urinating (e.g. *mojarse los melocotones*), menstruating, dying. Azevedo (1992) gives us the following common euphemistic expressions used to refer to death and dying: *perecer, fallecer, dejar de existir, pasar a mejor vida*.

Chun (in Lozano Domingo 1995: 124–26) carried out a small-scale study amongst young people in Madrid to see which *tacos* (swearwords) were most frequently used and whether there were differences in use between men and women. She rated them on a scale of 1–100 with 100 signifying the most frequent use. The scores she arrived at were as follows:

Word	Men	Women
joder	82	70
vete a tomar por culo	82	70
gilipollas	69	63
cabrón	74	57
hijoputa	62	38

Unsurprisingly, the results show that not only do men use swearwords, and in particular the more powerful ones, more than women, but working-class men and women swear more than university students.

Vigara Tauste (1994: 64) notes that one context where the use of swear-words is commonplace is in telling jokes. In her example, taken from Iñaki Ongay, Tele 5, 'Vip noche', 1991, we can also see the use of the euphemistic variants *jo* and *joer*:

> *Dice . . . Se encuentra uno con un amigo y dice:*
> *–Joder, estaba el domingo en la Zarzuela, viendo los caballos, tan tranquila-*
> *mente, y de repente, se monta un tío en la espalda ¡y me empieza a pegar con la*
> *fusta!*
> *–¡Jo! ¿Y qué hiciste?*
> *–¡Joer, lo que pude!: cuarto.*[18]

Swearwords also often form the basis of jokes which centre on a literal read-ing of their long-forgotten semantic core. Vigara Tauste (1994: 117) provides the following example:

> *Esto es un señor que tiene once hijos y, y se encuentra con otro, y dice, el que, el que*
> *tiene once hijos:*
> *–Hola ¿Qué tal estás?*
> *Y dice el otro:*
> *–Jo, yo estoy bien pero tú con once hijos cómo debes estar . . .*
> *Dice:*
> *–¡Me cagüen diez, para qué habré tenido once hijos . . . !*
> *Y dice el otro:*
> *–Pues por lo menos te queda uno limpio.*[19]

Swearing also can fulfil an important interpersonal function in conversation where, depending on context, it can range from being highly offensive to being positively 'polite'. We already noted (4.1.2) how it is frequently the in-group language of disaffected youth given its symbolic value as an anti-language. It can also function as in-group language amongst much wider groups of speak-ers where precisely the breaking of taboos signifies confidence and familiarity with the rest of the group. Briz (1998: 159) gives the following example taken from educated speakers over the age of twenty-five chatting during a picnic:

> B: *¡joder el del helicóptero tío!*
> A: *están infectando la – el ozono coño/y luego dicen que no nos echemos espráis*
> D: *porque tú te tiras cada ((cuesco))/que eso sí*
> B: *eso sí que destruye la capa de ozono*[20]

Let us now turn to a more recently tabooed area of public life and the political-correctness (PC) movement which reflects it. Here, what is taboo is language thought to belie 'unreconstructed' social attitudes. It is an area which 'minority' groups have taken extremely seriously in the developed nations where there has even been a move to recuperate previously tabooed terms from the euphemisms used in politically correct or 'polite' society to mask them, hence in English, 'queer studies' as the designation for the academic discipline relating to homosexuality.

We have already noted (2.1.4, 3.3) that the feminist campaign against sexist language has in Spain, as elsewhere, been particularly effective in changing language use despite the fact that its effects have not perhaps been as thoroughgoing as many of its proponents would like. We saw above that there is a considerable number of euphemistic and insulting terms relating to homosexuality. Perhaps the most commonly used of these is *maricón*. Both in Spain and Spanish-speaking America the male homosexual community has largely adopted the anglicism *gay* (plural *gais*), with *maricón* fulfilling the function 'queer' does in English, while the female community uses *lesbiana*, with other sexual orientations being referred to as *bisex* (abbreviation, in English 'bi') and *transexual* which would suggest the influence of English in this area.

Another area where PC is in evidence is that of disability, where language practice in Spain also appears closely modelled on Anglo-Saxon procedures. In line with a desire not to equate the individual with the disease or disability affecting them, there has been a move towards using the expression *persona con* as in *personas con síndrome de Down*, *personas con discapacidades*, *personas con deficiencias psíquicas*. The neologism *sidoso* (from SIDA (AIDS)) has acquired pejorative connotations and has been replaced by *persona que vive con sida*. It is interesting to note that some of the groups whose sensibilities have been attended to by means of prescribed language change are not always consulted in the process of change. The Spanish Association ONCE (*Organización Nacional de Ciegos Españoles*) was unhappy about the choice of the euphemism *invidente* which they felt gave the impression that they failed to be *videntes* (seers or fortune tellers). Their chosen term for self-reference is *ciego*. *Sordo* is the most frequent term used to refer to the deaf although *inhabilitado de audición* can also be found.

As an example, let us examine the paragraph relating to special needs provision in the education legislation (LOGSE). Chapter 2, subsection 3 is devoted to:

la escolarización de alumnos y alumnas con **necesidades educativas especiales asociados a un déficit auditivo**

As well as the lengthy reference to the nature of the disability it is interesting to note how here this document adheres to non-sexist language practices through its use of *alumnos y alumnas* (rather than the generic/masculine *alumnos*).

Interestingly also, the word *minoría (étnica)* functions as a euphemism for given ethnic groups where their designation is seen as pejorative in the eyes of sections of the community. Thus the help Web page for the gypsy community in Zaragoza, Spain, is accessed under *minoría* but not *gitano*, whereas in Latin

America this designation *minoría* is most commonly applied to the indigenous aboriginal populations.

In this short section on discourse it becomes apparent that the Spanish-speaking world, like the developed world in general, is aware of the power of certain discourses and their potential for influencing relationships between different sectors of society. In Chapter 2 we examined moves towards changing the discourses of public administration in order to project a more egalitarian relationship; we also examined moves to eradicate what was perceived to be sexism in the use and usage of the Spanish language. In Chapter 4 we saw how certain youth varieties functioned to reject the prevailing discourses of those who were perceived as empowered by society. This rejection included the deliberate flouting of linguistic and social taboos. In this section, we have focused on more generally on what society perceives as taboo, a concept which has widened in the late twentieth century to include what is not politically correct and we have looked at some forms of 'verbal hygiene' at work in the Spanish language today.

7.5 Conclusion

While many features of genre may be similar not only throughout the Spanish-speaking world but across language barriers (e.g. the tendency in news reporting to employ a wide variety of terms for coreference, or the tendency in political speeches to use abstract nouns as empty political symbols to be filled by the perceived ideology of the speaker), some may be, to a much greater extent, specific to Spanish (e.g. the scope provided by flexible word order to highlight information). What is more, we have seen that within a given genre, conventions may vary from country to country (for example the use of VSO word order in the Mexican press compared with SVO or SV + complement in the Spanish press). Furthermore, they may be influenced by those from, say, the English-language press (e.g. the use of 'telegraphese' and the increasing use of the passive in news reporting). We have considered elsewhere the extent to which campaigns for 'plain' or 'non-sexist' language have had an effect on actual language use; indeed the whole drive towards political correctness can be attributed to movements in the Anglo-Saxon world. These are discourses which are particularly evident in areas of public administration (e.g. education and healthcare).

8 Conversation, pragmatics and politeness

So far in this book we have included examples from planned discourse – such as most written texts, prepared speeches and monologues, jokes – as well as from unplanned discourse, for example, conversation, negotiation. The principal differences between planned and unplanned discourse have probably been quite apparent, with unplanned discourse displaying simpler structure, more repetition and redundancy, the use of intonation and pace to structure meaning allowing for fewer explicit connectors, the use of **deictics** (such as *este, aquí*), incompletion, overlap with another speaker and joint construction of meaning. Very often it is very hard to understand the transcription of unplanned spoken discourse because of everything that must necessarily be left out: mutual assumed knowledge between speaker and hearer, patterns of intonation and gaze, elements of context (the 'here and now' of the speech event). Nonetheless, natural languages share a series of rules governing the organization of discourse, rules which may be applied differently by different speech communities.[1] For example, some speech communities (e.g. Madrid) may have a much greater tolerance of overlap/interruption than others (e.g. Mexico). Similarly, some communities may also condone more active attempts to win a conversational turn by, say, 'upgrading' or talking increasingly loudly until one's conversational competitor desists. Others may prefer the convention of waiting until another speaker provides a signal that he or she is ready to give up a turn, perhaps by pausing, signalling closure by voice pitch or by selecting the next speaker by gaze. Unfortunately, very little work has been done on cross-cultural comparisons of speech style in Spanish, although there are increasing numbers of scholars investigating the organization of conversation as such.

8.0 Planned and unplanned discourse

As an example of formal, planned spoken Spanish, we shall take a transcript from a debate in the European Parlament (9 March 1993) where the Spanish member of the European Parliament, Sra García Arías defends the Spanish government's plans for restructuring the steel industry. The **field** is a debate regarding the planning of the steel industry within the context of Europe, the

mode is probably written to be read aloud, and certainly the text is planned. The interpersonal **tenor** is formal. Here, the participant, who is of high status, is ostensibly addressing a superior, the Chairman of the European Parliament, the distance between the speaker and addressees (the President and the remainder of those attending the session) is great, albeit reduced through common membership of the same institution, and the speaker is conforming to the norms of this speech event in order for her intervention to be given due weight.

Text 1: European Parliament debate

> *Señor Presidente, quiero señalar aquí la preocupación que existe en mi país y especialmente en dos de sus regiones por la situación a la que se ha llegado. Hace algunos meses el Gobierno español presentó un nuevo plan que adapta la dimensión de la siderurgia española a la situación del mercado y que, vista en el contexto de la siderurgía europea, podemos volver a insistir y señalar que es un plan coherente y valiente que, además, va a tener serias consecuencias en las dos regiones que se han citado aquí: el País Vasco y Asturias. (No. 3-429/59)[2]*

Before discussing the tenor of the text, it is interesting to note to what extent it approximates to the conventions of the written mode, particularly in the length, complexity and degree of subordination of the utterances although there are also some features of the spoken text present, for example, repetition and redundancy (*plan, insistir y señalar*).

Lexically, the text is characterized by:

- neutral vocabulary (*un plan, tener consecuencias*)
- a preference for nominalizations (*la preocupación*, rather than, say, the more colloquial *lo preocupados que somos, la situación del mercado* rather than *cómo está el mercado*)
- precise collocations (e.g. *que existe* rather than *que hay, citar* rather than *mencionar*).

and morpho-syntactically by:

- pre-position rather than post-position of adjectives (e.g. *serias consecuencias* rather than *consecuencias serias*), a feature more associated with the written text
- impersonalization (e.g. *a la que se ha llegado* (rather than, for example, *a la que hemos llegado*), *que se han citado*).

In contrast to the mixed mode of the text above, the two authentic sample texts we reproduce below illustrate the opposite ends of the spoken/written continuum. The two texts are taken respectively from a video-recorded interview with a male university student from Valladolid, Spain, aged approximately twenty-five years, informing a meeting of university students about recent events connected with student demonstrations against university reform and an account of the same incident published the following day by the regional newspaper, *El Norte de Castilla*.

Text 2: spoken student narrative

> . . . *bueno, cuando ya se había acabado unos cuantos, concretamente cuatro compañeros, nos metimos en un bar, estábamos tomándonos una cañita y unos vinitos y tal y entró la policía y nos pidió los carnets de identidad, nos llevaron a comisaría a comprobarlos; bueno, hablamos de todo menos del tiempo. Nada, fue aquello muy, muy informal y tal, vamos, no nos hizo ni puta gracia, como os podéis imaginar, pero bueno, nos soltaron en seguida; se conoce que como no teníamos ficha ni na(da), pues, a lo mejor sólo querían asustarnos, no sé, la cosa es que nos dejaron marchar.*[3]

(Stewart et al. 1991)

Text 3: newspaper report

> *Según han manifestado varios representantes de esta Facultad, 'una vez disueltos los estudiantes, una pareja de Policía Secreta entró en un bar donde estaban tomando un vino grupos de alumnos de la Facultad de Letras, pidiendo a tres estudiantes y a un joven indocumentado que les acompañasen a la Comisaría. Tras dar todos sus datos personales, la Policía los dejó marchar'.*

(El Norte de Castilla, 17.04.87)[4]
(Stewart et al. 1991)

As regards user variables, text one is marked as Peninsular Spanish by, for example:

- the use of *cañita* (a small draught beer). Indeed, the use of the diminutive *-ito* may restrict the geographic provenance of the speaker further, given the availability of other diminutives on a regional basis e.g. *-ín*, *-ico*, *-illo*.
- the use of the second-person plural familiar ending (*como os podéis imaginar*).

The use of the term *compañero* to refer to fellow students marks the speaker as young as well as having the interpersonal function of appealing to in-group solidarity through the use of a term used in a context of 'struggle' by the student body. The use of the expletive *puta* might arguably mark the speaker as male. In any case its use appeals to in-group solidarity by breaking the conventions of politeness normal in addressing a large group; expletives certainly would not be used in any standard press account of these events.

As regards relevant variables of use, this is a clear example of unplanned spoken discourse with:

- repetition (*nos soltaron, nos dejaron marchar*)
- fillers (*bueno, pues, vamos, y tal*)
- repair (*unos cuantos, concretamente cuatro*)
- a lack of subordination (note the use of the connector *y*).

Its tenor is extremely informal and this is marked by:

- the use of the informal *caña*
- diminutives (*unos vinitos*)
- fillers (*vamos*)
- reductions (*na* for *nada*)
- familiar address (*como os podéis imaginar*)
- personalization (*nos metimos, no teníamos*, etc.)
- ellipsis (*comisaría* and not *la comisaría, ficha* rather than *ficha policíaca*).

It is interesting that a number of the lexical items are clearly from the field of legal/police jargon (*comprobar (los carnets de identidad), ficha*); these precise collocates from a more formal register contrast with the colloquial account provided by the speaker (e.g. *nos llevaron a comisaría* as opposed to the more formal *nos pidieron que les acompañasen*, the equivalent form from the written account).

Text 3 is written in standard Spanish and as such bears few marks of user variation. The tenor is more formal and impersonal than the preceding text (e.g. *vino* is used rather than the diminutive *vinillo, la comisaría* retains the article, the neutral *estudiantes* is used rather than the affective *compañeros*). Features common to the written mode are:

- subordination (e.g. *una vez disueltos los estudiantes, . . ., pidiendo. . . que les acompañasen a la Comisaría*)
- explicitness and conciseness (e.g. *datos personales, una pareja de Policía Secreta, un joven indocumentado*)
- syntactically complete sentences without repetition.

The term *indocumentado* (amongst others) is very formal and clearly relates to the field of criminality where it would tend to collocate with marginalized groups in society; in any case, in this account it is presented as the defining feature of the individual in question.

8.1 Conversational Spanish

Although there have been a number of attempts, starting with that of Beinhauer (1978), to circumscribe and describe what is called *el español coloquial*,[5] not all of these have been based on spontaneous speech but rather have used as data the 'idealized' speech representations of novelists and playwrights (notably Steel and Beinhauer). More recently the need has been recognized to work on naturally-occurring speech. For example, the work carried out at the University of Valencia under the direction of A. Briz has yielded a rich corpus of 'conversational Spanish' (Briz 1995) which is providing valuable data for current research. We shall base our analysis of conversation on much of this recent research and focus on dialogue rather than monologue.

8.1.0 Adjacency pairs

One predictable feature of conversation is that certain kinds of utterances are likely to co-occur; greetings lead to greetings, questions to answers, summonses to responses. We shall see in 8.2.1, in an analysis of phone calls in Peninsular and Ecuadorian Spanish, that in response to an interrogation about identity (*¿Carmen?*) the expected response is a confirmation of that identity (e.g. *Soy yo*); what differs from one country to another is the level of formality adopted in providing that information (*con la misma* compared with *Soy yo*). Gallardo Paúls (1998) gives the following examples of adjacency pairs:

1
A: *¡Juan! ¡el café!*   Summons
B: *¡ya voy!*   Response

2
E: *¿me das un cigarro Gabriel?*   Request
G: *y dos también*   Acceptance

3
E: *cómete el yogur/ahí tienes natural*   Offer
L: *no tía no/si lo que no quiero es comer*   Rejection

The form that the second part may take is not predictable except in the case of extremely formulaic exchanges. However, the response given will be one of two kinds: preferred or dispreferred.

8.1.1 Preferred and dispreferred responses

In the case of all these adjacency pairs, there is a *preferred* response and a *dispreferred* one. In the first two examples above the preferred response is given, the summons is answered and the request is acceded to. In the last example, a dispreferred response is given, i.e. a refusal. Dispreferred responses can be interpreted as face-threatening acts (see 8.2) and therefore speakers often try to mitigate their effects. In Example 3 above, the face-threatening potential of the refusal is mitigated by the speaker using the affectionate address term *tía* and by giving a reason for the refusal. Dispreferred responses are frequently prefaced by *sí pero*, *bueno* and *pues*, for example:

A: *¿qué te parece este libro?*
B: **pues** *no sé qué decirte* (Briz 1998: 175)

Conversation is dependent to a considerable extent on the adjacency pair as we can see in the following example where the first speaker, a news journalist (PF), is indirectly suggesting that he go and cover a particular student protest. His boss (MD) prefaces his dispreferred response (i.e. a refusal) by an apparent agreement (*Sí*) and follows this up with a reason for his refusal before ending up by refusing point-blank (*y punto*).

PF: *Es que esta mañana, esta mañana, esta mañana en la zona de la universidad han . . . bueno, cuando hemos visto a los policías luego me han dicho que han vuelto a salir, y no sé si serían de medicina . . .*

MD: *Sí, pero si es que ya . . . ya, sí, hay que cubrir el tema por si pasa algo pero, en realidad, las manifestaciones ya interesan poco porque ya está la gente cansada de que. . . de contarles, pues, que se manifiestan, que van por un sitio, que tal. Si alguna vez se les ocurre una acción más imaginativa, más ingeniosa y que nos haga reir a todos pues bien; y, si no, pues damos la información normal que estamos cubriendo todos los días y punto.*[6]

This extract additionally provides a good example of a number of the features of spontaneous conversation:

- repetition (*Es que esta mañana, esta mañana, esta mañana . . .*)
- incompletion (*en la zona de la universidad han . . . bueno . . . , ya está la gente cansada de que. . . de contarles*)
- simple syntax (*que se manifiestan, que van por un sitio*)

8.1.2 Repairs

Repairs are essentially corrections of something which goes wrong in the conversation and can be initiated by the speaker (self-repairs) or by another participant in the conversation (other-repairs). Speakers tend to prefer self-repair. In the following example, the speaker, a junior reporter, is aware that her use of the T form could imply that she is making a general, and potentially authoritative, statement about how to prepare for an interview, rather than simply using the form to refer to herself and how she tends to go about the task. Therefore, she opts for self-repair using the filler *vamos*:

EM: *pues te informas un poco del tema . . . miras . . .* **vamos yo por lo menos** **pues miro** *si ha pasado en días anteriores . . .*

(Stewart *et al.* 1991)

8.1.3 Allocation of turns, interruption and overlap

Different speech communities have different conventions governing the allocation of conversational turns and different degrees of tolerance of speech overlap. Thus, what might be perceived as a rude interruption in one culture may be perceived as collaborative involvement in another. Overlap frequently occurs at the beginning of a turn when more than one speaker is competing for a turn and when both may upgrade (or speak louder and louder) until the turn is won. Very often this involves repetition, as in the following extract where both speakers repeat themselves until finally A2 wins the turn:

V: [*oy//pero también estamos en contra deeee- de Benidorm/y se ha hecho en Benidorm*]
A2: [*pero el pepé/el pepé/el pepé*] *que la haga en Benidorm*

(Briz 1998: 63)

Briz (1998: 63) argues that in the colloquial conversation that he has studied in Spain, overlap is virtually never interpreted as interruption but rather conversational involvement, even when this is one of disagreement as in the following example:

A6: *hasta que no vivan juntos no se conocen*
M7: *sí mujer*   [*sí/en un mes ya se conocen*]
A7:   [*no/no/no es igual/no es igual*]

(Briz, 1998: 61)

Kjaerback (1998) has compared Danish and Mexican Spanish conventions for turn-taking when a speaker wants to signal that they would like to contribute substantially to the negotiation. Her (simulated) data show that both Danes and Mexicans have strategies for signalling this; however, the Danes expect a response from other participants that they are willing to listen before embarking on an extended turn, while the Mexicans do not. The types of attention-getting devices that she argues signal a long turn include the items in bold below:

hm (.) sí claro **me permiten que yo intervenga** *(0.8) e: e en apoyo de mi compañero* (1998: 349)
mira *(0.6) si nosotros pedimos (0.6) la otra prueba*

(Kjaerback 1998: 352)

8.1.4 Closures

Very often speakers need to engage in active work to bring a conversation to a close using a variety of pre-closure signals to indicate imminent closure. Tusón Valls (1997) notes that elements such as *bueno, vale, muy bien* are likely to occur before the expected farewells such as *adiós* and *hasta luego*.

A: *tres noventa y cuatro/diez//cero dos*
B: *dos/vale/pues ya los aviso yo*
A: *sí/así se pone usté de acuerdo con ellos en la horaaaa*
B: *bueno/pues muchas gracias*
A: *vale/de nada*
B: *hasta luego*
A: *adiós/adiós*

B confirms the last digit of the number and could at this point take her leave. However, it is potentially face-threatening to close a conversation when the other speaker still wishes to continue. Therefore speakers, 'feel their way' towards closure, allowing each other to reactivate the conversation if desired. In the example above, both speakers reconfirm their previous understandings of the conversation; B offers thanks and this is accepted by B and finally they say farewell. A more abrupt closure could have created greater distance between the two speakers; here they are clearly violating the conversational maxim of quantity (only say as much as you need) (see Grice (1975)) in the interests of maintaining a good interpersonal relationship.

8.1.5 Pre-sequences

Speakers tend not to embark on any conversational move which might prove face-threatening, as in the case of the closure above. Therefore, in the case of potentially face-threatening acts such as requests, directives and criticisms, speakers 'work up to' the act through one or more pre-sequences. García (1993) is principally interested in linguistic politeness and has examined requests in this context. In the extract below, what is of interest is the complicated series of pre-requests which herald the speaker's implicit request that her neighbour teach her sister English.

Neighbor:	*y tu hermanita? todos bien?*
F10:	*Ay mi hermanita =*
Neighbor:	*= Qué pasa ah?*
F10:	*Tú sabes que ella ha sido siempre un dije, estudiando*
Neighbor:	
F10:	*= para variar me tiene un problema en un curso.*
	ahora se le salió – ya dejó las matemáticas, las tiene tranquilas =
Neighbor:	*= Ya*
F10:	*>Ahora me salió con inglés< =*
Neighbor:	*= Ya =*
F10:	*= No?*
Neighbor:	*Está mal con inglés? eso es ver– =*
F10:	*Mal es poco*
Neighbor:	*lo de todos los muchachos. No, las criaturas dicen que estoy mal pero no, captan rápido*

F10:   *Ojalá porque a mí me preocupa muchísimo no?*
Neighbor: *Tú sabes que yo doy clases de inglés?*
F10:   *Sí?*
Neighbor: *Sí: cuándo quieras?*

(García, 1993: 134–5)

The speaker (F10) first gives a dispreferred response to the enquiry about how her sister is keeping, implying that all is not well and indirectly inviting the neighbour to enquire what the matter is. Then she tells her neighbour what a good student her sister is and then implies that there is a problem with English, again inviting her neighbour to draw her out on the nature of the problem. Then as a final pre-request she tells her neighbour how worried she is which prompts her neighbour to 'spontaneously' offer English lessons. The speaker, in this extract, is not even required to make the request; the elaborate series of pre-requests is sufficient in itself. This text also gives a good example of what is called **'back-channelling'**, that is the small interventions made by a listener to signal that s/he is listening and willing to accept the speaker's extended turn. Here, the neighbour uses the token *ya* to back-channel and encourage F10 to complete her turn. We also see the cooperative nature of conversation where the participants build on each other's turns, for example *Está* **mal** *con inglés* (. . .) **Mal** *es poco.*

8.2 Pragmatics and politeness

In addition to the ability to select certain **forms** for their social meaning (as we have seen in the use of *tú/Vd.*), speakers also have the ability to use and understand appropriate grammatical forms for different **functions**. At the simplest level, and depending on the context in which it is said, an interrogative (form) such as 'Would you mind closing that door?' is not a request for information but much more probably a directive (function), i.e. 'Close that door'. Similarly, the imperatives 'Come in; sit down; have a cup of coffee' are not usually directives but rather invitations. The interrogative 'Where are your shoes?' addressed by a parent to a small child might be interpreted as a directive to put the shoes on in one variety of English (e.g. British); in another it might be interpreted as a request for information (e.g. American). Similarly, conventions of language use vary not only between languages but also within them. We shall examine in this section some of the ways which allow speakers of Spanish to make directives and requests and later note that there is an element of variation between Ecuadorian and Peninsular Spanish.

Closely related to the **pragmatics** of language is the whole area of **linguistic politeness** which we have touched on in the previous section. Politeness, while being a universal phenomenon only in the broadest of senses, is clearly rooted within society and may change over time and vary from community to community. We have seen, in the case of T/V in post-Franco Spain, how a process of democratization has been accompanied by an overwhelming trend towards the reciprocal use of pronouns and an increasing preference for T, the pronoun of solidarity rather than deference. However, this trend has not been mirrored to the same degree throughout the Spanish-speaking world. Given these changes, the use of V in certain contexts, for example to a middle-aged person in Spain, may even occasion offence, as its use is less associated with deference and more with respect for old age, a quality not highly valued in modern European society.

The term 'politeness'[8] is, in itself, misleading as it conjures up notions of conventional politeness: the concept is used in linguistics to refer to the ways in which speakers use language to create, maintain or modify interpersonal relationships. In addition to the dimensions of power and distance, there is what Brown and Levinson (1987) call the 'weight of the face-threatening act (FTA)', i.e. a speech act which threatens either the hearer's 'positive face' (the desire to be approved of) or 'negative face' (the desire for unimpeded freedom of action). FTAs of the first type might include insults or reprimands and of the second type requests or directives. An act which might be totally unthreatening to the negative face in one culture, such as asking one's interlocutor for a cigarette in Spain, might take on a more threatening dimension in another culture, for example in the UK or USA. Terms which can be used for positive politeness in Spain (e.g. the vocative *enano*) or in Latin America (racial terms such as *china, negrita, gringo, turco* (Carricaburo 1997: 50)), might be interpreted as insulting within another culture. The use of the vocative *niño* for 'waiter!' in parts of southern Spain is accepted practice; its use in other contexts (e.g. Barcelona) might be perceived as insulting.

Linguistic politeness refers to the linguistic strategies that speakers adopt to mitigate, or otherwise, these FTAs and to negotiate their relationship with others (compare, for example, the directness of a standard Peninsular request form, '*Dame un cigarrillo*' with the indirectness of the British English 'Could I have one of those please?'). While there is considerable research into cultures with highly developed politeness strategies (e.g. Japanese) there is very little research into this area in Spanish. Moreover, existing research tends to seek to describe a particular variety rather than compare and contrast different varieties, no doubt due to the methodological difficulties inherent in such studies. Nonetheless, a number of researchers do point to differences between say, Peninsular Spanish and British English (for example, Hickey and Vázquez Orta 1994), arguing that the former favours positive politeness whereas the latter tends to favour negative politeness. Others (Placencia 1994) point to the fact that certain deferential formulae are more habitual in one culture (e.g. Ecuadorian) than in another (e.g. Peninsular Spanish).

Let us consider two broad pragmatic areas of 'doing things with language', directives and requests. Subsequently I shall examine some of the politeness strategies adopted by speakers.

8.2.0 *Directives and requests*

Let us first examine a selection of linguistic forms that can be used as directives and requests (speech acts which inherently threaten the hearer's negative face and which open up the possibility of threat to the speaker's positive face if countered by a refusal).

The data is taken from a recording of two northern Spanish radio reporters participating in a regular meeting to decide what priority to give to different articles/bulletins they wish to publish and to share out responsibilities for other tasks. The senior reporter, Miguel de Dios (MdD), who does approximately 90 per cent of the talking, holds institutional **power** and is reponsible for allocating work duties to his junior colleague, Paco Forjas (PF), with whom he is obviously on good terms (low **distance**). As a model for some forms of directive language, this is a very rich text and it provides an interesting example of people doing things with Spanish. Extracts of the full text are provided below:

MdD: *Oye, me parece que . . . que lo que tienes que hacer es . . . te marchas tú a cubrir la información del Ayuntamiento, el pleno que va a haber esta tarde y la rueda de prensa que hay después y, entonces, me quedo yo con . . . con todo el tema de . . . de laboral. (. . .)*

MdD: *Y además, como después habrá rueda de prensa del alcalde para explicar en qué ha consistido la . . . la historia ésta, pues, bueno, pues lo que tienes . . . lo que se hace es . . . se cubre todo eso y, entonces, preparas como tres minutos para mañana, le dejas preparada a Pura una información para que la meta a las . . . a las siete y media, la suya, ya sabes, una cosa bastante más ligera, porque a esas horas está la gente todavía medio dormida, y después, pues, bueno, pues, pues montas, para el informativo de las dos menos cuarto nuestro, la información normal.*
(. . .)

MdD: *Está dado, lo dejas perfectamente para mañana, no hay . . . con ese . . . ese tema olvídate de él, en principio. Y después, el tema laboral, lo que sí puedes preguntarle al alcalde en la rueda de prensa también es qué pasa con el convenio colectivo.*
(. . .)

PF: *Movilizaciones, el comité de empresa de . . .*

MdD: *Eso, déjalos, olvídate de ellos porque vas a tener bastante con lo del (. . .)*

MdD: *Y después . . . después está el . . . espérate a ver, el tema de CC.OO. del hospital psiquiátrico sí que conviene que mañana por la mañana, ahora ya no, le des un telefonazo a la Diputación . . .*

PF: *¿De qué va eso?*

MdD: *Pues, una huelga que convoca CC.OO. en el Hospital Psiquiátrico por la política de personal. Entonces tú, como conoces muy bien a los de la Diputación, pues les das un telefonazo y que te cuenten la versión de la patronal, en este caso.[9]*

(Stewart *et al.* 1991)

MdD uses a relatively wide range of different forms essentially to achieve the same function. They are listed below in order of their degree of linguistic directness.

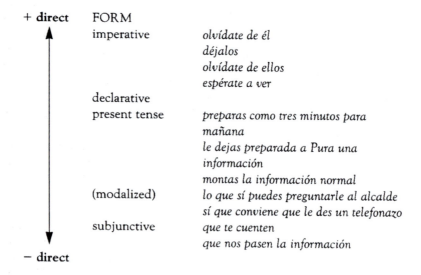

+ **direct**	FORM	
	imperative	*olvídate de él*
		déjalos
		olvídate de ellos
		espérate a ver
	declarative	
	present tense	*preparas como tres minutos para mañana*
		le dejas preparada a Pura una información
		montas la información normal
	(modalized)	*lo que sí puedes preguntarle al alcalde*
		sí que conviene que le des un telefonazo
	subjunctive	*que te cuenten*
		que nos pasen la información
− **direct**		

The form which most closely matches the directive function is the imperative and it is striking to see how few imperatives occur in this recording. Interestingly, the imperative is mainly used for directives which are in PF's best interests, that is, not at all face-threatening. Paco Forjas is asked, for example, not to bother to do certain jobs (*olvídate de él/ellos, déjalo*). Further on, the imperative is used for minor requests such as *pásame ese papel*.

Indeed the vast bulk of directive language in this recording does not use the imperative, the most common form used being the declarative present tense. This may or may not be modalized and may refer more or less directly to the person being directed to carry out the action. This is the form MdD uses when he is running through a series of standard requests for action: *preparas como tres minutos para mañana, le dejas preparada a Pura una información, montas la información normal*.

MdD renders these declaratives more indirect (and consequently less face-threatening) in two ways: modalization and impersonalization or agent deletion. Modalization includes 'conventional indirectnesses' of the type 'Could you pass me the salt' where a variety of modal devices (here the use of the conditional tense and of the modal verb 'to be able') allow both speaker and hearer to save face if the request is not complied with. This focus on ability rather than will gives hearers an 'out', enabling them to refuse by giving an excuse for non-compliance while, at the same time, implying that they would comply if they could (for example, they can say 'Sorry, I can't reach'). Even in a relationship as close as that between MdD and PF there are a number of modalized directives. For example, there are two actions required of PF in addition to the standard process of getting the news ready for the following day: asking the mayor about the collective agreement, and phoning the council. Both of these are heavily modalized: *lo que sí puedes preguntarle al alcalde* and *sí que conviene que (. . .) le des un telefonazo*. Both of these imply, by the use of *sí*, that they are a response to a question by PF of the type 'Should I do X?' However, no such question has been asked. Both of them also use modals with the main verb: in the first the conventional use of *poder*, in the second, the use of *convenir*. Thus, should Paco Forjas wish not to comply, a face-saving way out is to give reasons why he cannot or why it is not appropriate for him to do so rather than to offer a straight refusal.

In all the examples mentioned MdD addresses PF in the T form, mainly through verb endings. However, another way of making an indirect request is to use an impersonal form and not to mention the other person at all. In Spanish, the impersonal *se* form provides a productive resource for politeness. For example, MdD says *lo que se hace es se cubre todo eso*. Here it is up to the PF to infer that *se* refers to him and that the job is in fact incumbent on him. However, this strategy leaves him with an 'out' if he wishes to refuse; he can just act as if the request was not directed at him. An even more indirect way of suggesting that PF phone up a source for a briefing is to shift the focus away from him onto the people who are supposed to be providing the information. MdD uses the extremely indirect form: *que nos pasen la información*. What is ellipted from this is the fact that for this information to be passed on, PF must first contact the appropriate source and request it.

In analysing these extracts, we have looked at only one instance of directive speech. Nonetheless, we have seen a selection of ways of accomplishing this particular communicative goal, ways which are not always readily accessible in standard grammars of the language.

Carmen García has carried out a number of studies into the pragmatic strategies used by Peruvian Spanish speakers and in the case of requests she notes (1993: 147) that the Peruvian speakers in her study 'overwhelmingly preferred to express deference and respect towards their interlocutor in essence reflecting the desire not to impose.' She identifies a number of different strategies, some of which overlap with those identified above and others of which include what Brown and Levinson call 'off-record' strategies, i.e. the speaker does not actually make any request at all but rather drops a hint in the expectation that the service will be offered 'spontaneously'. As regards 'conventional' indirectnesses, she identifies modalization, either-speaker-focused for example, *quisiera que le dieras unas clases* (1993: 133), or hearer-focused as in the example below where the indirectness is grounded in a query about the interlocutor's ability/willingness to meet a request:

M8:   *Querida vecina, quiero pedirle un servicio, quiero que me: – si es posible, si usted puede darle clases de inglés a mi hermano que tiene once añitos? no sé.*[10]

(García 1993: 132)

García also identifies positive politeness as a strategy for making a request (used in her sample much less frequently than negative politeness) as in the example below where the speaker prefaces her request with a compliment:

Neighbor: *Qué me cuentas? qué gusto de verte!*
M3:   *Aquí pues paseando. Oye (0.2) conociendo que tú eres experta en idiomas, en inglés*
Neighbor: *Gracias*
M3:   *= Yo quisera que le dieras unas (0.2) uhm clases a Leni*
Neighbor: *Y:a*[11]

(García 1993: 140)

Although it is notoriously difficult to make rigorous comparisons between different varieties of Spanish in terms of the linguistic strategies and formulae used to express politeness, the following examples taken from Schwenter (1993), characterizing prototypical service encounters in Alicante (Spain) and in Mexico City, provide some insight into the different norms regulating discourse in both these communities. In both cases, the interlocutors are a sales assistant in a bread shop and a customer.

Extract 1 (Alicante)
C: *Hola*
D: *Hola, ¿qué quieres?*
C: *Ponme dos barras de pan y un paquete de galletas de chocolate.*
D: *(se lo entrega) Aquí tienes ¿algo más?*
C: *No, nada. Dime cuánto es.*
D: *Son 150 pesetas.*
C: *(le da el dinero) Aquí tienes.*
D: *Vale, gracias.*
C: *Hasta luego.*
D: *Adiós.*

(Schwenter 1993)

Extract 2 (México D.F.)
D: *Buenas tardes.*
C: *Buenas tardes.*
D: *¿En qué le puedo servir?*
C: *¿Podría darme Vd. una docena de tortas, por favor?*
D: *Como no señorita (se las entrega), aquí tiene. ¿Quisiera otra cosa?*
C: *No gracias, esto será todo.*
D: *Muy bien, son 3500 pesos.*
C: *(le da el dinero) Aquí tiene Vd.*
D: *Gracias, que tenga Vd. buenas tardes.*
C: *Igualmente, hasta luego.*

(Schwenter 1993)

In the extract from Spain, the use of T rather than V, the familiar *hola* as opposed to the more formal *buenas tardes*, the directness of *¿qué quieres?* when compared with *¿En qué le puedo servir?* and of the imperative forms in **Ponme** *dos barras de pan* and **Dime** *cuánto es* compared with the conventional politeness expressed by the use of the conditional with *poder* in *¿Podría darme Vd. una docena de tortas . . .* and the absence of tokens such as *por favor, gracias* and the pronoun of respect *Vd.* are just some of the features which distinguish these two varieties and which also go to show that while the different varieties of Spanish may share the same standard forms, the use which they typically make of them may be markedly different.

Koine (1994) compares the use of negation in requests, in English and Spanish, and shows how this can work very differently in each language. In English the invitation 'Won't you have another cup of tea?' allows the addressee scope to express polite refusal. In Spanish, not only does the use of the negative appear to be much less frequent, but it can also have a different illocutionary force from that which it enjoys in English. For example the suggestion 'Have you thought about reading this book' would need, in Spanish to be expressed negatively *'No has pensado en leer este libro'* to retain the force of suggestion. *'Has pensado en leer este libro'* invites yes/no confirmation. Conversely, the English equivalent 'Haven't you thought about reading this book' of the Spanish suggestion is more forceful than a suggestion and relays rebuke, the implication being that the addressee should have read the book. As we saw earlier, there is evidence in English that the same form may have different illocutionary force in different varieties, for example when a parent says to a child 'Where are your shoes?' in British English this may be interpreted as a request for action (i.e. 'Go and get them') while in American English this may be interpreted as a request for information, with the child replying, for example, 'in the cupboard' but not going to fetch them. Research still needs to be carried out into whether different varieties of Spanish show differences of this nature in the illocutionary force of similar utterances.

We have already noted that *muletillas* are a feature of colloquial informal spoken language and there is some evidence that their use is more widespread in Spanish than for example in English. Romero Trillo (1997) compares the use of the attention-getters *mira/mire, fíjate/fíjese, oye/oiga* and *escucha/escuche*, for example:

> ¡Ojalá, ojalá! ¡**mira** tú! ¡Ojalá! **Oye** y si tú crees . . .
> Y **mire**, cosa rara, la policía no me pidió nada . . .
> **fíjate** tú, si en lugar de . . .

with their equivalents in English and finds that in both languages they are more frequent in informal registers where no deference is being paid to the addressee and that references to 'looking' rather than 'listening' are more common. The reason he adduces for their much more frequent use in Spanish is that they replace prosody as an attention-getting device. A further reason could be that they are a positive politeness device aimed at involving the other speaker in the conversation. Berk-Seligson (1990: 126–7) notes that in court interpreting the *muletillas* are frequently a part of the Spanish testimony which is not conveyed, despite its importance in relaying the attitude of the speaker. She gives the following example of a highly agitated witness who has had his wallet stolen and who is emphatic about what happened. The text in bold was not translated by the interpreter, possibly because it was felt to be redundant. Berk-Seligson argues that these omissions render the witness's evidence less convincing.

> Witness: **Pues todo. Todo se llevaron con mi car-** . . . *El pasaporte,* **este,** *tarjeta que traíba de importancia, mi –* **Una prueba, más prueba voy a darle, mire:** *acabo de sacar el permiso de, del, de la emigración y aquí está,* **mire** (as he pulls out his wallet), *ahí está,* . . . *porque se llevaron todo. sss!*
>
> Interpreter: **Well** everything. **Everything was taken with my wall-** . . . My passport, **uh,** important cards that I was carrying, my – **Here's proof, I'm going to give you more proof, look:** I've just gotten my permit from Immigration and here it is, **look** [indicating his empty wallet], there it is! because they took everything, jeez!
>
> (Berk-Seligson 1990: 126–7)

There are a number of politeness strategies which are parallel across a number of languages. For example, the filler *bueno* fulfils a similar function to that of 'well' in English: to preface a dispreferred response, i.e. the response which the speaker does not wish to receive. For example, *–¿Vienes al cine? –Bueno, es que . . .*

8.2.1 Telephone calls

While each speech community may have its own conventions for carrying out certain routine activities such a making a telephone call, conventions which need to be acquired if incomers into the community are to function effectively, we are unable to cover here the range of conventions which exist. Consequently, in order to give some insight into variation of this kind, we shall focus on two varieties, which nonetheless are not chosen to represent both sides of the Atlantic. A comparative study by María Elena Placencia (1994) into telephone calls in Peninsular Spanish (PS) and Ecuadorian Spanish (ES) also points to greater levels of directness and informality in the former than in the latter. Placencia points to the scope for potential cross-cultural miscommunication that this opens up between both groups of speakers, with the Ecuadorians perceiving the Spanish as over-familiar and rude and the Spaniards perceiving the Ecuadorians as over-polite and distant. For example, in domestic phone calls speakers of ES answer the phone in a domestic context with *¿Aló?* while in PS the more potentially face-threatening imperatives *¿Diga?* and *¿Dígame?* as well as the direct request for information *¿quién es?* are frequently used by speakers. There are also differences in the resources used for confirming one's identity:

ES	PS
C: *¿Carmen?*	C: *¿Carmen?*
A: *Sí, **con la misma**.*	A: *Sí, **soy yo**.*

As Placencia notes, in ES the conventional response *con la misma*, ellipted from *habla con la misma* is significantly less direct, and more formal, than the PS equivalent. Similarly, a speaker of ES is likely to use more indirect and potentially deferential forms in identifying him or herself to the person called, for example, *Habla con Carmen*, *Le habla Carmen* and even *Le saluda Carmen* (using indirectness and the formal verb *saludar* rather than *hablar*) while in PS the direct *Soy Carmen* is standard usage. If the caller has to be requested to hold the line, in both ES and PS there are a variety of strategies which can be used by the speaker to acknowledge, minimize and compensate for the imposition this might cause the caller. For example, there is the use of the diminutive, *un ratito*, *un momentito*, apparently more common in Latin American varieties than the use of *ya* meaning 'right away', 'just'. Direct imperatives enjoining the caller to hold the line such as *espere/espera* are not acceptable in ES. While, as we have already seen, the present declarative is frequently used to express recommendations, requests and commands in PS (*Le dice que María llamó*), in ES the more indirect future tense can fulfil the same function (*Dirásle a la Gladys que no*). According to Placencia, this usage is influenced by contact with Quechua; the distancing in time (from present to future) is also a politeness device which makes the speech act less a force of command than one of recommendation.

A further study by Placencia (1995) compares telephone calls in Ecuadorian Spanish and British English (BE) and shows that prime considerations in ES are the expression of deference and the need to ellipt forms which are potentially face-threatening such as explicit requests. Thus, typical ways for a caller to ask a third party to put him or her through to the person called might be:

> *Tenga la bondad con el ingeniero Patricio Valencia.*
> *Hágame el favor María Cristina Valencia.*

Here the speaker uses the conventional politeness formulae (*Tenga la bondad/Hágame el favor*) and ellipts the request 'put me through to'. As in the comparison between ES and PS, Placencia shows that ES relies more heavily on deference and indirectness than BE.

8.3 Conclusion

In this chapter we have once again seen how speakers may use the same language system in very different ways to achieve similar ends. Not only are the linguistic strategies available to carry out certain functions, such as issuing directives, different in Spanish and in English (for example the use of the present tense declarative, *Preparas tres minutos*) but they also differ between different varieties of Spanish (note the Ecuadorian use of the future tense *Dirásle a la Gladys que no*). Evidence appears to point to communities which favour positive politeness (e.g. Spain) and those which place a premium on negative politeness (e.g. Ecuador and Peru). Scope for cross-cultural miscommunication is great and may explain some of the negative attitudes that some Spanish-speaking communities hold about others. Skills in a language, as we have seen, include a knowledge of the conventions which govern what constitutes a conversation. Here again, there is scope for cross-cultural miscommunication between speakers who do not share the same conventions, such as the need for pre-sequences in certain circumstances or the rule governing the negotiation of 'air-time' or the allocation of turns. This is an area where cross-cultural research could show up very interesting findings. It is also an area of great relevance to language learners who may have achieved a degree of mastery over the language system but may be unaware of crucial conventions of language use.

Part IV

Spanish in contact

9 Spanish in contact

We saw in Chapter 1 the range of different statuses which Spanish enjoys. It can be a sole national official language as it is in Spain, where it is also co-official in certain designated territories, and as it is in Mexico, where it is in contact with a large number of indigenous languages. It can be a co-official language as it is in Paraguay, where it it is co-official with the indigenous language Guaraní. It may also be a vernacular enjoying no official status, as it is in the United States. Spanish can also be used as a lingua franca between speakers of a number of languages none of which is Spanish; it has also formed the basis of a number of **pidgins** and **creoles** although it has proved less productive in this area than, for example, English and French. Spanish clearly, therefore, is spoken widely in contexts of bi- and multilingualism. While it is interesting to examine the factors which influence speakers to choose one code rather than another, the focus in this chapter will be on the consequences of language contact for a number of distinct varieties of Spanish. Hence, the far from exhaustive descriptions of these geographical varieties will focus on features deriving from contact alone, rather than other characteristic features unrelated to contact (for example, the particularly acute tendency in Catalan-speaking Spain to pluralize the impersonal había (habían), a feature which is not related to contact with the Catalan language, which, like Spanish, does not allow pluralization in the standard language).

We shall look initially at some examples of Spanish-based creoles, (zamboangueño, spoken in the Philippines, papiamento spoken in the Dutch West Indies and palenquero spoken on the Atlantic coast of Colombia). Then we shall examine Spanish in contact with an indigenous minority language in Spain (Catalan), with an indigenous minority language in Latin America (Maya), with a non-indigenous minority language in Argentina (Italian), with a national language of equal status along the border between Uruguay and Brazil (Portuguese) and in contact, as the vernacular rather than the dominant language, in the United States (English). It should be remembered that the creoles, unlike the other contact varieties referred to, have crystallized into an autonomous linguistic code, albeit also subject to change. Finally, we shall examine one aspect of language behaviour common in bi- and multilingual societies: **code-switching**. Code-switching is a widely recognized phenomenon whereby individuals, for a whole range of reasons, draw on the resources of more than one language in everyday interaction. Specifically, we shall look at code-switching between English and Spanish in the United States and between Spanish and Catalan in Spain.

9.0 Spanish-based creoles

In some cases creoles are based on pidgins, which are languages which develop as a means of communication between people who do not have a common language. Pidgins tend to develop as trade languages and to draw on the lexical resources of a third, generally colonial, language such as French, English, Spanish, Portuguese or Dutch. Indeed, the majority of the world's pidgins and creoles are the result of the massive colonization drive between the sixteenth and nineteenth centuries by the European nations speaking these languages. Pidgins tend to have a restricted range of functions such as buying and selling, as the speakers have at least one other language to carry out other functions such as establishing and maintaining social relations. Creoles, on the other hand, have native speakers of their own; the children of pidgin speakers may learn them as a first language; adult speakers may restructure the lexifiers to communicate with each other. Over time their range of functions becomes extended and elaborated through more complex structures and a wider range of vocabulary. Often, after time, creoles may undergo a process of decreolization where they gradually assimilate features of the lexifier as the high-prestige variety. There are surprisingly few creoles lexified by Spanish compared with English- and French-based creoles. McWhorter (1995) attributes this to three main factors: the small size of the initial Spanish sugar plantations, which allowed the slaves to acquire Spanish and then pass it on; the fact that Spain often colonized areas previously occupied by the Portuguese and inherited Portuguese-based pidgins from them, and the absence of Spanish trade settlements in West Africa from which Spanish-based pidgins could subsequently be exported. Indeed, McWhorter does not accept the Spanish-based creoles that we shall examine in this chapter as being truely based on Spanish. In his view they are largely Spanish relexifications of Portuguese pidgins. This is certainly the case with *papiamento*, which, nonetheless, has been subject to such a degree of relexification from Spanish that, for the purposes of this book, we shall discuss it as a Spanish-based creole.

Hancock (1971, in Crystal 1987: 338–9) identifies the following Spanish-based pidgins and creoles, although, in line with the definition provided above, a number of them could be more properly classified as contact varieties: *pachuco* (Spanish-English contact language in limited use in Arizona and parts of southern California (see p. 191)), Nahuatl-Spanish creole (used in Nicaragua and now probably extinct), *papiamento/u* (see p. 183), pidgin Spanish (a Spanish-based trading language mainly used by two tribes in Venezuela), Spanish creole (varieties of creole used in northern Colombia, of which *palenquero* (see p. 184) is one), Trinidad and Tobago creole, *cocoliche* (a variety of Italianized Spanish spoken in Buenos Aires, Argentina, see 9.1.4), Franco-Spanish pidgin (a contact language used in Buenos Aires sometimes referred to as 'fragnol'), *inglés de escalerilla*, (a Spanish-English-based pidgin used in some Mediterranean ports such as La Línea de Concepción), *caviteño* and *ermitaño* (Spanish-based creoles used in the area around Manila in the Philippines), *chabacano*, *davaueño* (a Spanish-based creole used in the Philippines), Bamboo Spanish (a Spanish-based pidgin used by the Japanese and later by the Chinese in the Philippines), and *ternateño* (used in the Moluccas between Spanish and Portuguese speakers).

9.0.0 *Philippine creole Spanish (Zamboangueño), Papiamento, Palenquero*

In this section[1] we are going to examine briefly the three principal Spanish-based creoles, *chabacano* from the Philippines, *papiamento* from the West Indies and *palenquero* from the Colombian coast.

Philippine Creole Spanish (PCS), known locally as *chabacano* was formed in the sixteenth and seventeenth centuries under the Spanish colonization of the Philippines, began a process of decreolization just before Spanish influence disappeared with the American occupation, and curiously, given the absence of contact with Spanish speakers, continues to absorb elements from Spanish.

PCS, initially a number of dialects of which the only one to truly survive is *zamboangueño*, is spoken by several hundred thousand people, and despite having absorbed elements from local indigenous languages, has retained its character as a Spanish-language creole. It is the first language of the majority of the inhabitants of the city of Zamboanga, is the preferred language in almost all informal situations and is the predominant language of local broadcasting. Although English is the official medium of instruction, along with obligatory classes in Pilipino, teachers frequently use *chabacano*. While speakers often believe that *chabacano* is a form of 'broken Spanish' and 'has no grammar', creolists point to the fact that creoles do have their own developed grammatical structures. In the case of *chabacano*, the language differs from Spanish to the extent that, as Lipski points out, some speakers of Spanish might have difficulty in recognizing the language as a Spanish derivative. *Chabacano* has borrowed lexically from early Spanish (e.g. *endenantes*, earlier in the same day), Visayan, an indigenous language (e.g. *anak*, son/daughter), later Spanish (e.g. *aeropuerto*) and English (e.g. *valuable*).

Papiamento is currently spoken in the islands of Curaçao, Aruba and Bonaire of the Dutch West Indies, where according to the 1981 census some 80 per cent of the population were creole speakers. It is probably derived from an earlier Portuguese-lexified creole.[2] It is the only Spanish-based creole with a rich and vital literary and audiovisual culture and high prestige amongst speakers of all social classes. It also acts as a powerful symbol of cultural and national identity. Within *papiamento* there are a number of distinct geographical and stylistic varieties where differences relate primarily to lexis. For example, in Curaçao, there are three principal geographical varieties, one with a strong Hispanic base spoken by descendants of the Sephardic Jews, another Dutch-based variety spoken by descendants of the Dutch colonizers and an intermediate variety spoken by the majority black population. These differences can be exemplified by the following lexical pairs derived respectively from Spanish and Dutch: *ekonomisá/spar* (*economizar*), *imprimí/drùk* (*imprimir*), *pusha/stot* (*empujar*) (Munteanu, in Alvar, 1996a: 69). The varieties spoken in Aruba and Bonaire display greater influence from Spanish and in the case of Bonaire also from English. Influence from African languages can be seen in the phonology of *papiamento* (like *palenquero*, it is tonal, with a high tone used to distinguish between some minimal pairs where stress would be used in cognate languages), in preferred pronunciations (e.g. *kabaron* for *camarón*), and most importantly in its morphosyntax (e.g. the plural marker is *-nan*, *kas* (*casa*), *kasnan* (*casas*)), and the verbal system, based on aspectual distinctions, differs markedly from that of Spanish and is clearly derived from African languages.

Currently speakers of *papiamento* show a clear preference for borrowing from Spanish rather than the official language, Dutch, which may be rejected for anti-colonial motives, or English, which has a strong media presence but which may be more culturally alien. This borrowing is taking place to such an extent that some experts speak of the decreolization and Hispanicization of *Papiamento*, although this process is mainly taking place at a lexical and not at morphosyntactic level with some phonological Hispanicization occurring.

Palenquero is a Spanish-based creole spoken by a community of some 2,500 descendants of slaves in San Basilio de Palenque on the Atlantic coast of Colombia which, with the exception of pre-nasalization (e.g. *ndejá* (*dejar*) and its distinctive intonation pattern, is very similar phonetically to the Caribbean Spanish of the north coast to which it is gradually approximating. De Granda (1994: 402–6) identifies, in addition to pre-nasalization, the following features of *palenquero* which he notes are derived from African languages from south of the Sahara: the subsitution of /r/ and /ɾ/ by /l/, for example, *balé* for *barrer*, *blaso* for *brazo*, the substitution of /d/ by /ɾ/, for example, *arió* for *adiós*, the substitution of the semi-consonantal glide /j/ by the palatal nasal /ɲ/ such as *ñamá* for *llamar*, nasalization of the vowel succeeding as well as preceding a nasal consonant; a CVCV (consonant-vowel consonant-vowel) syllable structure, and *sandhi*, that is the elision of the first vowel when two vowels come into contact, for example, *lengua ele* becomes *lengwéle*.

Morpho-syntactically, *palenquero* is similar to other creoles in, for example, the loss of inflection to mark person, tense, aspect and mood and its substitution by particles, as in *Pueblo mí ta pelé lengua ané* (My people are losing their language) where *ta* is a particle derived from *estar* and *pelé* equates to the infinitive *perder*. The personal pronoun system is derived from Bantu (*enú* 'you plural formal', *ané*, 'they'), Portuguese (*bo* 'you singular', *ele*, 'he/she') and Spanish (*suto* 'nosotros') and *utere* 'ustedes'). Negation operates very differently from that of Spanish, with the negative particle *nu* normally being placed at the end of the clause, for example, *I ta ablá kayetano* **nu**, 'Yo no estoy hablando castellano' (Patiño Rosselli 1989: 341–52). The survival of *palenquero* is in great doubt: there is widespread code-switching into English; the community clearly sees Spanish as the prestige variety and fewer families are passing the creole on to the younger generations.

In the case of these three Spanish-based creoles, although it could be argued that *chabacano* is, to a certain extent, an exception, perhaps the most salient fact common to most creoles throughout the world, is their low status within their communities which is leading in many instances to their gradual loss, whether through processes of rehispanicization or through widespread adoption of other varieties, generally Spanish, which enjoy greater prestige. Thus most Spanish-based creoles can be seen as linguistic relics of a long-past colonial age.

9.1 Contact with other languages

9.1.0 *Spanish/Catalan*

It is generally true to say that the less dominant language is likely to be subject to greater language change in a situation of contact and that thus Catalan is likely to undergo greater change than Spanish.[3] Nonetheless, the Spanish spoken in the Catalan-speaking communities of Catalonia, the Balearic Islands and Valencia has been affected to differing extents by its proximity to Catalan. Given the high numbers of bilingual speakers (passive bilingualism is particularly prevalent and facilitated by the degree of lexical cognacy between Spanish and Catalan which Green (1990a: 123) sets at approximately 80 per cent) and the high levels of societal bilingualism especially in the first two of these communities, opportunities for contact are great. In this section we shall look briefly at some salient features of the phonetics, morpho-syntax and lexis of the Spanish spoken in areas where there is contact with Catalan.[4]

Phonetically the most salient feature characterizing the Spanish spoken in Eastern Spain is the retention of intervocalic /d/ in words ending in *-ado*, particularly past participles. According to Blas Arroyo (1992: 20) this tendency is due to the influence of Catalan, where the tenser articulation of consonants leads to the past participle of *-ar* verbs being pronounced as [t]. Catalan speakers of Spanish consequently tend to articulate word-final /d/ in line with Catalan to the extent of rendering what in Castilian is a voiced consonant as the unvoiced [t], for example, *Madrit* for *Madrid*, again running counter to the wider national trend towards relaxing the articulation of the final consonant. Catalan speakers may also pronounce the word-final /l/ of *-al* endings as a velar or 'dark' 'l'. In certain dialects of Catalan there is a distinction between /b/ and /v/ which does not exist in Spanish; consequently speakers may make this distinction (e.g. *vino* for *bino* when speaking Spanish). Another interesting influence deriving from Catalan relates to the *seseo*. Given that no distinction exists between /s/ and /θ/ in Catalan (which in this respect is similar to Galician and Basque), Catalan speakers, particularly of rural extraction, have difficulty in making this distinction in Spanish and revert to the use of *seseo* – which is seen here, unlike in Andalusia and Latin America, as a stigmatized form used only by those incapable of making the distinction.

As far as **morpho-syntax** is concerned, a number of features are worthy of interest. The practice in Catalan-speaking areas of using a determiner with a proper name *¿Está la Julia?* (rather than *¿Está Julia?*) may be due to contact with Catalan which in many cases uses a determiner, although at the same time the determiner is being lost in Catalonia, perhaps under pressure from Spanish. It should be added that this feature is also shared by speakers of other varieties of Spanish, notably Andalusian and Aragonese and is stigmatized to a greater or lesser extent. The practice of creating adverbs ending in *-mente* where Spanish would use an adverbial phrase (*malamente* for *de una manera mala*), although a feature of non-standard Spanish more generally, may here too be promoted by contact with Catalan. In Catalan, as in French, the future tense is used in subordinate clauses to refer to future time, while Spanish employs the subjunctive *cuando pases. Cuando pasarás* is frequently employed in Catalan-speaking areas. Prepositional use can also be affected through contact with Catalan, for example, the extension of the use of *en* to replace in certain contexts *a, de,* and *con,* such as *Corta el pan **en** (con) el cuchillo* (Gómez Molina, in López Morales, 1989: 160). Non-standard double negation is also a feature of this variety of Spanish; standard Spanish allows double negation when the particle *no* precedes the verb (**No** lo ha visto nadie) but not when it is postposed (**Nadie **no* lo ha visto*). The latter form occurs in the Spanish of Catalan-speaking areas (Gómez Molina, in López Morales, 1989: 160).

Lexically, the influence of the contact language is greatest and can be seen in numerous borrowings and calques from the contact language (e.g. *bajoca* for a green bean (*judía verde* in standard Spanish), *Voy **derecho** a Barcelona* from the Catalan *dret* rather than the Spanish *Voy **directo** a Barcelona*), **hacer** *tarde* from the Catalan *fer tard*.

9.1.1 Spanish/Portuguese

Portuguese, another language highly cognate with Spanish, comes into contact with Spanish on the border between Spain and Portugal and on the border between Brazil and a number of Latin American nations. Rona (1965, in López Morales, 1989: 154) has studied the language continuum between the Spanish spoken in Uruguay and the Portuguese spoken on the other side of the border with Brazil. He identifies two varieties, a Spanish-based *fronterizo* and a Portuguese-based *fronteiriço*, spoken either mono- or bilingually by the inhabitants of that zone. These varieties on occasion prove to be incomprehensible to monolingual speakers of both standard Spanish and standard Portuguese. Both these border varieties in turn fragment into four sub-varieties. *Fronterizo* is phonetically very similar to Spanish, has some morphosyntactic influence from Portuguese and much lexical borrowing. Nonetheless, the latter does not predominate over the Spanish-based lexicon. Interestingly, the selection criterion according to which lexical items are retained is based in the proximity of the term to both languages. For example, from the following three terms for 'pig' in Spanish *cerdo/puerco/chancho, puerco* is retained as being closest to the Portuguese *porco* (Rona, in López Morales, 1989: 156). Where no such term is available, Spanish is favoured, for example, *pinha* from the Spanish *piña* and not the Portuguese *abacaxi*.

9.1.2 Spanish/Maya (Yucateca)

Maya is spoken in the Yucatán Peninsula and the Tehuantepec Isthmus of Mexico as well as in part of Guatemala and in the north of Honduras. Maya is unlike the Romance languages we have looked at previously. It is unrelated to Spanish and is an agglutinative language (building up meanings through, for example, prefix- and suffixation) and is, in many ways, similar in nature to Basque with which Spanish is in contact in the Iberian Peninsula. Maya, however, unlike Basque, is phonetically very dissimilar to Spanish. Maya had a written language before the arrival of the Spaniards; however, the hieroglyphs used by the ancient Mayas have only very partially been deciphered to this day. It was the Franciscans who, shortly after the conquest, created the Mayan alphabet. It has a rich literature and has been amply codified. In this section we shall concentrate on the Spanish spoken in Mérida, the capital city of the Yucatán Peninsula.[5]

In Mérida, literacy campaigns have meant that there are now comparatively few monolingual speakers of Maya, the majority of the population being either bilingual or monolingual in Spanish. Nevertheless, contacts between the city and its agricultural and predominantly Maya-speaking hinterland are such that Spanish and Maya are in close daily contact. What is more, given a lack of basic communication between Mérida and the capital until the 1950s (the main route was by sea and from 1928 onwards by air), it is only during the last half of the twentieth century that there has been sustained contact with other varieties of Spanish. The eminent Mexican linguist Juan Lope Blanch has singled out the variety of Spanish spoken in the Yucatán Peninsula as one of the most distinctive in Mexico (in Suárez Molina 1996: xvii).

Phonetically, this variety shows very clear evidence of influence from Maya: the characteristic intonation pattern with its slow rhythm and pauses, the use of stress for emphasis and the use of the glottal stop in certain contexts, for example *no'* as a stressed refusal, *hija'* as a vocative, are all derived from Maya. The unvoiced plosive stops [p], [t] and [k], unaspirated in standard Spanish, are marked by the force of their articulation. Another defining feature of Yucatecan Spanish is the substitution of [m] for word-final [n], as in *el pam* (*pan*), *el balcóm* (*el balcón*). Amongst less educated speakers of Spanish there is also a tendency to substitute [p] for [f] (*peliz* for *feliz*) given that the phoneme /f/

does not exist in Maya. Similarly the absence of *jota* and *ñ* in Maya mean that the former is not pronounced as a fricative, a tendency to be found elsewhere although for other reasons, and the latter is pronounced *ni*, for example, *ninio* rather than *niño*. A sound frequently found in toponymics as well as borrowings which does not exist in standard Spanish is [tʃ] preceding a number of consonants, *xkikil*, for example; also it is possible to find word-finally a variety of consonants which do not occur in Spanish, such as *bob*, *tux*, *lek*.

Morpho-syntactically, there is very little influence from Maya, given that the language is quite different in structure from Spanish. One feature of note, however, is the tendency of Maya to use syllabic reduplication for emphasis. In Yucatecan Spanish it is common to find reduplications such as *buenisísimo*, *feisisísimo*. Mayan word order also influences the use of certain adverbs borrowed from Mayan as these precede the verb in Mayan, for example, Me *hach gusta tu traje*. Constructions such as *Le tomaron su pelo por José* for *Le tomó el pelo José* are a reflection of Mayan, which favours passive constructions. Other features, not exclusive to Yucatecan Spanish, may be due to the influence of Maya. For example, the pleonastic use of possessives, e.g. *su casa de Juan*, frequent also in other varieties of Spanish, may be due to the requirement in Mayan to prepose the genitive *u*, normally translated as *su*.

Lexically, there is a wide range of borrowings from Mayan, particularly in fields relating to regional customs, agriculture, flora and fauna. Many of these are direct borrowings, for example, *xux* (wasp). Others are adapted to Spanish phonology, such as *cenote* (from *ts'onot*, an underground deposit of water) and others are are blends of both languages (e.g. *chocolomo* from the Mayan *choko* (hot) and the Spanish *lomo* (loin) to refer to a regional meat stew, *hacer loch*, (to hug somebody)). A number of the interjections used in the Yucatán are also influenced by Mayan, for example ¡*way*! for 'ouch' (¡*ay*! in standard Spanish) and the emphatic *chuch*, as in ¡*Chuch, qué linda estás!* Mayan is also responsible for semantic extension and shift in Yucatecan Spanish, for example, the verb *acotar*, which in standard Spanish means to mark out the boundaries of an area or to fence in, in Yucatecan Spanish means to enclose with a wall or a hedge under the influence of the Mayan *kotah*, which means to build walls.

9.1.3 Spanish/Italian

Italianisms are frequent in many varieties of Latin American Spanish and most particularly in those of Argentina and Uruguay. Notably they are a major ingredient of *lunfardo*, an underworld slang spoken in the River Plate area and spread by the Italian community, which also contains terms from Peninsular Spanish, Portuguese, French slang and argot and English.[6]

Cocoliche, however, is a spontaneous mixture of these two languages spoken, to an increasingly lesser degree, by a number of speech communities in the River Plate area of Argentina and Uruguay. As such it is often difficult to tell which is the base language, for example, whether a speaker is Hispanicizing an Italian construction or Italianizing a Spanish one. Speakers of *Cocoliche* are unaware of using a language other than their native Italian or Spanish and yet through accommodating to the language of a speech community which is not the speaker's own, for example, through the accommodation of Italian immigrant workers to River Plate Spanish, they spontaneously combine both languages. Therefore, it could be said that there is no fixed speech variety but rather as many as there are speakers (Meo Zilio 1989: 209).[7]

However, some consistencies can be detected. The type of *cocoliche* spoken depends on linguistic factors (e.g. presence or absence of formal and semantic equivalence between the two languages) and individual factors (for example, the degree of language awareness of the immigrant, their native dialect, the length of time spent in the host country). For example, while newly arrived immigrants may speak a variety closer to Italian, more established groups will incorporate more elements of Spanish. Also, different groups develop *cocoliche* in different ways. The first wave of immigrants, prior to the Second World War, were mainly composed of young, impoverished and uneducated manual labourers from the south who spoke southern dialects and standard Italian with difficulty if at all. They had little access, on the one hand, to standard Italian through the media and, on the other, to standard Spanish, as the nature of their employment and the importance of family ties isolated them from the language of their host country. The *cocoliche* spoken by these groups is prototypical. These speakers over time lose their native language without consciously learning that of the host country. Thus it is extremely difficult to determine when they cease to speak Italian (with Spanish influence) and start speaking a Spanish heavily influenced by Italian.

The second wave of immigration after the Second World War was composed of more highly educated, older people who were speakers of standard Italian, who had a degree of linguistic consciousness and who saw a need to learn Spanish in order to exercise their chosen professions. What is more, the fact that they were from the north of Italy, where language varieties are phonetically closer to Spanish, facilitated their learning of the language. Thus the *cocoliche* spoken by these groups approximates much more closely to standard spoken Spanish when addressing Spanish speakers and to standard spoken Italian when addressing speakers of that language.

Given that immigration has now virtually ceased and that these communities are becoming integrated into Argentine life with their descendants learning native Spanish, *cocoliche* is dying out. Nonetheless, at the end of the twentieth century it still survives within some homes and neighbourhoods as Lavandera's actual recording of spontaneous *cocoliche* demonstrates:

El hombre se interesó michísimo e, ya había tomato informe, el dueño que me había tomato a trabajar estaba muy contento diche que yo muchacho é un muchacho que trabaja entontse el jombre me dijo, dice sí, dishe, hacete valere, diche, hacete valere porque el hombre sta muy contento, muy conforme. A mí el hombre me había dicho, diche, Roque, dice, vo te quedá tre día . . .[8]

(in Lipski (1994: 179))

9.1.4 *Spanish/English*[9]

We saw in Chapter 1 the extent and diversity of the Spanish-speaking communities in the United States. The country of origin (principally Mexico, Cuba and Puerto Rico), length of residence in the United States, extent of contact with English-speaking communities, age, socio-economic group are only some of the factors which determine the status and the range of social functions of the minority language in the often very different communities which speak it. Even within the largest group of speakers, the *chicanos* of Mexican descent mainly living in the south west of the United States, a number of distinct varieties of Spanish have been identified. For example, Elías-Olivares (in Amastae and Elías-Olivares, 1982: 335) describes and exemplifies four varieties in the Spanish of East Austin, the major Chicano barrio in Austin, Texas:

1 'Español correcto' or Northern Mexican Spanish: *se fue a la escuela en su bicicleta.*
2 'Mejicano' or popular Spanish: *se fue [hwe] a la escuela [ehkwela] en su bicicleta.*
3 'Español regüelto/'Spanglish' or mixed Spanish: *se fue [hwe] a la escuela [ehkwela] en su* bicycle.
4 Caló or Pachuco: *se fue [hwe] al escuelín [ehkwelin] en su yonca* (or *chisca*).

In addition to these varieties, the same community also commands a similar range of varieties of English and also draws on the linguistic resource of code-switching, that is the combining of both English and Spanish, in their interaction. Elías-Olivares (in Pfaff in Amastae and Elías-Olivares, 1982: 265) provides the following figure of the Spanish/English continuum:

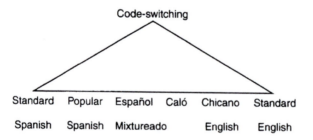

Figure 9.1 Spanish/English code-switching in East Austin, Texas (based on Amastae and Elías-Olivares (1982))

In this section, we shall look first briefly at *caló* or *pachuco*, the variety most distant from standard Spanish, then at popular Chicano Spanish and finally consider some of the features which are common to most of the standard varieties of Spanish spoken in the United States. In 9.2 we shall examine the lexical borrowing which is a characteristic of *español mixtureado* or Spanglish and focus on code-switching between English and Spanish and between Spanish and Catalan.

Caló

Caló, also known as *pachuco* or argot, is the name given to a non-standard variety of Spanish spoken in the southern states of the United States (we have already mentioned gypsy *caló* in our discussion of youth varieties in Spain). It is different from the anti-languages we have examined so far (*cheli* and *lunfardo*) insofar as it may be the only variety of Spanish available to a speaker (who uses English in more formal circumstances). It is a blend of Hispanicized gypsy speech and delinquent cant grafted onto informal popular Mexican Spanish and is frequently used by predominantly male marginal groups to mark ethnic identity and as a symbol of rejection of the dominant Anglo-Saxon culture. Speakers may simply adopt expressions from *caló* into their spoken Spanish to signal attitude, or they may be extremely creative within the variety. For instance, they may add nonsense syllables to words (*otro* may become *otrofo* or even *ofotrofo*), play with taboo and euphemism exploiting, say, the verb *chingar* (see Chapter 8), use irony and playfully improvise (anything beginning with 'n' might be used to say no) (Webb in Amastae and Elías-Olivares (1982: 127)).

Sánchez (in Amastae and Elías-Olivares, 1982: 15) provides a transcript of the speech of a *vato loco* (cool dude):

> *Guacha, ¿Por qué no me alivianas con un aventón y me dejas en el chante? Y mientras que vas por el Chente, yo tiro clavao, me rastío la greña y me entacucho.*[10]

> (Sánchez, in Amastae and Elías-Olivares, 1982: 15)

This very short extract is mainly characterized by non-standard lexis such as *el chante*, *entacucharse* and some non-standard pronunciation, for example, *clavao*. It is interesting to note the possible influence of English in the noun *aventón* (a lift), which is not lexicalized in standard Peninsular Spanish.

Popular Chicano Spanish

What characterizes popular Chicano Spanish are to a large extent the features commonly found in popular varieties of Spanish elsewhere, such as the addition of [s] to the preterite second-person singular, *fuistes* for *fuiste*, the archaic subjunctive form *haiga* for *haya*, the regularization of radical changing verbs, *vuélvamos* for *volvamos*, the use of the rural archaic *asina* for *así*, the substitution of *nos* for *mos* as the first person plural marker as in *nos juntábanos*. As regards pronunciation, vowels are so lax that they are frequently lost. For example, unaccented vowels in initial position may be lost, for example, *acordar* is pronounced *cordar* and, similarly, sounds are lost at the end of a word, as in *pa* for *para*. Consonants also tend to be lax (intervocalic and final [b], [d], [g] and [j] are frequently lost, for example, *abuelo* – [awelo], *lado* – [lau], *luego* – [lue'o] [lo'o] [lo], *muy* – [mu]. Along with this there is the aspiration of sibilant [s] in any position as in *sí señor* – [hi heɲoʀ], *este* – [ehte], of the voice-less fricative [f], for example *fuerte* – [hweɾte] and of what is now orthographic 'h', *se huyó* – [se hujo].

However, unlike popular varieties in monolingual communities, the presence of English is salient lexically, for example, *no sabe* **espelear** and struc-turally, for example, *me llamó* **pa tras**. Nouns and verbs are assimilated (see 4.0.1 for a general description of this phenomenon) with verbs taking an *-ar* (pronounced *-iar*) ending, such as *dostear* (to dust), *chainear* (to shine) and nouns being assigned number and gender although these may vary from variety to variety, for example, *un plogue/una ploga* (a plug), *un troque/una troca* (a truck). Also, proximity to English leads to extensions of meaning, for example, *una librería* (*biblioteca* in standard Spanish) is used to refer to a library and not a bookshop, as it would in standard Spanish.[11]

Sánchez (in Amastae and Elías-Olivares 1982: 15) provides the following transcript of two neighbourhood housewives talking:

–*Fíjate que anoche llegó Juan echándole trancazos a la Filomena. Hizo una rejolina que ¡Válgame Dios! Y pa cabarla de remolar pos no se le antojó a Pedro irse a meter al borlote quesque pa pararle el alta al Juan. A ése ni quien lo pacigüe pero Pedro es mu cabezudo.*
–*¿Y a poco se le rajuelió todo?*
–*Ande, si ni chanza tuvo, porque lo-lo vino la chota y cargó con toos. Diay la Filomena se dejó venir.*
–*¿A poco quería que se lo juera a sacar?*
–*Pos sí, . . .*[12]

In this extract, we can see the lax pronunciation (*pa* (para), *cabar* (acabar), *pos* (pues), *lo* (luego), *mu*, (muy), *pacigüe* (apacigüe), *toos* (todos), *diay* (de ahí), *juera* (fuera), influence from English, *chanza*, (chance), the 'regularization' of the preterite of the irregular verb *rajolear* (to back down) to *rajuelió* and the use of Chicano slang, for example, *la chota* (the police).

Standard Spanish in the United States

The main influence on the Spanish spoken in the United States, particularly in bilingual communities, is that of contact with English which is easiest to observe in the lexicon, but which permeates phonology and morpho-syntax as well. In 5.0 where we examined, for example, the gradual loss of the subjunc-tive mood and the extension of *estar* at the expense of *ser*, we already saw how external contact with English could accelerate a change in progress internal to the language, that is one which is also occurring in monolingual Spanish-speaking communities.

If we look at the Spanish spoken by speakers who are in close contact with English we can see a range of similar features. Morales (1986, 1981, 1979, in López Morales 1989: 167–70), in her study of Puerto Rican Spanish, found a particularly high frequency of use of the subject personal pronoun. However, she does not attribute this to the pressure of English, where these are obligatory, as it is a tendency common to the Caribbean in general, where contact with English is less direct. She has also studied the low frequency of the use of subjunctive mood where choice is determined by semantic and pragmatic considerations. This particularly affects the expression of doubt and regret *No creo que **hace/haga** bien la asignación* and *Lamento que **viene/venga***. Furthermore, she notes an increased use of the infinitive, for example, *Ellos son tremendos amigos pero a la hora de **nosotros salir***, a tendency also common to Caribbean Spanish in general but possibly accelerated here through contact with English. Other processes similar in nature are the use of the gerund as noun, **Nadando** *es bueno para la salud*, as an adjective, *La junta emitió un decreto **nombrando** director* and the use of *para* + infinitive in subordination expressing purpose, *El propósito de la reunión es **para** la policía **dar** a conocer su opinión*.

Another tendency when two languages come into contact is not for the converging language to adopt 'alien' structures but rather to use more frequently structures which parallel those used the contact language and to use less frequently the structures normally used in these contexts. Such is the case of the present and imperfect continuous tenses, the usage of which is markedly different in English and Spanish. Klein (1980, in Silva-Corvalán 1989: 187) studied the use of these tenses in the Spanish of monolingual and bilingual Puerto Rican speakers in New York. She found that, while the monolinguals tended to use the standard simple tense, as in *Y una vez cuando **iba** de regreso de la escuela a la casa*, the bilinguals would frequently use the past progressive mirroring the preferred English construction, for example, *Y una vez cuando **iba caminando** a casa*.

9.2 Borrowing and code-switching

Wherever there is bi- or multilingualism, there tends to be borrowing and code-switching. While borrowing, broadly speaking, involves incorporating and frequently assimilating individual words from one language into another, for example, *Es posible que te **moqueen*** (they might mug you) (Poplack in Amastae and Elías-Olivares, 1982: 232), code-switching involves the use of two or more languages, or codes, by the same speaker within a single turn or interaction or between turns. Poplack and Sankoff (in López Morales 1989: 171) provide the following example of code-switching between Spanish and English from a Puerto Rican speaker in New York:

> But I used to eat *bofe*, the brain. And then they stopped selling it because *tenían, este, le encontraron que tenía* worms. I used to make some *bofe*! *Después yo hacía uno d'esos* concoctions: the garlic *con cebolla, y hacía un mojo, y yo dejaba que se curara eso* for a couple of hours. Then you be drinking and eating that shit. Wooh! It's like eating anchovies when you're drinking. Delicious!
>
> (Poplack and Sankoff in López Morales, 1989: 171)

Code-switching tends to be viewed fairly negatively both by those bilinguals who use it, and are often unaware that they are doing so, and especially so by the monolingual language communities who do not use it, hence the profusion of derogatory terms such as Tex-Mex and Spanglish which they use to describe it. They view code-switching as evidence of the inability of bilingual speakers to command either code, in this case English and Spanish, sufficiently well to be able to maintain a conversation in either. They also see it as the beginning of the end of the subordinate language. In the words of one Yale professor the use of Spanglish 'poses a grave danger to Hispanic culture and to the advancement of Hispanics in mainstream America' (*The Guardian*, 2.9.97). Despite the extremely negative attitudes which surround code-switching, its use can be vibrant and expressive. Indeed, in the case of the United States, with the growing confidence of Spanish speakers, it is increasingly used by the different Hispanic communities in an ever wider range of contexts, for example, newspaper small ads, radio talkshows and pop music. Linguists (for example, Poplack in Amastae and Elías-Olivares (1982), far from seeing code-switching as a sign of language deficit, point to the sophisticated skills that bilinguals deploy in effective code-switching and note that while monolinguals shift styles in interaction, bilinguals are able to draw on the resources of two codes for stylistic purposes. While the monolingual may be able to shift stylistically between the standard language and its regional and social variants as well as different styles related to use, the proficient bilingual can call on twice this range of resources. What is more, code-switching is a universal phenomenon arising in situations of language contact; in itself it provides no evidence of 'grave danger' to the subordinate language.

Code-switching can be prompted by reasons external to the interaction, whether these are situational, for example, English may be favoured in the place of work, or metaphorical. The latter may be topic-related (for example, the making of a specifically Mexican garlic sauce might prompt the use of Spanish as in the extract above, or a socio-culturally English language concept such as 'bussing' might prompt a switch to English), language-preference related (speakers might converge towards the language preference of their addressee from politeness, or alternatively diverge, a point which we shall discuss below) or to do with ethnicity and group membership (for example, speakers who wish to put on record their Hispanic identity might choose to do so by switching into Spanish). Code-switching may show where a speaker's affections and loyalties lie, with, for example, Spanish being used when the Hispanic speaker is personally involved with what they are saying and English chosen in the case of greater detachment. Timm (1993: 101) provides a telling example of this: 'Why, I questioned myself, did I have to daily portray myself as a gringo *cuando mi realidad tenía más sangre y pasión*'. The choice of one code rather than another may fulfil a rhetorical function and redefine a situation, for example marking a transition from seriousness to humour, formal to informal or equanimity to anger. Holmes (1992: 46) notes that in Paraguay, Guaraní, the low variety, is considered more appropriate for joking and humorous anecdotes and that when discussing a serious political issue in Spanish, a speaker may switch to Guaraní for a witty or humorous aside. Spanish speakers in the Catalan-speaking parts of Spain may use Catalan to swear in as it is felt to soften the force of the invective, for example *Oye chaval . . . ¡y no seas pesao!* **Ves-tén a la merda!** *¡Anda ya, y no fastidies!* (Casamiglia and Tuson 1980: 70 in Blas Arroyo 1995: 14).

Code-switching may also be prompted by a whole series of linguistic factors, for example, direct speech is likely to be relayed in the original language, repetition may often occasion a switch, interjections such as *hijole* may be inserted into strings of English, one language may be favoured for lexical precision or for the connotations of a particular term in one language or another, for example, picketing, *mestizos*, training.

Of course, not all those who code-switch have equal proficiency in both languages. Poplack (1982) identifies three levels of code-switching. First there are what are called 'emblematic' switches involving tags, interjections, set expressions and single nouns, for example, '*vendía arroz*'n shit' which are favoured by speakers who are not proficient in the 'tag' language. Then there is inter-sentential switching where a speaker changes code after a complete utterance, for example, 'It's on the radio. *A mí se me olvida la estación.* I'm gonna serve you another one, right? (Poplack in López-Morales 1989: 173). While this type of change requires a speaker to be able to maintain an interaction in each of the two codes, it does not in itself require any code-switching skills. Lastly, there is what is called intra-sentential code-switching where the speaker is able to move seamlessly from one code to the other without violating in any way the grammatical structures of either, for example, 'Why make Carol *sentarse atrás pa'que* everybody has to move down *pa'que se salga* (Poplack in Amastae and Elías-Olivares 1982: 237). This type of code-switching requires the greatest degree of bilingual ability and is favoured by balanced bilinguals.

Code-switching may play a valuable role in resolving questions of identity in societies where monolingual and bilingual communities coexist. For example, in the case of Spain, monolingual Spanish-speakers in minority language areas may use emblematic code-switching (for example, in Catalonia, the almost universal use of *Bon dia* (good day) and *adeu* (goodbye), or in the Basque country the use of the equivalent greetings *Kaixo* and *Agur*) to put on record their desire to accommodate to the preferred language of the other speaker despite being unable to do so. Conversely, where bilingual speakers are required to use Spanish with a monolingual, they may wish, nonetheless, to use minority language tags as a signal of their identity. Blas Arroyo (1995: 7) provides the following transcript of part of a conversation between himself (B) and a regional government official (A) who replies in Catalan to his telephone enquiry:

A: Bon dia, diguem?
B: *Sí, ¿es la inspección de enseñanza primaria?*
A: *Sí, aquí es, dígame, dígame*

(. . .)

B: *Bueno:: pues muchas gracias por la información.*
A: *De nada,* adeu, bon dia.[13]

What is interesting here, is not so much that speaker A has been prepared to switch to Spanish in response the B's choice of that language, but rather his choice to revert to Catalan at the end of the interaction to mark his loyalty to Catalan.

As Woolard (1988: 54) notes, the overarching social effects of code-switching can often only be understood with reference to the notions of 'we/they'. She examines code-switching between Catalan and Spanish in Barcelona (Spain) at a particularly tense time in the development of the relationship between the Catalan-speaking natives and the Spanish-speaking immigrants. Indeed, this was a time when polarization was such, with speakers preferring the language to which they were politically affiliated, that extended code-switching was limited. Woolard investigates the effects of code-switching and mixing, locally known as *la barreja*, by a stand-up comedian, Eugenio, whose act was a massive popular success in the 1980s with bilingual Catalans and monolingual Spanish-speakers at the same time. She notes that the audience, whether Catalan or Spanish, could not identify the base language of his act, although it was in fact 80 per cent Spanish, and indeed, all the punchlines were Spanish. Spanish was the primary language of narration and Catalan used for embellishment. However, the mistaken impression that both languages were used equally came principally from Eugenio's use of Catalan pronunciation and intonation patterns, some borrowings and morpho-syntactic interference and the repeated use of Catalan set phrases and single lexical items. In fact the type of code-switching he engages in is different from the language use in the community and allows barriers to be broken down and both native Catalan speakers and Spanish speakers to derive special enjoyment from the event; the former because Catalan is being used in front of a broad public audience and the latter because they are given the impression of listening to Catalan and 'getting it'. Woolard (1988: 64) gives the following example of Eugenio's use of both codes:

> *Dice,* 'Oiga, padre,' **diu,**
> 'Usted es el que aparta a las mujeres del mal?'
> **Diu,** 'Sí, hijo, sí.'
> **Diu,** 'Apártame dos para el sábado, **si us plau**'.[14]

It is obvious here that it is not the jokes but rather the way they are told, and here the code in which they are told, which is the secret of Eugenio's success.

While code-switching is predominantly an oral activity, there is evidence that this form of talk is acquiring greater status through its incorporation into published literature, principally poetry, but also children's stories and novels. Timm (1993: 104) illustrates this by a fragment of a poem which draws on the bilingual and bicultural context which it represents for the force of its imagery. The poem is entitled 'Wheat paper *cucarachas*' and is by the widely regarded Chicano poet, Alurista.

> wheat paper *cucarachas*
> *de papel trigo*
> *y la cosecha del sol*
> winged in autumn
> *de vuelo al sol*
> *y las alas de trigo*
> *a volar*
> *en la primavera*
> spring of youthful bronze
> melting in the lava of our blood
> *la cucaracha muere*
> *y muerde el polvo*
> powder wheat
> *de atole con el dedo*
> and they bleed
> crushed by florsheims[15]

That code-switching will continue to provide a rich linguistic resource for the Hispanic communities in the United States which wish to maintain their dual identity as Hispanics and members of mainstream culture is summed up in the following extract provided by Pfaff (in Amastae and Olivares, 1982: 295), taken from a class lecture by Alurista, also an instructor at the University of Texas, Austin:

> This is the way we speak. *Así hablamos en los barrios en las comunidades.* You know, we have to use English to survive and Spanish to preserve our heritage. Why you use the one or the other *eso tiene mucho que ver con* what kind of impact you give to your words. *Ves, hay palabras en inglés que tienen mucha fuerza emocional, como práctica. El idioma anglo-sajón es muy práctico.* It's a business language.

9.3 Conclusion

Geographically, the Spanish language, occupying as it does part of each of the five continents, having an extensive colonial history and providing work and workers for adjacent communities, has come into contact to varying degrees with vast numbers of other languages, some highly cognate and others linguistically unrelated. This contact allows Spanish-speaking communities to define their identity in relation to the contact community. The Italian of north Italian immigrants to Buenos Aires may converge onto Spanish because of a desire to assimilate to the dominant and economically powerful host country;

alternatively, in the use of *caló* both the dominant culture of English and the immigrant (of whatever generation) culture of Spanish may be rejected in favour of a hybrid anti-language. On the whole, the many varieties examined here are of limited significance for the Spanish language which is in most contexts of contact, the dominant language. The only language where the effects of contact may be more thorough-going and influential in the longer term is English, which frequently takes the role of dominant language.

Conclusion

Spanish is indubitably a world language of considerable vitality and variety. We have considered forces at work towards unification, such as the commitment of the Spanish-speaking media to identifying and promoting a panhispanic norm, most recently through the ambitious *Proyecto Zacatecas*, which aims to create a style guide to standardize usage on both sides of the Atlantic. Along similar lines are the strenuous efforts currently taking place to make corpus-based lexicography (e.g. CREA) reflect a panhispanic norm while respecting its broad diversity. We have also considered tensions leading to fragmentation and have noted that contact with other languages, even with the powerful English language, has a minimal effect on Spanish except primarily as a source of renewal and revitalization through, for example, borrowing and derivational processes. Obviously the pressures of globalization are ever present and work towards the consolidation of English as the world language. This is a challenge which faces all other major languages along with Spanish.

Evidently there are numerous sub-varieties of Spanish, the fortunes of which rise and fall with those of their speakers – hence rural varieties are dying out in Spain at the same time as the increased importance of globalization, technology, the professions and leisure is creating new jargons and, most significantly, new words. There is a perceptible need for contrastive studies to be carried out into different varieties of the language, not merely at the more traditional levels of phonetics, lexicology and morphosyntax, but at those of pragmatics, politeness, discourse and conversational analysis. We have seen how cross-cultural miscommunication may arise not because speakers do not share a common language system, but rather because the conventions for its very use vary from community to community. We have also seen how the conventions governing different genres of language use, for example news reporting, may differ significantly from one community to another, even when both broadly share a supranational variety of the language.

Language change both reflects and influences social change. The changing patterns of use of T/V pronouns of address bear witness to a complex negotiation of new social relationships, whether 'from below' over a prolonged period of time or 'from above' when, for example, a regime, or an organ of state tries to impose language change. We have examined change internal to the Spanish language and change motivated or accelerated by contact with other languages and cultures: this is most evident in the case of English and is particularly salient in terms of the large communities of Spanish speakers in the United States.

The interplay between language and society is the key to gaining some understanding of the variety and richness of the Spanish language today, rather than an idealized 'panhispanic norm' recognized by many but used by none, hence the need for studies of authentic language use firmly located within a defined social and cultural context.

Notes

Notes to Chapter 1

1 For a sociolinguistic account of the Castilianization of Latin America, see Mar Molinero (1997), Chapter 2.
2 For a detailed analysis of the post-Franco linguistic situation in Spain, see Siguan (1992).
3 All figures relate to 1991 and are in Quilis (1992).
4 For a description of the Spanish spoken in Equatorial Guinea, see Quilis (1992).
5 See 3.2 for an extract of *ladino* in Roman letters.
6 For a discussion of this creole, see Chapter 9.
7 For a discussion of lexical creation see Chapter 4.
8 For a discussion of the status of Spanish in international organizations, see Marqués de Tamarón (1995).

Notes to Chapter 2

1 For a comprehensive discussion of standardization and related issues, see Milroy and Milroy (1991).
2 For a discussion of prestige norms in Latin America see Lipski (1994: 136–40).
3 In this book I shall use the term 'Castilian' to refer to the geographical variety of Spanish spoken in the north of Spain. While *castellano* and *español* may be used interchangeably on both sides of the Atlantic to refer to the Spanish language, they have each acquired a symbolic dimension which varies according to the context in which they are used.
4 For a superb history of the Spanish language see Penny (1991).
5 For a brief account of the development of the Latin American *academias* see López Morales (1994).
6 See Section 3.2 on spelling.
7 For a comprehensive overview of dictionaries of Spanish, see Haensch (1997).
8 For further information about work in progress in Mexico, see Lope Blanch (1994), and for information about dictionaries of Latin American Spanish, see Haensch (1997).
9 See Haensch (1997: 227–30) for a more detailed account of the project.
10 See Section 3.2.
11 Cárdenas Nanneti (1959) *Manual de Selecciones (Normas generales de redacción)*.
12 See Lipski (1994: 143–46).
13 See also 2.0.3.
14 The transition to a democratic regime in Spain after Franco.
15 e.g. *dequeísmo* and *sindequeísmo*, see Section 5.2.1.
16 For further discussion of these issues, see Chapter 3.

17 For example, new intransitive usages for formerly transitive verbs e.g. *calentar* for *calentarse*, the conditional of allegation.
18 For a detailed description of one representative element of administrative language, the language of the *Boletín Oficial del Estado* (Official State Gazette), for the period immediately prior to the transition to democracy, see Calvo Ramos (1980).
19 For a further discussion of this area, see 2.0.3.
20 See 2.0.3.
21 [It is a reassuring thought, in a manner of speaking, and it is also a disturbing one, in fact it is more disturbing than reassuring, that while men are killing each other and everything around them, the public administration in Spain sees fit to reinvent grammar, tamper with the spirit of the language and reorganize the vocabulary used by civil servants.] (My translation)
22 [The fact is that it was long overdue. It is not particularly difficult to introduce the feminine form on application forms, to do away with the assumption that the male is the sole head of family, to include the woman as something other than wife, etc.] (My translation)
23 For a discussion of sexism and the Spanish language, see García Meseguer (1988) and (1994).
24 For further discussion, see Chapter 7.
25 For a detailed presentation of the study of spoken Spanish and an extensive bibliography of related studies, see Cortés Rodríguez (1994); for a discussion of dialect atlas projects, see Lipski (1994: 153–61); and for an up-to-date collection of contributions on Latin American and Spanish dialectology, see Alvar (1996, a and b); and for a list and discussion of twenty-eight corpus projects currently in progress in Spain, see the *Corpus orales y escritos disponibles y en desarrollo en España (Instituto Cervantes)*.
26 For a list of published linguistic atlases of Spanish see Haensch (1997: 83).
27 See, for example, Briz (1995).

Notes to Chapter 3

1 More detailed observations about the phonetics of Latin American Spanish can be found in Lipski (1994). For a more detailed overview of the phonology of the Castilian norm, see MacPherson (1975), Green, (1990a: 80–90) and D'Introno, del Teso and Weston (1995).
2 For a more detailed but concise discussion of the phonology of Spanish, see Green, (1990a: 80–90).
3 See Battye and Hintze (1992: 95).
4 [predominant usage in Madrid over the last fifty years amongst upper middle-class families long-established in Madrid and in the majority of educated and university circles.] (My translation)
5 See Williams (1987: 65–79).
6 See Silva-Corvalán (1989).
7 For information on the development of this phenomenon see Penny (1991: 86–90), Lipski (1994: 43–4), Green (1990a: 82–3), Narbona *et al.* (1998: 128–38).
8 For a discussion of stress see Butt and Benjamin (1994: 488–93).
9 See Quilis (1997: 76–85, Alarcos Llorach (1994: 49–56), Green (1990a: 80).
10 For a fuller examination of this area, see Butt and Benjamin (1994: 493–98).
11 See Penny (1991).
12 [and when she rode, in order to cover the things which might cause her shame, should they be revealed as she was riding, she had to find a way of keeping them covered so that as she was riding she need not be troubled that she was doing so without due care . . .] (Translated by C. Dixon)
13 For a discussion of phonological change in Spanish since the Middle Ages, see Penny (1991: 27–97).

14 See, for example, Marcos Marín (1979: 102).
15 For a discussion of the principal letter–sound correspondence of Castilian, see Green (1990a: 90–2).
16 [My dear friend, Your letter, which I received when I was getting water from the boarding-house dining-room, upset me greatly. I must say that I never expected such inconsiderate behaviour on your part . . .] (My translation)
17 [these two letters have been assassinated through pressure from and economic colonization by the English-speaking world]. (My translation)
18 Such a reform would nonetheless maintain the phoneme /ɲ/ rather than replace it by [ni] for this would be a conventionalized spelling rather than a phonemic transcription.
19 [. . . 500 years after the expulsion, Judeo-Spanish is still a language which can be understood quite easily by Spanish speakers in different parts of the world. Not only that but it awakens in them a great interest, on account of phonetic distinctiveness and its success in retaining many elements of medieval Spanish as well as many songs, tales and refrains which constitute a veritable treasure trove for those who devote themselves to the history of the Spanish language and literature.] (My translation.)
20 See Butt and Benjamin (1994: 494), Casado (1993: 25–6).

Notes to Chapter 4

1 See Chapter 8.
2 For further information on suffixes which differ from those commonly used in English, see *Collins Spanish Dictionary* (Smith 1993: 821–25).
3 For a discussion of emotive suffixation see Lang (1990: 91–122) and Gooch (1970).
4 C: ['Poor me! all I've eaten is a sandwich (DIM.) of three salt cod (DIM.) with a little (DIM. + DIM.) garlic oil on the bread and and a
   P: well the garlic oil (you shouldn't have)
   C: some peppers (DIM.) or something but the salt cod (DIM) down on its own without heating it up or anything either if you make up a little (DIM.) fried vegetables (DIM.).
   P: Yes, of course, it's tastier (DIM.)
   C: You put a little (DIM.) fried vegetables, and some tomato sauce (DIM.) but there was nothing else, everything was meat and stuff, I couldn't put anything on, Oh cousin (DIM.) I have been very happy to see you.'] (My translation)
5 See Rodríguez González (1993b) and Casado Velarde (1985).
6 See Casado Velarde (1985).
7 ['The truth is that seeing Mariano Rubio the other day slumping off to the (bull's) favourite spot of the Bank of Spain (...), backing up into the fence and spilling blood through the mouth (...) Blasco Ibáñez the bull is in the front row of seats.'] (My translation.)
8 ['The most obvious mistake was an easy smash over the net, where the ball went past the edge of Steffi's racket. It was the only time when Arantxa was able to get back into the game. And she made the best of it. She made her only two breaks of the match and equalized on five all.'] (My translation)
9 See Gregory and Carroll (1978).
10 For a discussion of the cultural context and an extensive bibliography of this area see Rodríguez González (1989: 9–21).
11 Two useful 'dictionaries' of *cheli* in particular and slang in general are Umbral's *Diccionario cheli* (1983) and León's *Diccionario de argot español* (1994). There are numerous dictionaries of vocabularies used by criminal subgroups throughout the Spanish-speaking world and particularly of the varieties of *caló* and *lunfardo* (spoken in the River Plate area).

12 [Grandmother: Wow! These bubbles really freak me out. Don't they turn you on?
[...]
Grandmother: I'm heavily into my knitting. You piss me off.
Tony: Grandmother, we could set up a farm in the village, couldn't we?
Grandmother: Right on, man!]. (My translation.)
13 See Casado Velarde (1985: 81–91).
14 For further discussion see Herrera in Rodríguez González (1989: 179–201). See also
7.5.
15 See Català in Rodríguez González (1989: 203–16).
16 [The thug starts telling stories of trips, of Gorbachovs, raspberries and supermen.
He says his best trip was with his pals from the army, some rookies, I think.
'Have you done your military service yet?' asks Roberto.
'Man, I'm telling you. But military service is not what it was. I had to do it in
Madrid, like almost everyone these days, and nothing, you left every Friday at mid-
day and by four o'clock you were back home, just as if it were any old job. Military
service is dead easy these days, a nonsense'.
The thug starts to talk to his girlfriend while I roll a joint.]
17 See Montgomery (1995: 103).

Notes to Chapter 5

1 For a discussion of the forms used with the pronoun *vos*, see 6.0.
2 For a discussion of the passive and the use of *se*, see a standard grammar of
Spanish, for example Butt and Benjamin (1994: 362–74).
3 For a discussion of typical usage, see, for example, Butt and Benjamin (1994:
375–81).
4 See Butt and Benjamin (1994: 223–26).
5 See Lope Blanch (1995).
6 See Butt and Benjamin (1994, Chapter 15).
7 See also Chapter 9.
8 For a discussion of standard expression of modality, see, for example, Butt and
Benjamin (1994).
9 JB: No, it's . . . it's obvious that given that in this city, which taking in the province
has half a million inhabitants, there's only one newspaper, and, of course, if
there were (*-ra* form) two, we'd be more on the ball, we'd . . .
FF: Yes, but I think that that wouldn't . . . or rather doesn't affect the quality, I
think, well, even if there were (*-se* form) another newspaper, well of course, as
Julián says, it would make you be a bit more alert. (My translation)
10 See Silva-Corvalán (1989: 128–39).
11 A comprehensive description of this area of morpho-syntax can be found in standard grammars of Spanish, for example, Butt and Benjamin (1994), Alarcos Llorach
(1994).
12 See, for example, Fernández Ramírez (1951) Barrenechea and Alonso (1973),
Rosengren (1974), Silva-Corvalán (1982), Haverkate (1984), Enríquez (1984),
Bentivoglio (1987).
13 See Chapter 6.
14 [Look the thing is . . . there's a whole question which I find important . . . what you
just said . . . the question of inertia . . . I don't know if you've noticed . . . I at least
have . . . have seen it that in general amongst the students women are quite a bit
more conscientious than the men. . . .] (My translation)
15 See Chapter 8.
16 See Lavandera (1982) for her study of variation between *vos/usted* and *uno* in Buenos
Aires Spanish.
17 [then when in the morning you know that there's going to be a student demonstra-

tion or . . . well something like that you find out a bit about what it's about . . . you look, well, I at least look. . . .

'you get to class . . . so in the class of the three hundred students who are registered for it . . . well normally there are a hundred and fifty, a hundred and sixty . . . you get to class you give your class and you leave] (My translation)

18 For a much fuller description of gender, see, for example Butt and Benjamin (1994: 1–16).

19 See Butt and Benjamin (1994: 312–18) for a comprehensive review of the contexts in which 'personal *a*' can be used.

20 See Butt and Benjamin (1994: 464–75) for a discussion of word order.

Notes to Chapter 6

1 For a comprehensive discussion of forms of address in Spanish, see Carricaburo (1997).

2 [The reciprocal use of *tú* is very Spanish. It is almost an emblem of the new Spain. Is it a sin? There are people who see in this deluge of the use of *tú* the beginning of the end of authority and respect.] (My translation)

3 For a historical account of forms of address in Spanish, see Penny (1991: 123–5).

4 See Lipski (1994) for a more detailed country-by-country discussion of pronominal use and usage in Latin America.

5 [Now that those of us who are between thirty-five and forty-five would use *tú* with the Leviathan itself, that is with national and regional ministers, using *tú* with somone has lost any emotional charge.] (My translation)

6 See, for example, Pitt-Rivers (1971).

7 See Beinhauer (1978: 27).

8 See Carricaburo (1997: 52–3).

9 [MA: And in the studio we have three guests who are the representatives of what we see as the three most important Holy Week committees of the region, although we'd better tread carefully because we all know what the jealousies and the competition can be like in an activity even such as this one. I start on my right, Salvio Barrioluenga, good afternoon!

SB: Good afternoon!

MA: Secretary of the Holy Week committee of León. How are you?

SB: Very well, very well, I'm delighted to be here with you (fam.).

MA: Francisco Fernández Santamaría, secretary of the Holy Week committee of Valladolid. Good afternoon!

FF: Good afternoon!

MA: And Eduardo Pedrero, who is the only chairman, rather than secretary of the Holy Week committee of Zamora, isn't that right?

EP: Yes, indeed.

MA: Do you (fam.) agree that these are the three most important or is there another? Have I left anyone out?

SB: Well, I think that that would be . . .] (My translation)

10 [B: Of course don Gildo (don + first name), now I'll give you what you (formal) asked for on the telephone.

A: Many thanks Carlos Alberto (both first names) Rest (fam.) assured that this money will be put to good use. You (fam.) can be absolutely sure of it.

B: I know, don Gildo. That is why I can give it to you without you needing to tell me what it is for.

A: I have no reason to hide it from you, boy. This money is going to help a young girl who after a long time has gone back to studying again. Oh, and, if that time in Tampico I wasn't very pleasant to you I did it because I'm an interfering old man who thought he was doing the right thing, man. Forgive me, boy.

B: Would that in the life of all men there were always an interfering old man to rebuke you just as you did to me, don Gildo.

A: You've always had a good heart, Pineda, Pinedita (+ dim.) as our dearly departed Nestor would have said, God rest his soul from the irritation that we all have caused him, with no respect for his memory. Well, son, this old crock is on his way. I have a lot to do.

B: Wait for me, don Gildo. I have thought a great deal about you recently. Look, here in the company there are always technical problems. I feel I should insist on your working for us as soon as possible, Engineer don Gildo Soberanes.]
(My translation)

Notes to Chapter 7

1 The Plain English campaign is one of a number of advocates of the use of 'plain language', i.e. lay vernaculars, rather than arcane professional jargon, with the aim of making texts accessible to a considerably wider readership. For a discussion of plain language, see Cameron (1995).

2 [ILLUSTRIOUS SIR

Sir............................. born in ...., province of .... of ....
years of age, resident in .... province of ...., street of
............................., n° ...., National Identity Card n° ....
delivered in .... date .... of .... of 19...........,
to Your Worship states:

That he has finished at the University School of Languages (of Translators and Interpreters) the studies that fulfil the degree of .... and wishing to pay the statutory fees for the issue of the relevant Diploma, to Your Worship:

BEGS that you will deign to dispense the enclosed application which he submits to the superiority in supplication that to him may be issued the aforementioned Diploma of ....

        May God keep Your Worship for many years,
        Bellaterra, ... the .... of 19........
                    (signature of the interested party)]
(My translation)

3   [Official Academic Certificate
Sir..
Secretary of ....

I CERTIFY: That on account of the records held in the Secretariat of this Centre it follows that .... born in .... province of .... born on the day .... of .... of ...., of nationality .... has followed and passed all the courses which make up the Diploma of Translation and Interpreting (.....................................), according to the curriculum of 21-7-86 (BOE 4-9-86).
Passed the whole course on the day of .... of .... of ...., obtaining the qualification of PASS.
Paid the fees for the issue of the Diploma on the .... of .... of .... Fulfilled all the requirements under current regulations, is issued this certificate with the authorization of the most illustrious sir Dean in order for the

relevant diploma to be issued to you, in Bellaterra on the .... of .... of
....

Authorization

The Dean,   The Official,   The Secretary.] (My Translation)

4 [The undersigned ('the Sender') acknowledges that, by virtue of this document, notwithstanding the agreement provided by DHL Internacional España, on our request that the charges that they incur in respect of the services provided under the protection of the aforementioned aerial cognizance will be met by the addressee, that we shall continue to assume complete responsibility to meet all charges payable by the Sender in respect of the services provided under the protection of the afore-mentioned aerial cognizance, inclusive of freight charges, taxes, customs duties, administrative charges and charges in respect of storage and return of delivery to ourselves, these to be determined exclusively by themselves, engaging ourselves to meet the abovementioned charges without delay upon your request.] (My translation)

5 [Dear (+ first name):

I am sorry to have to inform you (fam.) that for unforeseen personal reasons, the Sports Coordinator of this District Council will not be able to attend the meeting to be held next Saturday, 24 October, concerning the games to be held in that city in 1993.

Nonetheless, he has requested me to inform you of the intention of this District Council to take part in the aforementioned games in accordance with the provisions that you communicated to us, although it will not be possible for us to participate under the rubric golf, given that this sport is not played in our locality.

I take advantage of this opportunity to send you my warmest regards.

(name of town), 21 October 1992

DIRECTOR OF CULTURAL ACTIVITIES

P.S. Please send me a fax to confirm that you have received this and that you under-stand what I mean by it.] (My translation)

6 [In Lima on the ninth of February nineteen hundred and ninety-three, appear in the courtroom Mr (+ name), identified by his electoral card (+ number), on the electoral register, born in Lima, twenty-five years old, cohabitee, second year of secondary education, trader and Ms (+ name), identified by her military certificate (+ number), twenty-two years old, born in Lima, cohabitee in his house, fourth year of sec-ondary education, (both) resident in (+ address) being present in these proceedings the Provincial Attorney, Dr (+ name), identified by her papers issued by the Ministry of Public Affairs, all gathered together to carry out the formalities of Consent which must be completed by the birth parents of the minor subject of these proceedings, which are carried out in the following terms:

In these proceedings, on not possessing an electoral card the lady, that is at her twenty-two years she declares she does not have an electoral card, she will be cited at a new date for her appearance, will be taking place ONLY THE DECLARATION OF THE BIRTH FATHER who is duly identified, . . .]

(. . .)

[RULING ON RECORD TWO HUNDRED AND FOUR. -Lima, Twenty second of May of nineteen hundred and ninety-three. -Being in relation to the rightfulness in the foregoing: May the Judgment of the date of the seventeenth of May of nine-teen hundred and ninety-three, relating to records two hundred and two hundred and one and decreeing the text of record two hundred and three be taken as agreed, May it be informed in accordance with arrangements.——————— It is a faithful copy of the original in reference and to which I refer in case of need. -I issue the present document in original form duly corrected and collated in accordance with the Law. -Lima, on the twenty-sixth day of the month of May of nineteen hundred and ninety-three.—————] (My translation)

7 [III. –That by this act gives
   CONSENT
   that were it necessary in law, in its particular case, to the aforementioned testamentary will, given that in the case of such a bequest she should receive nothing, and the sole bequest in favour of the wife of the deceased, mother of the person appearing before me now is in accordance with the law.
   In it is ratified, after a reading that I, the Notary, have given of the legal document, which she also reads understanding the Spanish language in which it is drafted, by signature. I identify her by means of the documentation shown. Of which and of the content of the legal document which I draw up on two sheets of paper stamped by the State, exclusively for notarial documents, series . . . , numbers . . . , I, the Notary, testify. Signed and sealed:
   Mark, signature and flourish:
   With the seal of the Notary's Office] (My translation)

8 See Cillán Apalategui (1970) for a discussion of the content and style of a number of Franco's speeches to the Spanish Cortes from 1943–67.

9 [We must show also, with the same clarity, with the same incontrovertible conclusiveness of the facts, that a modern State with authority is not an arbitrary State, nor a brutal State, nor a police State, nor a dictatorial State. A modern State with authority can be, and Spain is one, a State of Law, in which the citizens feel to be guaranteed their civil rights, protected their life, their property, their family, their job, their wish to live as they please, within a respect for the common good and the good of each one of their compatriots. A State with full authority over the interests of the individual and of the group, on which its existence does not depend and gives to each what should be his own; it is at all times in a position to say 'no', as much to the irresponsible demands of demagoguery as to the canvassing of the pressure groups of the powerful. All this is possible thanks to an executive power which has been and will continue to be vigorous and effective, and to a judicial power of absolute integrity and independence, which fairly chastises or absolves the individual or the State, the corporation or the member, with no other aim but the proper application of the law. We have now these Cortes renewed and rejuvenated, emanation and representation of the people, which through them lets their voice be heard and expresses their hopes, their desires, their ambitions, their fears or their indignation. Each of you has entered into a sacred bond of fidelity with the Spanish people, of whom those who elected you are part. Your assiduous and diligent work on committees, your close and constant contact with those who elected you, your sense of duty, of responsibility and of justice are the only conditions which in the eyes of your compatriots can justify the fulfilment of the mandate which you exercise through the will of the people.] (My translation)

10 [We should all think of the present and the future of Spain, albeit in different ways. To make these different ways compatible and combine them in the service of the common interest is what the citizens demand of us through their overwhelming vote.
   Our aspiration as socialists, with the responsibility to govern for all Spaniards, is constantly to increase the freedoms of the individuals and the communities of Spain.] (My translation)

11 [We understand that the chronification of structural unemployment by 7.5 (. . .) is not sufficient argument not to accept the consolidation at least of the idea for debate in later tax years (. . .) It is not possible to approach in a capitual manner, in short, a problem which demands integrated solutions, global solutions, whether they be macroeconomic, microeconomic or promotional in nature.] (My translation)

12 [In view of the importance of small and middle-sized businesses as a source of employment, growth and competitivity, efforts have been made to facilitate their greater access to information, training and research, by removing obstacles to their good functioning.

As regards energy, substantial progress has been made on the directive on common norms in the electricity sector.

Regarding research and development, efforts have been concentrated on adapting the IV framework programme as a result of enlargement.

As regards the environment, of note is the common position arrived at regarding the revision of the LIFE programme, as well as the important debate on water policy.

In the field of transport, amongst other achievements, it has been possible to agree a common stance in respect of the directive relating to size in road transport and there has been the adoption of the directive on baggage handling for air transport.

In agriculture efforts have centred on those market organizations awaiting revision, approving the one for rice and achieving progress in the one relating to wine. We are awaiting the ruling of this Assembly on the reform of the market organization for fruit and vegetables so that it may be adopted as soon as possible.

Finally, regarding fisheries, the most important achievement has been the full integration of Spain and Portugal and, in the ambit of foreign relations, the agreement reached with the Kingdom of Morocco.] (My translation)

13 [Honourable Congress of the Union, Mexican people:

With the respect which is customary amongst the Powers of the Union, I attend the opening of the first ordinary period of session of the Congress. At the same time, I now deliver the report on the general state of the public administration of the country. In this way, I have fulfilled the terms of the constitution. It is particularly pleasing that this duty be met in the rebuilt seat of the Chamber of Deputies, the new refurbishment of which makes it, at one and the same time, a more appropriate space for the work of legislation and a place more fitting for democracy.

Aims and achievements

In the last government report, I expressed my firm commitment to continuing with the change that the Mexican people have demanded: change to consolidate links abroad, and, within the country, change to promote a new relationship between the State and society. In this way, we are seeking a greater presence of Mexico in the world, a greater and more secure exercise of liberties in our fatherland, a greater stability in the conditions affecting productive life and more opportunity to achieve well-being, especially for those who need it most.] (My translation)

14 [I would ask you one question. If the Helms-Burton law, the Torricelli law and whole lot of them, if the cynical politicians who are this day in charge of that Northern neighbour, were to continue to act the way they have up until now for many more years and were to continue with the blockade and their hostilities for fifty years, would you be prepared to give in? Would you be prepared to hand over your fatherland? The Revolution? Socialism? That strong and vibrant 'no' is the only response that can be expected of you and the only response that we expect from you.

Socialism or death!

Fatherland or death!

We shall overcome!] (My translation)

15 ['Democracy is not chaos'

MEXICO – Now that there is a balance of power, we are also obliged to admit to the people, that democracy does not imply chaos or violence and that Mexico has lost its fear of democracy, observed today the member of the federal parliament, Porfirio Muñoz Ledo.

Muñoz Ledo, convenor of the parliamentary group of the Party of Revolutionary

Democracy in the Chamber of Commons, in a radio interview rejected the idea
that rebellion implies violence.
The legislator from the PRD . . .] (My translation)
16 [The central government representative in Extremadura calls the PSOE the 'travelling companions of terrorists.'
The central government representative in Extremadura, Oscar Baselga, declared yesterday that nobody is going to teach him lessons about democracy much less 'those
who for so long were travelling companions of State terrorists and barrack-room
mutineers' alluding to the socialists, informs EFE.
Baselga made these declarations after the socialist parliamentary group asked for
him to appear before the Commission for Justice and Home Affairs to report on
the actions of the security forces on what has been called the Madrid march in
defence of state education, held last Saturday. The trades unions denounced the
fact that members of the Civil Guard had appeared in a number of school institutions some days previously in order to discover who would be participating in the
march.] (My translation)
17 See Cameron (1995: 125).
18 [It goes . . . A man meets a friend and he says:
Joder, on Sunday I was at the Zarzuela (racecourse), watching the horses, minding
my own business, when suddenly a guy gets on my back and starts to beat me with
a whip!
Jo! And what did you do then?
Joer, the best I could! I came in fourth.] (My translation)
19 [This is one about a man who has eleven children and, and he meets another man
and says, the one who has eleven children says:
Hello, how are you doing?
And the other says:
Jo, I'm fine but you, what with your eleven children must be . . .
He says:
Me cagüen diez (lit. 'I defecate on ten'), why ever did I have eleven children . . . !
And the other says:
Well, at least there's one of them still clean.] (My translation)
20 [B: joder the one in the helicopter tío (man)
       A: they're polluting the ozone coño and then they go and tell us not to use aerosols
       D: because you (fart) like fury/so you do
       B: and that does destroy the ozone layer] (My translation)

Notes to Chapter 8

1 For an introduction to conversational analysis, see Sacks, Schegloff and Jefferson
  (1974) and Wardhaugh (1998: Chapter 12). For an introduction to discourse analysis,
  see Brown and Yule (1983).
2 [Mr President, I wish to make known to this House the concern that exists in my
  country, and especially in two of its regions, at the situation that has arisen. A few
  months ago the Spanish government put forward a new plan scaling down the
  Spanish steel industry to take account of market conditions, a plan which, seen in
  the context of the European steel industry is, may we again insist and affirm, a
  coherent and bold plan which, furthermore, is going to have some serious consequences for the two regions that have been referred to here, the Basque Country and
  Asturias.] (No. 3-429/54)
3 [. . . well, when it had finished some of us, as a matter of fact four of us went into a
  bar, and we were having some beer and some wine and stuff and the police came in

and asked for our identity cards, and took us to the station to check them; well, we talked about everything but the weather. Nothing, it was all very, very informal and stuff, well it didn't bloody amuse us, as you can imagine, but anyway they let us go right away; it is known that as we didn't have a criminal record or anything, well, they probably only wanted to frighten us, I don't know, the thing is that they let us go.] (My translation)

4 [According to the declarations of a number of representatives from this faculty, 'once the students had broken up, two secret police entered a bar where groups of students from the Faculty of Arts were drinking wine, and asked three students and a young man not carrying identification to accompany them to the police station. After they provided all their particulars, the Police allowed them to leave'.] (My translation)

5 See for example Briz (1995, 1998), Cortés (1986), Narbona (1998), Steel (1976), and Vigara (1980, 1992).

6 [PF: The thing is this morning, this morning, this morning in the university area they . . . , well, when we saw the police they went and told me that they're out again, I'm not sure if it's the medical students . . .

MD: Yes, but the thing is that well . . . well yes, the story has to be covered in case anything happens but, the truth is that demonstrations no longer interest anyone because the people are already tired of . . . telling them that, well, here they are demonstrating, here they are going somewhere, and so on. If at some point they think of something a bit more imaginative, more ingenious, something that gives us all a good laugh, then fair enough; and if not, well let's give the normal news that we cover on a daily basis and that's it.] (My translation)

7 Neighbor: And your little sister? Everybody's okay?
  F10: Oh my little sister =
  Neighbor: = What's wrong?
  F10: You know she's always been a jewel, studying
  Neighbor:
  F10: = she has problems with one of her courses, for a change. Now she's hit me with – not with Math any more, she's okay there =
  Neighbor: = Okay =
  F10: >now she's hit me with English< =
  Neighbor: = okay =
  F10: = you see?
  Neighbor: She's not doing well in English? that is true– =
  F10: Not doing well is putting it mildly
  Neighbor: = all the kids are the same. No, kids say I'm not doing well but no, they learn fast
  F10: I hope so because I'm very worried
  Neighbor: Do you know I give English classes?
  F10: Yeah?
  Neighbor: Yeah: whenever you want? (Translation by García (1993: 134–5))

8 For a discussion of the major area of linguistic politeness, see Brown and Levinson (1987).

9 [MD: Hey, it seems to me that . . . that what you've got to do is . . . you go off and cover the news at the Town Hall, the plenary that's going to be held this afternoon and the press conference that's afterwards and, then, I'll deal with . . . with the whole area of labour relations.
  And, what's more, as afterwards there'll be the mayor's press conference to tell what the whole story's been about, well, then, what you have to . . . what is done is . . . that's all covered and, then, you prepare about three minutes for tomorrow, you leave a news bulletin ready for Pura for her to use it at . . . at seven thirty, in her slot, you know, something a lot lighter because at that time

people are still half asleep, and then, well, well, well, well you put together, for
our news slot at a quarter to two, the normal news bulletin.

That's been covered, you can leave it perfectly well for tomorrow, there's
no . . . with that . . . that item, forget about it in principle. And then, the
labour issue, what yes you can ask the mayor in the press conference is what's
happening about the collective agreement.

(. . .)

PF: Demonstrations, the works committee for . . .

(. . .)

MD: That, leave them, forget them because you're going to have enough with the
thing about . . .

And then . . . then there's the . . . wait and see, the issue about the union
(Comisiones Obreras) at the psychiatric hospital yes it is appropriate that
tomorrow morning, not now, you make a phone call to the council . . .

PF: What's that about?

MD: Well a strike called by Comisiones Obreras at the psychiatric hospital on
account of staffing policy. So, you, as you know the folk at the council very
well, then you give them a phone call and let them tell you the employers'
side of things on this issue.] (My translation)

10 M8: Dear neighbour, I want to ask you a favour, I want you to – if it's possible,
if you could give my brother who's eleven, some English classes? I don't
know.

(Translation by García 1993: 132)

11 Neighbor: What's new? How nice to see you!

M3: Just taking a walk. Oh (0.2) knowing that you're an expert in languages,
in English

Neighbor: Thank you =

M3: = I'd like you to give Leni (0.2) uhm some classes

Neighbor: okay

(Translation by García 1993: 140)

Notes to Chapter 9

1 For an introduction to pidgins and creoles see Fasold (1990, Chapter 7); for an
introduction to Romance creoles, see Green (1990b: 420–73); for a discussion of
zamboangueño, see Lipski (1987a and b); for a discussion of *papiamento* see
Munteanu in Alvar (1996a); and for a discussion of *palenquero* see Joaquín Montes
in Alvar (1996a).

2 For a fuller description of *papiamento* see Munteanu in Alvar (1996a: 68–78).

3 See, for example, Gómez Molina (1986) for a discussion of the numerous influences of Spanish on *valenciano*, a variety of Catalan.

4 For a discussion of the varieties of Spanish spoken in Castellón, see Blas Arroyo
(1992).

5 For a detailed description of this variety, see Suárez Molina (1996).

6 See Lipski (1994: 175–76).

7 For an account of Spanish/Italian language contact see Meo Zilio (1989).

8 [The man was very interested and, he had already found out, the boss who had
taken me on to work was very happy he says that I boy is a boy who works then the
man said, he says yes, he says, make yourself useful, he says, make yourself useful
because the man's very happy, very pleased. The man had said to me, he says,
Roque, he says, you stay three days . . .] (My translation)

9 For further reading on this area see Amastae and Elías-Olivares (1982) and Bergen
(1990).

10 [Guacha (person from Mexico city), why don't you help me with a lift and leave me

home? And while you go for *el Chente*, I'll have a wash, brush my hair and get dressed up.] (My translation)

11 See Sánchez in Amastae and Elías-Olivares (1982) for a detailed description of Chicano Spanish.

12 [–See last night Juan arrived shutting the latch against Filomena. He made such a rumpus that, God spare me! And to cap it all well didn't Pedro decide to go and raise hell to put a stop to Juan. There's no one who can calm him down but Pedro is very stubborn.

    –Really, so he made him back right down?

    –Come on, he didn't get a chance, because right away the police arrived and laid into everybody. From there Filomena let herself come out.

    –Really, so she wanted them to come and get her?

    –Well, yes, . . .] (My translation)

13 [A: Good day, can I help you?

    B: Yes, is that the primary school inspectorate?

    A: Yes, here it is, can I help you?

        (. . .)

    B: Well, then, thank you very much for the information.

    A: Not at all, goodbye, good day] (My translation)

14 [He says, 'Listen, Father,' he says,

    'are you the one who saves women from sin (sinful women)?'

    He says, 'Yes, son, yes.'

    He says, 'Save me two for Saturday, please.'] (My translation)

15 Timms provides the following translation of the Spanish sections: l. 1 'cockroaches' (marijuana cigarettes), ll. 2–3; 'of wheat paper/and the harvest of the sun', ll.5–8: 'flying to the sun/and the wings of wheat/to fly/in the spring time', ll. 11–12: 'the cockroach dies/and bites the dust', l.14 'of *atole* [cornmeal gruel] with the finger.

Glossary

Acronym A word derived from the initial letters of the words that make up a name, e.g. *la ONU* (The United Nations Organization).

Adjacency pairs Certain kinds of utterances which tend to co-occur, such as questions and answers, summonses and responses. The second part can be a **preferred response,** e.g. that a request will be acceded to, or a **dis-preferred response**, e.g. a refusal to meet a request.

Affixes These are morphemes which can be attached to the beginning of a **root (prefixes)**, e.g. *euro*diputado, (Euro MP) or to its end (**suffixes**), e.g. *eurocracia* (Eurocracy), to form a new word.

Affricates Air obstructed by a complete closure made at some point in the mouth on release creates a plosive sound followed by **fricative**, e.g. [d].

Allophone The phonetic variants of a phoneme are known as allophones. The phoneme /n/ is pronounced differently in, for example, *cuando* and *nada*.

Alveolar Refers to a consonant sound made by the tongue against the alveolar ridge (just behind the upper teeth), e.g. [l].

Apodosis The consequence of an 'if' clause, usually following the **protasis**, e.g. *Si como mucho* (protasis) *me engordo* (apodosis).

Assimilation The adaptation, in whole or in part, of a borrowed item to the phonology/prosody, orthography and morphology of the host language, e.g. *márketing*.

Back-channelling A minimal intervention in a verbal interaction supportive of another speaker's **turn**.

Bilabial This refers to a consonant sound made by the coming together of the lips, e.g. [b].

Bilingualism Societal bilingualism refers to communities where individuals can use either of two languages; individual bilingualism refers to individuals who can use two languages.

Borrowing Word transferred from one language to another, e.g. *pub*.

Calque A 'loan translation' where the component parts of a borrowed word or phrase are translated into another language, e.g. *rascacielos* (from skyscraper).

Clitic A form which resembles a word but which cannot stand on its own, e.g. *le* (to him).

Code-switching Switching from one language to another.

Cognate Languages which share a common ancestor can be said to be cognate. Hence Spanish is cognate with Catalan, Portuguese and Italian amongst others.

Collocate A word which is commonly combined with another, e.g. to draft (and not write) a bill.

Compound The creation of a new word through the combination of independent words already existing in the language, e.g. *cazatalentos* (talent spotter).

Creole Creoles are similar to pidgins except that they have native speakers of their own and their range of functions is more extended and elaborated through more complex structures and a wider range of vocabulary.

Deictics Features of language which refer directly to the context of utterance, i.e. the situation (time, place, participants) in which the words are used, e.g. *ahora, aquí, yo*.

Dental Refers to a consonant sound made by the tongue against the teeth, e.g. [t].

Derivation A process of word formation employing **affixes**.

Description Describing the language as it is used (cf. **prescription**).

Dialect A variety of a language, generally geographical but also social.

Dialect levelling The elimination of distinctive features of local or regional varieties of a language.

Discourse The ways in which certain social groups use language to convey their attitudes towards certain areas of socio-cultural activity, e.g. racist discourse, officialese, sexist discourse.

Dispreferred response See **adjacency pair**.

Distance Degree of common interests between speakers (based, for example, on family, birthplace, profession).

Domain An institutionalized social situation such as a business meeting, church sermon.

Ellipsis That part of a sentence or utterance which is succinctly referred to or left out but can generally be recovered by reference to context.

Face(-threatening-act) See **politeness**.

Field See **register**.

Form Linguistic units such as sentences, morphemes, lexemes, nouns, etc.

Fricative A sound where audible friction is heard caused by the proximity of two vocal organs to each other, e.g. [f]. High frequency fricatives are known as **sibilants**, e.g. [s].

Function (In contrast with **form**) what language accomplishes, e.g. making a request, expressing an attitude.

Gemination A stylistic strategy, consisting of repetitive use of sets of terms for related concepts, e.g. *estas Cortes* **renovadas y reverdecidas, emanación y representación** *del pueblo*.

Genre   Conventionalized communicative events (written and/or spoken) recognized as such by the professional communities which adopt them, for example, the genre of a political speech.

Glide   A semi-vowel i.e. a sound in between a consonant and a vowel such as [j] and [w].

Graphemes   See **orthography**.

Homonyms   Words with the same spelling and the same sound but with different meanings, e.g. *mi* (my) and *mí* (me, disjunctive pronoun).

Hypercorrection   Occurs where a speaker of a non-standard variety produces inappropriate 'corrections' to their speech in an attempt to approximate to the prestige norm, e.g. they may pronounce *bacalado* for *bacalao*, perceiving the *-ao* ending to be that of the past participle in its stigmatized form (and not that of a noun) and 'correcting' it to the prestige form *-ado*.

Illocutionary force   The intended communicative effect of an utterance, e.g. a request.

Lateral   A sound made by air being released around the sides of a partial closure, e.g. [l].

Lexis   Vocabulary.

Lexicalization   The creation of words to cover a particular semantic field, e.g. computer terminology.

Lexeme   See **root**.

Marked   A feature which is distinctive (cf. **unmarked**).

Metathesis   The transposition of phonemes in a word, e.g. *estógamo* for *estómago*.

Modality   The attitude of a speaker towards a proposition, as expressed by items such as 'perhaps', 'may', 'should'.

Mode   See **register**.

Morpheme   See **morphology**.

Morphology   The system of word structure in a language based on **morphemes** which are the minimal distinctive units of grammar.

Muletillas   'Empty' words and set phrases.

Nasal stop   See **stop**.

Negative Politeness   Strategies whereby a speaker attends to the negative face (see **politeness**) of the hearer. For example, when making a request a speaker strives not to impose on the hearer 'If it's not too much bother, I wonder if you could give me a lift'.

Neologism   A new coinage.

Oral stop   See **stop**.

Orthography   Spelling, made up of graphemes or single letters used to relay vowel and consonant sounds. Spanish also has digraphs, that is double letter combinations used to relay single phonemes and employs **diacritics** which are symbols used, for example, to indicate **stress** e.g. *ira* and *irá* ('anger' and 'will go') or to differentiate between **homonyms** e.g. *él* and *el* ('he and 'the').

Palatal Refers to a consonant sound made by the front of the tongue and the hard palate, e.g. [ʎ].

Phonetics The description and classification of speech sounds.

Phoneme See **phonology**.

Phonology This refers to the description of the sound system of a particular language, describing its **phonemes**, or minimal units in the sound system of the language, and the ways they combine with each other.

Pidgin Pidgins tend to develop as trade languages and to draw on the lexical resources of a third colonial language such as French, English, Spanish, Portuguese or Dutch.

Planned discourse Discourse where a speaker knows in advance what will be said, either because he or she is working from a written script (as in a speech) or a memorized one (as in reciting poetry).

Plosive See **stop**.

Politeness In Brown and Levinson's model (1987), all speakers have a **positive** and a **negative face**, i.e. the desire to be approved of and the desire for unimpeded freedom of action. An act may threaten the face of the speaker or the hearer, e.g. a directive would threaten the hearer's negative face. Speakers may adopt linguistic strategies to mitigate these **face-threatening acts**. How they do so is influenced by factors such as **power**, **distance** and the perceived weight of the face-threatening act, e.g. asking for a large sum of money is generally more threatening than asking for a small sum.

Positive Politeness Strategies whereby a speaker attends to the positive face (see **politeness**) of the hearer. For example, when making a request a speaker may appeal to the hearer's better nature: 'Be a sweetie; give me a lift'.

Power The power of individuals is based on factors such as age, social class, wealth, physical strength, institutional role.

Prosody This is loosely a synonym for **suprasegmentals** and refers to variations in pitch, loudness, tempo and rhythm in speech.

Pragmatics The ways in which speakers use language for different communicative purposes, e.g. to give directives or to make requests.

Preferred response See **adjacency pair**.

Prescription Views on how a language ought to be used.

Prestige norm A variety of a language considered by a speech community to be the linguistic **standard** and valued as such, e.g. 'good' Spanish.

Protasis See **apodosis**.

Register This can be defined in terms of **field**, **mode**, and **tenor**. Field refers in general terms to what the text is about. **Mode** refers to the continuum between discourse which is written to be read through to unpreplanned spontaneous spoken discourse. **Tenor** refers both to the degree of formality in the relationship between speaker and hearer (e.g. formal, colloquial, intimate) also known as **interpersonal tenor** and also to the language function the speaker is engaged in (e.g. instructing, directing, requesting, thanking) or **functional tenor**. The main components of the interpersonal relationship are the relative statuses of participants, the degree of intimacy or distance between them and the purpose and domain of the interaction.

Repair   This takes place when a speaker self-corrects (self repair) or corrects another speaker (other repair).

Root   A base form of a word to which **affixes** may be attached.

Semantic extension   A word in a host language acquires additional meaning through contact with a donor language, e.g. *versátil* (originally 'inconstant' now 'adapatable').

Semantics   The study of meaning.

Semiotic   A dimension of context whereby an element of language choice may act as a sign, e.g. the choice of the Catalan spelling *la Generalitat* rather than the Hispanicized *la Generalidad* may connote pro-Catalan feelings.

Sibilant   See **fricative**.

Solidarity   See **distance**.

Standard language   See **prestige norm**.

Stops   These are sounds produced when air builds up behind a closure in the vocal tract and then released explosively. They can be **oral (plosives)** e.g. [t] or **nasal**, e.g. [m].

Stress   This refers to the prominence of a particular syllable or syllables within an utterance and is achieved usually by an increase in loudness of the syllable but also by increases in length and pitch. Grammatical stress refers to that stress which is determined by a series of linguistic constraints and over which the speaker has no control.

Suprasegmentals   These are features which continue over several successive phonemes and which mould meaning for the hearer, e.g. intonation (see **prosody**).

Syntax   The rules governing the combinations of words in sentences and between them.

Tenor   See **register**.

Turn   A speaker's intervention in verbal interaction (this is more extended than **back-channelling**).

Turn-taking   The participation of speakers in a conversation.

Unmarked   Not displaying any distinctive feature (cf. **marked**).

Unplanned discourse   Spontaneous speech where a speaker does not use a script whether written or memorized (see **planned discourse**).

Use variables   See **register**.

User variables   See **variety**.

Velar   Refers to a consonant sound made by the back of the tongue against the soft palate, e.g. [k], [g].

Variety   A variant of a language distiguishable by grammatical, phonological and lexical features. A variety may be determined by **user variables** (e.g. geographical provenance, age, sex, socio-economic group, ethnic group) and by **use variables** (see **register**).

Vibrant These sounds include flaps, or single taps by one articulator on another, e.g. *pero*, and trills, a series of rapid taps, as in *perro*.

Selected bibliography and further reading

ABC (1993) *Libro de estilo de ABC*, Barcelona: Prensa Española.

Agencia EFE (1989a) *Manual de español urgente*, Madrid: Agencia EFE.

Agencia EFE (1989b) *Normas básicas para los servicios informativos*, Madrid: Agencia EFE.

Alarcos Llorach, E. (1994) *Gramática de la lengua española*, Madrid: Espasa Calpe.

Alba de Diego, V. and Sánchez Vidal, J. (1980) 'Tratamiento y juventud en la lengua hablada. Aspectos sociolingüísticos' BRAE LX: 95–129.

Alberto Miranda, J. (1993) *Usos coloquiales del español*, Salamanca: Publicaciones del Colegio de España.

Alcina, J. and Blecua, J. M. (1980) *Gramática española*, Barcelona: Ariel.

Almela Pérez, R. (1991) 'La construcciones del tipo "delante suyo"' in C. Hernández *et al.* (eds.) *El español de América*, vol. 1, Valladolid: Junta de Castilla y León, 435–44.

Alvar, M. (1993) *La lengua de . . .*, Alcalá de Henares: Ediciones de la Universidad.

Alvar, M. (Dir.) (1996a) *Manual de dialectología hispánica: el español de América*, Barcelona: Ariel S.A.

Alvar, M. (Dir.) (1996b) *Manual de dialectología hispánica: el español de España*, Barcelona: Ariel S.A.

Alvar Esquerra, M. (Dir.) (1994) *Diccionario de voces de uso actual*, Madrid: Arco Libros.

Alvar Esquerra, M. (1995) *La formación de palabras en español*, Madrid: Arco Libros.

Alvarez, M. (1995) *Tipos de escrito III: epistolar, administrativo y jurídico*, Madrid: Arco Libros.

Alvarez de Miranda, P. (1994) in M. Seco, and G. Salvador, (coord.) *La lengua española, hoy*, Madrid: Fundación Juan March, 269–79.

Amastae, J. and Elías-Olivares, L. (eds.) (1982) *Spanish in the United States: Sociolinguistic Aspects*, Cambridge: Cambridge University Press.

Austin, J. L. (1962) *How to do things with words*, Oxford: Clarendon Press.

Azevedo, M. (1992) *Introducción a la lingüística española*, Englewood Cliffs NJ: Prentice Hall.

Bajo Pérez, E. (1997) *La derivación nominal en español*, Madrid: Arco Libros.

Ball, R. (1997) *The French speaking world*, London: Routledge.

Barrenechea, A. and Alonso, A. (1973) 'Los pronombres personales sujetos en el español hablado en Buenos Aires' in J. M. Lope Blanch *Los pronombres personales sujetos en el español hablado en las principales cuidades de América*, México: Universidad Nacional Automa de México.

Battye, A. and Hintze, M.-A. (1992) *The French Language Today*, London: Routledge.

Beinhauer, W. (1978) *El español coloquial*, 3rd edition, Madrid: Gredos

Bentivoglio, P. (1987) *Los sujetos pronominales de primera persona en el habla de Caracas*, Caracas: Universidad Central de Venezuela.

Bergen, J. J. (ed.) (1990) *Spanish in the United States: Sociolinguistic Issues*. Washington DC: Georgetown University Press

Berk-Seligson, S (1990) *The Bilingual Courtroom: Court Interpreters in the Judicial Process*, Chicago: University of Chicago Press.

Blas Arroyo, J. L. *et al.* (1992) *Variedades del castellano en Castellón*, Castelló: Diputació de Castelló.

Blas Arroyo, J. L. (1995) 'La función interpersonal del cambio de códigos en la interacción verbal' paper given at *II Simposio de pragmática y gramática del español hablado*, Universitat de València, 14–16 November 1995.

Bobes Naves, M. (1971) *Las personas gramaticales*, Santiago de Compostela: Universidad de Santiago de Compostela.

Bookless, T. (1994) 'Can Spanish take the strain? The neological pressures facing contemporary Spanish', *ACIS 7*: 8–9(2)

Briz, A. (coord.) (1995) *La conversación coloquial (materiales para su estudio)*, Valencia: Universitat de València.

Briz, A. (1998) *El español coloquial en la conversación*, Barcelona: Ariel.

Brown, G. and Yule, G. (1983) *Discourse Analysis*, Cambridge: Cambridge University Press.

Brown, P. and Levinson, S. (1987) *Politeness*, Cambridge: Cambridge University Press.

Brown, R. and Gilman, A. (1960) 'The pronouns of Power and Solidarity' in P. P. Giglioli (ed.) (1972) *Language and Social Context*, Harmondsworth: Penguin.

Butt, J. and Benjamin, C. (1994) *A New Reference Grammar of Modern Spanish*, 2nd edn, London: Arnold.

Calero Fernández, M. A. (1991), 'Los sexos y el sexo en los tacos, una cuestión etnolingüística' in *Actas de las VIII jornadas de investigación interdisciplinarias*, Madrid: Instituto Universitario de Estudios de la Mujer, Ediciones de la Universidad Autónoma de Madrid.

Calvi, N. V. and Monti, S. (1991) *Nuevas palabras–parole nuove*, Paravia: Turin.

Calvo Ramos, L. (1980) *Introducción al estudio del lenguaje administrativo: gramática y textos*, Madrid: Gredos.

Calzada, M. (1997) *Transitivity in Translating: The Interdependence of Text and Context*, unpublished PhD thesis, Heriot-Watt University.

Cameron, D. (1995) *Verbal Hygiene*, London: Routledege.

Canal Sur Televisión (1991) *Libro de estilo Canal Sur Televisión*, Sevilla: Canal Sur Televisión.

Carbonero Cano, P. (1982) 'Usos de las formas verbales *-ra* y *-se* en el habla de Sevilla (nivel popular)' in V. Lamíquiz (coord.) *Sociolingüística andaluza 1*, Sevilla: Universidad de Sevilla, 45–58.

Cárdenas Nanneti, J. (1959) *Manual de selecciones (Normas generales de redacción)*, La Habana: Reader's Digest.

Carrera de la Red, M. and Zamora Salamanca, F. J. (1991) 'Americanismos en la prensa bonaerense' in C. Hernández *et al.* (eds) *Actas del III congreso internacional de el español de América*, vol 1, Salamanca: Junta de Castilla y León, 1101–9.

Carricaburo, N. (1997) *Las fórmulas de tratamiento en el español actual*, Madrid: Arco Libros.

Casado Velarde, M. (1985) *Tendencias en el léxico español actual*, Madrid: Coloquio.

Casado Velarde, M. (1988), *Lenguaje y cultura*, Madrid: Síntesis.

Casado Velarde, M. (1993) *El castellano actual*, Pamplona: Eunsa.

Castañón Rodríguez, J. (1991) 'Hispanoamericanismos en el lenguaje futbolístico español', in C. Hernández *et al.* (eds) *El español de América*, vol. 2, Valladolid: Junta de Castilla y León.

Castañón Rodríguez, J. (1997) 'El fútbol y los libros de estilo' in R. Soca, *La página del idioma español*, http://www.el-castellano.com/duq.html.

Cillán Apalategui, A. (1970) *El léxico político de Franco en las cortes españolas*, Zaragoza: Dr. Casas.

Clyne, M. (1995) *The German Language in a Changing Europe*, Cambridge: Cambridge University Press.

Contreras, H. (1976) *A Theory of Word Order with Special Reference to Spanish*, Oxford: North Holland.

Cortes Generales, *Diario de sesiones del congreso de los diputados, pleno y diputación permanente*, Año 1995, V Legislatura, Núm. 180.

Cortés Rodríguez, L. (1986) *Sintaxis del coloquio: aproximación sociolingüística*, Salamanca: Universidad de Salamanca.

Cortés Rodríguez, L. (1994) *Tendencias actuales en el estudio del español hablado*, Almería: Universidad de Almería.

Cortés Rodríguez, L. (ed.) (1995) *El español coloquial*, Almería: Universidad de Almería.

Criado Costa, J. and Criado Costa, M. (1992) *Estudios de dialectología andaluza: el habla de San Sebastián de los Ballesteros*, Córdoba: Diputación Provincial de Córdoba.

Crystal, D. (1987) *The Cambridge Encyclopaedia of Language*, Cambridge: Cambridge University Press.

De Bruyne, J. (1995a) *A Comprehensive Spanish Grammar*, Oxford: Blackwell.

De Bruyne, J. (1995b) *Eutrapelias del alfabeto español*, Madrid: Visor.

De Granda, G. (1994) *Español de América, español de Africa y hablas criollas hispánicas*, Madrid: Gredos.

De Jonge, B. (1993) 'Pragmatismo y gramaticalización en el cambio lingüístico: *ser* y *estar* en expresiones de edad', *Nueva revista de filología española* XLI (1): 99–126.

De Kock, J. (1991) 'Pretéritos perfectos simples y compuestos en España y América' in C. Hernández *et al.* (eds.) *El español de América*, vol. 1, Valladolid: Junta de Castilla y León, 481–94.

De Mello, G. (1992a), 'Adjetivos adverbializados en el español culto hablado de diez ciudades', *Lingüística española actual* XIV: 225–42.

De Mello, G. (1992b) '*Se los* for *se lo* in the spoken cultured Spanish of eleven cities', *Hispanic Journal*, 13(1): 165–79.

De Mello, G. (1993) 'Pronombre relativo con antecedente humano' *Nueva revista de filología española* XLI (1): 75–98.

Díaz Barrado, M. P. (1989) *Análisis del discurso político*, Mérida: Editora Regional de Extremadura.

Díaz-Castañon, C. (1975) 'Sobre la terminación *-ado* en el español de hoy' in *Revista española de lingüística*. V(I): 111–20.

Díaz Rojo, J. (1994) 'Las metáforas sobre la situación política española en la primavera de 1994 a través de los medios de comunicación', *Español actual* 62/1994, Arco Libros S.L., 55–66.

Diego Quesada, J. (1997) 'Obituary: adiós de passive in Spanish', *La Linguistique*, 33(1): 41–62.

D'Introno, F., del Teso, E. and Weston, R. (1995) *Fonética y fonología actual del español*, Madrid: Cátedra.

Selected bibliography and further reading   223

The Economist (1996) The World in 1997, London: The Economist Publications.
El correo español, El pueblo vasco Libro de estilo, Bilbao: Bilbao Editorial.
El Mundo (1996) Libro de estilo, Madrid: Temas de Hoy.
El Mundo Deportivo (1995) Libro de estilo, Barcelona: El Mundo Deportivo.
El País (1980) El País: Libro de estilo, Madrid: PRISA.
El País (1990) El País : Libro de estilo, Madrid: Ediciones El País.
Enríquez, E. (1984) El pronombre personal sujeto en la lengua española hablada en Madrid, Madrid: CSIC.
Entwhistle, W. J. (1966) The Spanish Language together with Portuguese, Catalan and Basque, London: Faber and Faber.
Fasold, R. (1990) Sociolinguistics of Language, Oxford: Blackwell.
Fernández Calvo, R. (1996) Glosario básico de internet, Barcelona: ATI.
Fernández Ramírez, S. (1951) Gramática española: los sonidos, el nombre y el pronombre, Madrid: Revista de Occidente.
Fleischmann, S. and Waugh, L. (eds.) (1991) Discourse Pragmatics and the Verb, London: Routledge.
Flores Farfán, J. A. (1990) 'Ethnography of drug addicts in Mexico and Spain: some comparative findings on drug argots', Proceedings of the Community Epidemiology Group, Maryland: US Department of Health and Human Services.
Fontanella de Weinberg, B. (1973) 'Comportamiento ante -s de hablantes femeninos y masculinos del español bonaerense', Romance Philology 27: 50–8.
Fontanella de Weinberg, M. B. (1995) El español de América. Madrid: Mapfre.
Fontanillo, E. and Riesco, M. (1994) Teleperversión de la lengua, Barcelona: Anthropos.
Fuertes Olivera, P. (1992) Mujer, lenguaje y sociedad: los estereotipos de género en inglés y en español, Alcalá de Henares: Ayuntamiento de Alcalá de Henares.
Fundación Germán Sánchez Pérez (1990) El idioma español en las agencias de prensa, Madrid: Fundación Germán Sánchez Pérez.
Gallardo Paúls, B. (1998) Comentario de textos conversacionales, Madrid: Arco Libros.
Galván, R and Teschner, R (1991) El diccionario del español chicano, Lincolnwood: National Textbook Company.
García, C. (1992) 'Refusing an invitation: a case study of Peruvian style', Hispanic Linguistics 5(1–2): 207–43.
García, C. (1993) 'Making a request and responding to it: a case study of Peruvian Spanish speakers', Journal of Pragmatics (19): 127–32.
García, E. (1986) 'El fenómeno (de)queísmo desde una perspectiva dinámica del uso comunicativo de la lengua' in J. Moreno de Alba (ed.) Actas del II congreso internacional sobre el español de América, Mexico: Universidad Nacional Autónoma de México, 46–65.
García Meseguer, A. (1988) Lenguaje y discriminación sexual, 3rd edn, Barcelona: Montesinos.
García Meseguer, A. (1994) ¿Es sexista la lengua española?, Barcelona: Paidós.
García Mouton, P. (1994) Lenguas y dialectos de España, Madrid: Arco Libros
Gómez Font, A. et al. (1992) Vademécum del español urgente, Madrid: Agencia EFE.
Gómez Molina, J. (1986) Estudio sociolingüístico de la comunidad de habla de Sagunto, Valencia: Institut Alfons el Magnánim.
Gómez Molina, J. (1995) 'La variación lingüística en el español hablado en Valencia', paper given at II Simposio de pragmática y gramática del español hablado, Universitat de València, 14–16 November 1995.
Gooch, A. L. (1970) Diminutive, Pejorative and Augmentative Suffixes in Modern Spanish, Oxford: Pergamon.

Green, J. (1990a) 'Spanish' in M. Harris and N. Vincent (eds.) *The Romance Languages*, London: Routledge.

Green, J. (1990b) 'Romance creoles' in M. Harris and N. Vincent (eds.) *The Romance Languages*, London: Routledge.

Gregory, M. and Carroll, S. (1978) *Language and Situation: Language Varieties and their Social Contexts*, London: Routledge.

Grice, H. P. (1975) 'Logic and Conversation' in P. Cole and J.L. Morgan (eds) *Syntax and Semantics*, vol.3, *Speech Acts*, New York: Academic Press, 41–58.

Guerrero Ramos, G. (1995) *Neologismos en el español actual*, Madrid: Arco Libros.

Gutiérrez, M. J. (1992) 'The extension of *estar*: a linguistic change in progress in the Spanish of Morelia, Mexico', *Hispanic Linguistics* 5(1–2).

Haensch, G. (1997) *Los diccionarios del español en el umbral del siglo XXI*, Salamanca: Universidad de Salamanca.

Halliday, M. A. K. (1978) *Language as a Social Semiotic: the Social Interpretation of Language and Meaning*, London: Edward Arnold.

Harris, T. (1996) 'The current status of Judeo-Spanish in the United States and Israel' in *Donaire* 6, London: Consejería de Educación y Ciencia.

Hart-González, L. and Feingold, M. (1990) 'Retention of Spanish in the home' in *International Journal of the Sociology of Language* 84: 5–34.

Haverkate, H. (1984) *Speech Acts, Speakers and Hearers*, Amsterdam: John Benjamin.

Hickey, L. (1983/4) 'Some trends in contemporary Spanish' in *Vida hispánica*, Winter, 25–32.

Hickey, L. (1994) 'Word order in Spanish: four perspectives', *Occasional Papers Series* 14, Bristol: University of Bristol.

Hickey, L. and Vázquez Orta, I. (1994) 'Politeness as deference: a pragmatic view', *Pragmalingüística*, 2, Cádiz: Universidad de Cádiz.

Hodge, R. and Kress, G. (1993) *Language as Ideology*, 2nd edn, London and New York: Routledge.

Holmes, J. (1992) *An Introduction to Sociolinguistics*, London: Longman.

Jaramilla, J. (1990) 'Domain constraints on the use of TÚ and USTED.' in J. J. Bergen (ed.) *Spanish in the United States: Sociolinguistic issues*, Washington DC: Georgetown University Press.

Kjaerbeck, S. (1998) 'The organization of discourse in Mexican and Danish business negotiations', *Journal of Pragmatics* 30: 347–62.

Klein, F. (1979) 'Factores sociales en algunas diferencias lingüísticas en Castilla la Vieja', *Revista de sociología* II: 45–64.

Koine, D. A. (1994) 'Negation in Spanish and English suggestions and requests: mitigating effects', *Journal of Pragmatics* 21: 513–26.

Lambert, W. and Tucker, G. (1976), *Tu, vous, Vd*, Rowley, MA: Newbury House.

Lamíquiz, V. (Dir.) (1987) *Sociolingüística andaluza 4: encuestas del nivel popular*, Sevilla: Servicio de Publicaciones de la Universidad de Sevilla.

Lang, M. (1990) *Spanish Word Formation: Productive Derivational Morphology in the Modern Lexis*, London: Croom Helm.

Lara, L. F. (Dir.) (1982), *Diccionario fundamental del español de México*, Ciudad de México: El Collegio de Mexico.

Lara, L. F. (Dir.) (1986) *Diccionario básico del español de México*, Ciudad de México.

Latorre, G. (1991) 'Anglicismos en retirada: contacto, acomodación e intervención en un sistema léxico' in C. Hernández *et al.* (eds.) *El español de América*, vol. 2, Valladolid: Junta de Castilla y León, 765–73.

Lavandera, B. (1982) 'Creative variation: shifting between impersonal and personal in Spanish discourse', unpublished BA thesis Mimeo, Buenos Aires.

La Vanguardia (1986) *La Vanguardia: libro de estilo*, Barcelona: La Vanguardia TISA.

León, V. (1994) *Diccionario de argot español*, Madrid: Alianza.

Lipski, J. (1985) '/s/ in Central American Spanish', *Hispania* 68: 143–9.

Lipski, J. (1987a) 'Modern Spanish once-removed in Philippine Creole Spanish: The case of Zamboagueño', *Language in Society* 16: 91–108.

Lipski, J. (1987b) 'El español en Filipinas: comentarios sobre un lenguaje vestigial' in *Anuario de lingüística hispánica*, Valladolid: Universidad de Valladolid, 123–42.

Lipski, J. (1994) *Latin American Spanish*, Harlow: Longman.

Llorente Maldonado, A. (1977) 'Las construcciones de carácter impersonal en español' in M. Conde et al. (eds.) *Estudios ofrecidos a Emilio Alarcos Llorach*, vol. 1. Oviedo: Universidad de Oviedo.

Lope Blanch, J. (1994) 'El Colegio de México y la lengua española' in M. Seco and G. Salvador (coord.) *La lengua española, hoy*, Madrid: Fundación Juan March, 281–90.

Lope Blanch, J. M. (1995) 'El problema de la lengua española' in *Nueva revista de filología española*, XLIII (1): 17–36.

López García, A. and Morant, R. (1991) *Gramática femenina*, Madrid: Cátedra.

López Morales, H. (1989) *Sociolingüística*, Madrid: Gredos.

López Morales, H. (1994) ' 'in Seco, M. and Salvador, G. (coord.) *La lengua española, hoy*, Madrid: Fundación Juan March, 281–90.

Lorenzo, E. (1966) *El español de hoy, lengua en ebullición*, Madrid: Gredos.

Lorenzo, E. (1995) 'La derivación nominal en el español actual', *Donaire* 4: 35–41.

Lozano Domingo, I. (1995) *Lenguaje femenino, lenguaje masculino*, Madrid: Minerva.

Lunn, P. and Cravens, T. (1991) 'A contextual reconsideration of the Spanish *-ra* "indicative"' in S. Fleischmann and L. Waugh (eds.) *Discourse Pragmatics and the Verb*, London: Routledge.

MacPherson, I. R. (1975) *Spanish Phonology*, Manchester: Manchester University Press.

McWhorter, J. (1995) 'The scarcity of Spanish-based creoles explained', *Language in Society* 24: 213–44.

Mañas, J. A. (1994) *Historias del Kronen*, Barcelona: Destino.

Marcos Marín, F. (1979) *Reforma y modernización del español*, Madrid: Cátedra.

Mar-Molinero, C. (1997) *The Spanish-speaking World*, London: Routledge.

Marqués de Tamarón, (1995) *El peso de la lengua española en el mundo*, Valladolid: Secretariado de Publicaciones de la Universidad de Valladolid.

Marsá, F. (1986) *Diccionario normativo y guía práctica de la lengua española*, Barcelona: Ariel.

Martín Rojo, L. (1994) 'The jargon of delinquents and the study of conversational dynamics', *Journal of Pragmatics* 21: 243–90.

Medicina Clínica (1993) *Medicina Clínica: Libro de estilo*. Barcelona: Ed. Doyma S.A.

Meo Zilio, G. (1989) *Estudios hispanoamericanos: temas lingüísticos*, Roma: Bulzoni Editore.

Millán Garrido, A. (1997) *Libro de estilo para juristas*, Barcelona: Bosch.

Milroy, J. and Milroy, L. (1991) *Authority in Language*, 2nd edn, London: Routledge.

Ministerio de Administración Pública (1990) *Manual de estilo del lenguaje administrativo*, Madrid: MAP.

Ministerio de Asuntos Sociales/Instituto de la Mujer (1989) *Propuestas para evitar el sexismo en el lenguaje*, Madrid: Ministerio de Asuntos Sociales/Instituto de la Mujer.

Ministerio de Educación y Ciencia (Plan para la Igualdad de Oportunidades para la Mujer).

Ministerio de Educación y Ciencia (1988) *Recomendaciones para el uso no sexista de la lengua*, Madrid: Ministerio de Educación y Ciencia.

Ministerio de Relaciones con las Cortes y de la Secretaría de Gobierno (1987) *Vocabulario normalizado de informática*, Madrid: Ministerio de Relaciones con las Cortes y de la Secretaría de Gobierno.

Moliner, M. (1966) *Diccionario del uso del español*, 2 vols, Madrid: Gredos.

Montgomery, M. (1995) *An Introduction to Language and Society*, 2nd edn, London: Routledge.

Moreno Fernández, F. (1986) 'Sociolingüística de los tratamientos. Estudio sobre una comunidad rural', *Anuario de Letras*, vol. XXIV, México.

Moya Corral, J. and García Wiedemann, E. (1995) *El habla de Granada y sus barrios*, Granada: Universidad de Granada.

Mühlhaüsler, P. and Harré, R. (1990) *Pronouns and People: The Linguistic Construction of Social and Personal Identity*, Oxford: Blackwell.

Narbona, A., Cano, R., Morillo, R. (1998) *El español hablado en Andalucía*, Barcelona: Ariel.

Navarro Alcalá-Zamora, P. (1979), *Mecina*, Madrid: CSIC.

Orwell, G. (1966, first published 1938) *Homage to Catalonia*, Harmondsworth: Penguin.

Patiño Rosselli, C. (1989) 'Una mirada al criollo palenquero' in *Estudios sobre español de América y lingüística afroamericana*, Bogotá: Publicaciones del Instituto Caro y Cuervo, LXXXIII.

Paz, O. (1959) *El laberinto de la soledad*, 2nd edn, Mexico: Fondo de Cultura Económica.

Penny, R. (1991) *A History of the Spanish Language*, Cambridge: Cambridge University Press.

Pfaff, C. (1982) 'Constraints on language mixing: intrasentential code-switching and borrowing in Spanish/English' in J. Amastae and L. Elías-Olivares (eds.) *Spanish in the United States: Sociolinguistic Aspects*, Cambridge: Cambridge University Press.

Pitt-Rivers, J. A. (1971) *The People of the Sierra*, London: University of Chicago Press.

Placencia, M. A. (1994) 'Pragmatics across varieties of Spanish', *Donaire* 2: 65–76.

Placencia, M. A. (1995) 'Explicitness and ellipsis as features of conversational style in British English and Ecuadorian Spanish', *International Review of Applied Linguistics in Language Teaching* 33(2): 129–41.

Prego, V. (1995) *Así se hizo la transición*, Barcelona: Plaza y Janés.

Quesada Pacheco, M. A. (1996) 'El español de América central' in M. Alvar (Dir.) *Manual de dialectología hispánica: el español de España*, Barcelona: Ariel S.A.

Quilis, A. (1992) *La lengua española en cuatro mundos*, Madrid: Mapfre, S.A.

Quilis, A. (1997) *Principios de fonología y fonética españolas*, Madrid: Arco Libros.

RTVE (1985) *Manual de estilo de RTVE*, Barcelona: Labor.

Ramoncín (1993) *El tocho cheli*, Madrid: Temas de hoy.

Real Academia Española (1931) *Gramática de la lengua española nuevas normas de prosodia y ortografía* (1952), Madrid: Real Academia Española.

Real Academia Española (1973), *Esbozo de una nueva gramática de la lengua española*, Madrid: Espasa Calpe.

Rodríguez González, F. (ed.) (1989) *Comunicación y lenguaje juvenil*, Madrid: Fundamentos.

Rodríguez González, F. (1991) *Prensa y lenguaje político*, Madrid: Fundamentos.

Rodríguez González, F. (1993a) ' ' in *Prensa y lenguaje político*, Alicante: Instituto de Estudios Juan Gil Albert, 101–52.

Rodríguez González, F. (1993b) 'Las siglas como procedimiento lexicogenésico', *Estudios Lingüísticos de la Universidad de Alicante* 9: 9–24.

Rodríguez González, F. and Lillo Buades, A. (1997) *Nuevo diccionario de anglicismos*, Madrid: Gredos.

Rodríguez Izquierdo (1982) 'Economía y redundancia en el uso de sustitutos gramaticales' in P. Carbonero (ed.) *Sociolingüística andaluza 1*, Sevilla: Universidad de Sevilla.

Romero Gualda, M.V. (1991) 'Rasgos morfosintácticos de la prensa americana' in C. Hernández *et al.* (eds.) *Actas del III congreso internacional del español de América*, Vol. 1, Salamanca: Junta de Castilla y León, 541–9.

Romero Trillo, J. (1997) 'Your attention please: pragmatic mechanisms to obtain the addressee's attention in Spanish and English conversation', *Journal of Pragmatics* 28: 205–21.

Rosengren, P. (1974) *Presencia y ausencia de los pronombres personales en el español moderno*, Stockholm: Actas Universitatis Gothoburgensis.

Sacks H., Schegloff, E. and Jefferson, G. (1974) 'A simplest systematics for the organization of turn-taking in conversation', *Language* 50(4): 696–735.

Sala, R. (1991) 'Sobre la normalización lingüística en Cataluña', *ACIS* 4 (2): 18–23.

Schwenter, S.A. (1993), 'Diferenciación dialectal por medio de pronombres: una comparación del uso de tú y usted en España y México', *Nueva revista de filología hispánica* XLI (1): 127–49.

Seco, M. (1986) *Diccionario de dudas y dificultades de la lengua española*, Madrid: Espasa Calpe.

Seco, M. and Salvador, G. (coord.) (1994) *La lengua española, hoy*, Madrid: Fundación Juan March.

Shaul, M. (1996) 'El djudeo-espanyol: pasado, prezente i perspektivas para su futuro', *Donaire*, 6, London: Consejería de Educación y Ciencia.

Siguan, M. (1992) *España plurilingüe*, Madrid: Alianza Editorial.

Silva-Corvalán, C. (1982) 'Subject expression and placement in Mexican-American Spanish' in J. Amastae and L. Elías-Olivares (eds.) *Spanish in the United States: Sociolinguistic Aspects*, Cambridge: Cambridge University Press.

Silva-Corvalán, S. (1986) 'Bilingualism and language change: the extension of *estar* in Los Angeles Spanish', *Language* 62: 587–608.

Silva-Corvalán, S. (1989) *Sociolingüística: teoría y análisis*, Madrid: Alhambra.

Silva-Corvalán, S. (1994) 'The gradual loss of mood distinctions in Los Angeles Spanish', *Language Variation and Change* 6 (3): 255–72.

Smith, C. (1993) *Collins Spanish–English, English–Spanish Dictionary*, 3rd edn, Glasgow: HarperCollins.

Smith, C. (1995) 'El español en el periodismo de hoy' *Donaire* 4, London: La Consejería de Educación, Embajada de España.

Solé, C. A. (1991) 'El problema de la lengua en Buenos Aires: independencia o autonomía lingüística' in C.A. Klee and L.A. Ramón-García (eds) *Sociolinguistics of the Spanish-speaking world: Iberia, Latin America, United States*, Tempe, AZ: Bilingual Press/Prensa bilingüe.

Steel, B. (1976) *A Textbook of Colloquial Spanish*, Madrid: SGEL.

Stevenson, C. H. (1970) *The Spanish Language Today*, London: Hutchinson.

Stewart, M., Mason, I. and McDowall, W. (1991) *Camino a Castilla*, Edinburgh: Edinburgh University Language Learning Centre.

Stewart, M. (1992) *Personal Reference and Politeness Strategies in French and Spanish: A Corpus-based Approach*, unpublished PhD thesis, Heriot-Watt University.

Suárez Molina, V. (1996) *El español que se habla en Yucatán*, Mérida: Universidad Autónoma de Yucatán.

Telemadrid (1993) *Libro de estilo de Telemadrid*, Madrid: Ediciones Telemadrid.

Timm, L.A. (1993) 'Bilingual Code-switching: An Overview of Research' in B. J. Merino, H. T. Trueba and F. A. Samaniego (eds.) *Language and Culture in Learning*, London: Faber Press.

Tinsley, T. (1992) 'El lenguaje administrativo: a case study in sociolinguistic change', *Association for Contemporary Iberian Studies* 5(1): 23–9.

Tusón Valls, A. (1997) *Análisis de la conversación*, Barcelona: Ariel Practicum.

Umbral, F. (1983) *Diccionario cheli*, Barcelona: Grijalbo.

UPI (1988) *Manual de estilo y referencia*, Washington DC: United Press International.

Uruburu, A. (1990) *Estudios sobre la lengua española en Córdoba*, Córdoba: Diputación Provincial.

Vaquero de Ramírez, M. (1996) *El español de América II*, Madrid: Arco Libros.

Vigara Tauste, A.M. (1980) *Aspectos del español hablado: aportaciones al estudio del español coloquial*, Madrid: SGEL.

Vigara Tauste, A. M. (1992) *Morfosintaxis del español coloquial: esbozo estilístico*, Madrid: Gredos.

Vigara Tauste, A. M. (1994) *El chiste y la comunicación lúdica: lenguaje y praxis*, Madrid: Ed. Libertarias.

Wardhaugh, R. (1986) *An Introduction to Sociolinguistics*, 2nd edn, 1998 Oxford: Blackwell.

Whitehead, M. (1998) 'A case of language contact generating language change', paper given at the Annual Conference of the Association of Contemporary Iberian Studies, Edinburgh.

Williams, L. (1987) *Aspectos sociolingüísticos del habla de la ciudad de Valladolid*, Valladolid: Secretariado de Publicaciones/Universidad de Exeter.

Woolard, K. A. (1988) 'Code-switching and comedy in Catalonia' in M. Heller (ed.) *Code-switching: Anthropological and Sociolinguistic Perspectives*, Berlin: Mouton de Gruyter, 77–96.

Other sources

Almodóvar, P. (Dir.) *¿Qué he hecho yo para merecer esto!* (film).

Castro, F. (1997) Speech to the Young Communists, www2ceniai.inf.cu/pcc/d4_4_97.html.

Bradley, D. *Corpus of Spanish neologisms*, unpublished corpus.

Departamento de Español Urgente (DEU), regular bulletins, 1995.

Salinas de Gortari, C. (1995) Speech to the Mexican Congress, www.cddhcu.gob.mex.

Stewart, M. *et al.* (1987) *Videotaped corpus of spoken Spanish from Valladolid/Madrid*, unpublished corpus.

European Parliament, speech no. 3–429/59 and translation no. 3–429/54.

My own corpus of newspapers, etc. (1990s): C16 (*Cambio 16*), EP (*El País*), EPS (*El País Semanal*).

My own corpus of realia.

My own corpus of recordings.

Index